Montréal

Patricia Harris and David Lyon
Photography by Benoît Aquin

Compass American Guides: Montréal

Editor: Paula Consolo
Designer: Tina R. Malaney
Compass Editorial Director: Daniel Mangin
Compass Creative Director: Fabrizio La Rocca
Compass Senior Editor: Kristin Moehlmann
Editorial Production: Linda Schmidt
Photo Editor and Archival Researcher: Melanie Marin
Map Design: Mark Stroud, Moon Street Cartography

Cover photo: Festival Montréal en Lumière, Place des Arts, by Benoît Aquin

First Edition
ISBN 1–4000–1315–1
ISSN 1543–1576

The details in this book are based on information supplied to us at press time, but changes occur all the
time, and the publisher cannot accept responsibility for facts that become outdated or for inadvertent errors
or omissions.

Compass American Guides are available at special discounts for bulk purchases for sales promotions or
premiums. Special editions, including personalized covers, excerpts of existing guides, and corporate
imprints, can be created in large quantities for special needs. For more information, contact your local
bookseller or write to Special Markets/Premium Sales, 1745 Broadway, M-D 6-2, New York, NY 10019.

Compass American Guides, 1745 Broadway, New York, NY 10019
PRINTED IN CHINA

10 9 8 7 6 5 4 3 2 1

For Gilles—epicure, savant, bon ami

C O N T E N T S

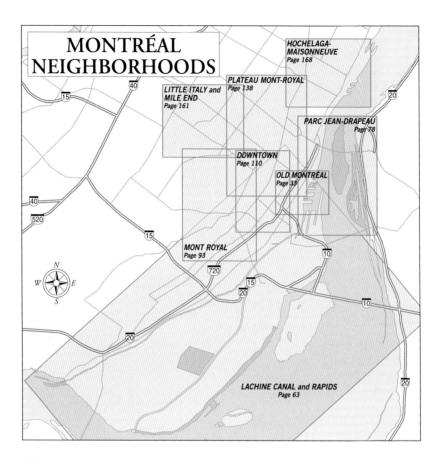

MONTRÉAL NEIGHBORHOODS

HOCHELAGA-MAISONNEUVE
Page 168

LITTLE ITALY and MILE END
Page 161

PLATEAU MONT-ROYAL
Page 138

PARC JEAN-DRAPEAU
Page 78

DOWNTOWN
Page 110

OLD MONTRÉAL
Page 33

MONT ROYAL
Page 93

LACHINE CANAL and RAPIDS
Page 63

Maps

Literary Extracts

Topical Essays and Sidebars

INTRODUCTION

"*Bonjour*-hi!" exclaims the baker at our avenue Laurier *boulangerie* when we go in at 7 A.M. to score a loaf of multigrain before it's all sold out. Even in the predominantly francophone Plateau neighborhood, it's the quintessential Montréal salutation: French? English? A bit of both? The daily texture of Montréal life is like the rich crunch of Jean-François's bread—toothy, solid, chewy, a little nutty, always satisfying.

One of us mutters "*un multigrain, s'il-vous-plaît,*" and he reaches for a long loaf and holds it up.

"*Tranché?*" he asks, gesturing to the slicing machine.

"*Non, merci.*"

We love the way Montréal smells in the morning—the buttery, grainy aroma of a thousand croissant bakeries, the in-your-face insouciance of dark-roasted coffee, the metallic tang of hot maple syrup. But the fresh breeze that sweeps down from the piney Laurentians reminds us that we're in Canada, not France.

Montréal is often called the Paris of North America because it's the largest French-speaking city on the continent and, for that matter, the second-largest francophone city in the world. But Montréal is no provincial Paris. The Montrealers have bigger dogs, smoke less, spend more time outdoors, and, if you ask them, speak better French. All of which is to say that Montréal is a child of France that long ago left home and grew up to be a complex metropolis with its own character, quirks, charms, and frustrations. In 1990, the travel writer Jan Morris opined in *City to City* that Montréal is "unquestionably the most exciting of Canadian cities," calling it "the grit, so to speak, in the Canadian oyster, which may or may not develop into its pearl."

The rest of Québec province begrudges (and envies) the facile bilingualism of the Montrealer, and the rest of Canada regards Montréal with the same suspicion that Americans bring to Manhattan. Cosmopolitan and international, Montréal is the urban antithesis of a country that pulls on plaid woolens and lumberjack boots to run down to Tim Horton's for doughnuts. For the most part, Montrealers don't regard the rest of Canada at all. They relish their role as the national grit and bask in the reflected nacre of their city. The pearl has definitely formed.

(preceding pages) Montrealers defy the winter dark at the Festival Montréal en Lumière.
(left) A living statue captivates the crowd.

We first started visiting Montréal more than twenty years ago as a romantic get-away, and it has never disappointed. Above all, Montréal is a city of sensual pleasures. Daylight lingers deliciously on long summer days as the Montrealers gather in sidewalk cafés for drinks and conversation, their sun-touched cheeks aglow in the salmon-colored half-light of a loitering high-latitude sunset. The crystalline edge of a boreal January day fails to deter skaters on the Bassin Bonsecours from spraying a flurry of ice as they bank into the turns of a tight figure eight and wind up their routines with an Olympic spin. When the golden autumn light slants through the birches and maples of Mont Royal, families on bicycles labor up the Olmsted path as lovers in thick sweaters repose on a grassy incline to behold the spectacle of a single falling leaf. Spring announces itself in Park Lafontaine with a flourish of daffodils, each yellow cup a trumpet's bell in the fanfare of seasonal resiliency.

For years, as we traveled the globe for work, Montréal kept calling us back for pleasure. It beckoned with its contrasts and contradictions, its combination of complex history and an almost innocent optimism about the future. Montréal, above all, is that rare city blessed with both memory and hope. Solid little gray limestone houses from the ancien régime squat next to Victorian hat factories, and both stand proudly in the shadows of glass skyscrapers. The old public baths in erstwhile immigrant neighborhoods have been reborn as community swimming pools. The canal where Canadian industry sprang up has become a linear park for boaters and bicyclists alike. A conversation with a stranger over coffee may range from Rabelais to Camus to the latest Keystone Cops escapades of the language police arresting a junkyard owner for his English-only sign. Like Jean-François's bread, taste and texture are everything.

After decades of dating Montréal a few times a year and finally exhausting all the usual tourist activities, we moved in. We rented a flat—a five-and-a-half, in local parlance—on the Plateau to become, if only for a while, on intimate terms with a city we love. Away from the commercial bustle of downtown, away from the clip-clopping carriage horses and fire jugglers of Old Montréal, we settled into the domesticity of a neighborhood, waking twice a week to the pre-dawn garbage pickup and playing auto roulette with street parking restrictions.

We found that some parts of daily life are immutable. The low glow of triple-decker houses at night does nothing to diminish the great white sweep of the Milky Way across the sky. From open windows along the street, Céline Dion and Edith Piaf wage a war of plaintive laments. Everyone walks to the store—and drives to church. Every Sunday and twice on Saturdays, wedding parties gather on the parish church lawns for photos. On sunny Monday mornings, clothesline pulleys squeak as families hang out the wash. Late on Friday afternoons, the lines at the *dépanneur* (corner store) are impossibly long as workmen load up on cases of beer for the weekend.

We grew to know our neighbors and shopkeepers at least enough to nod on the street, and we learned that despite the flurry of elbows as everyone pushes onto the Métro, large crowds bring out the best in the Montrealer. Politesse prevails when fifty thousand people gather at Place des Arts to hear Les Cowboys Fringant rock the streets. As rare anglophones in a sea of Québecois *pur laine* (pure wool, i.e., of original French stock), we've been welcome to wave our fleur-de-lis balloons during the parade down rue Notre-Dame that celebrates la fête Jean-Baptiste, Québec's National Day. We've climbed Mont Royal on the hottest afternoon in thirty years, only to find that half of Montréal was already there. And we've spent the evening with ten thousand of our newest acquaintances, sharing oohs and aahs (the same in French and English) from the Jacques Cartier Bridge as fireworks splattered the sky for no other purpose than to celebrate exuberance in a metropolis charged with spirit.

This book takes the form of a guide to Montréal. But consider it instead a roman à clef, the decades-long saga of a love affair with a city worth loving. *Merci à vous* for reading.

—Patricia Harris and David Lyon

Explorer Jacques Cartier was the first European who made a documented landing at the site of

H I S T O R Y

Even geologists can't pinpoint when the Champlain Sea shrank down to become the St. Lawrence River (between seven thousand and nine thousand years ago), but since the retreat of the glaciers, most of the raindrops that have fallen in Canada east of the Rocky Mountains have eventually flowed past Montréal on their way to the sea. The St. Lawrence is the gateway to the Great Lakes and the continental interior, and the island of Montréal sits at the first major bottleneck to navigation, the Lachine Rapids.

The Ottawa River, the watery highway into the north country of Ontario and Québec, joins the St. Lawrence just west of Montréal, making the spot a natural trading crossroads for First Nations tribes who ranged over central and eastern Canada in the centuries before European contact. Anthropologists assume occupation of the St. Lawrence and Ottawa Valleys began about four thousand years ago, but the first extensive archaeological record appears around 1300 A.D., when Iroquois peoples expanded northeast from the Great Lakes into the areas inhabited by Algonquian-speaking tribes. By 1350, the precise spot where Montréal would be founded three centuries later—the spit of land at the mouth of the Little Saint Pierre River—was already established as a seasonal trading post.

■ EXPLORATION AND COLONIZATION: 1534–1663

Europeans sought fish and whales in the Gulf of St. Lawrence from at least the mid-fifteenth century, but the first documented exploration dates from the voyages of Jacques Cartier, who circumnavigated Newfoundland and explored the Gulf of St. Lawrence in 1534, planting a cross on the Gaspé Peninsula to claim New France.

The next year, Cartier followed the St. Lawrence River inland to the Iroquois village of Stadacona, where Québec City now stands. He continued upriver to another village, Hochelaga, where the Iroquois took him to the summit of the mountain that he christened Mont Royal. But Cartier was less interested in the natives than in finding a passage to the Far East, or at least some of the gold and gems the Spanish were extracting from their American colonies. When he instead discovered tumultuous rapids, he returned to Stadacona to spend the winter of 1535–36, where 25 of his crew of 110 perished from scurvy.

AT HOCHELAGA

And we having arrived at the said Hochelaga, more than a thousand persons presented themselves before us, men, women, and children alike, the which gave us a good reception as ever father did to child, showing marvelous joy; for the men in one band danced, the women on their side and the children on the other, the which brought us store of fish and of their bread made of coarse millet, which they cast into our said boats in a way that it seemed as if it tumbled from the air. Seeing this, our said captain landed with a number of his men, and as soon as he was landed they gathered all about him, and about all the others, giving them an unrestrained welcome.

And the women brought their children in their arms to make them touch the said captain and others, making a rejoicing which lasted more than half an hour. And our captain, witnessing their liberality and good will, caused all the women to be seated and ranged in order, and gave them certain paternosters of tin and other trifling things, and to a part of the men knives. Then he retired on board the said boats to sup and pass the night, while these people remained on the shore of the said river nearest the said boats all night, making fires and dancing, crying all the time "Aguyaze!" which is their expression of mirth and joy.

–James Phinney Baxter, *A Memoir of Jacques Cartier,
Sieur de Limoilou: His Voyages to the St. Lawrence. A Bibliography and a
Facsimile of the Manuscript of 1534 with Annotations, etc.,* 1906.

Cartier returned on an ill-fated voyage in 1542, but his expeditions failed to bring back either riches or a trade route. Consequently, New France languished for sixty years—until Samuel de Champlain explored the coasts of present-day Maine, Nova Scotia, and New Brunswick and ventured up the St. Lawrence as far as the rapids at Montréal in 1603. By then, warfare between the Algonquin and Iroquoian peoples had pushed the Iroquois back toward their historic heartland around the Great Lakes. Stadacona was now an Algonquin village, and Hochelaga was nowhere to be found.

Champlain's attempts to plant colonies in Maine and New Brunswick failed, but in 1608, he was granted a monopoly on the fur trade in exchange for erecting a settlement, Ville de Québec. It would remain little more than a trading post for several years, although Champlain returned repeatedly to France to recruit settlers. Old enemies France and England were at war again, and in 1629, the English took Québec, returning it to Champlain in 1632 with the conclusion of the fighting. The epic struggles among the European powers in the seventeenth century had both religious and economic roots. The French sent religious orders to secure New France as a Catholic land, beginning with the Recollets in 1615 and following with the more militarily minded Jesuits in 1625. The traders and the missionaries did not always see eye to eye, but Québec, which was founded for the principal purpose of collecting beaver pelts, soon became the Catholic religious center of the fledgling colony.

This missionary zeal of the Counter Reformation reached its apex in New France in 1642, when Ville-Marie de Montréal was founded where the Little Saint Pierre River flows into the St. Lawrence. Although Paul de Chomedy, Sieur de Maisonneuve, and his small band of colonists came to save souls, they soon learned to trade for pelts. New settlers arrived at Montréal in 1653 and 1659, but the community struggled at the edge of the wilderness, functioning as a buffer between Québec and the Iroquois, who inhabited the lands south and west of the island. Warfare between the Iroquois and the Algonquin allies of the French hampered the free flow of furs that would make New France a going economic concern.

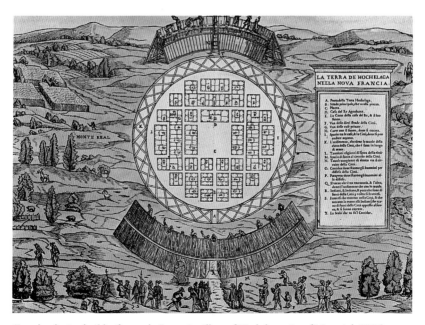

French colonists build a fort at the Iroquois village of Hochelaga, site of Montréal, 1556.

■ OVERSEAS PROVINCE: 1663–1760

Intended to be a moneymaker and soul-saver, New France instead proved a beggar on the royal treasury. In 1663, Louis XIV brought the failing colony under royal administration. He dispatched 400 soldiers to defend the settlers from the Iroquois (and, with some prescience, the British) and gave title to the entire island of Montréal to the priests from the Seminaire de St-Sulpice, the first of whom had arrived in 1657. Moreover, the king began to dispatch single young women to help populate the colony. Known as the *filles du roy,* or "daughters of the king," they were given dowries and encouraged to marry and multiply. Between 1663 and 1673, approximately eight hundred *filles du roy* arrived at Montréal alone. Quickly married off, they proved more fruitful than even a king might have imagined. The provincial government made cash awards for every child born, and farming families along the St. Lawrence between Montréal and Québec typically had a dozen children or more.

The Sulpicians proved apt administrators of Montréal, bringing order to the city street patterns and to the rural roads and farm grid. By 1670, a revitalized Montréal had emerged as the hub of the fur trade, while Québec remained the provincial capital and seat of power. Montréal's economic dominance was sealed in 1701, when Louis-Hector de Callière, governor first of Montréal and later of New France, negotiated a peace treaty with thirty-nine tribes. By establishing the French governor as arbiter of all First Nations disputes, the treaty effectively gave French traders a monopoly on the fur trade in interior North America. French missionaries and adventurers had already penetrated nearly to the Rocky Mountains, explored the length of the Mississippi River, and established missions and outposts along the Gulf Coast.

The expansion did not go unnoticed by the British, who were also trading for furs by following the northerly route into Hudson's Bay. Back in Europe, the two nations were locked in intermittent warfare that would become ever bloodier before the final defeat of Napoleon in 1815. French and British colonists and their Indian allies were impressed as surrogate warriors.

For Montréal and Québec it all came to a head in 1759 and 1760. The British Gen. James Wolfe laid siege to Québec through the summer of 1759, writing home to his mother, "These colonies are deeply tinged with the Vices & bad Qualities of their mother Country & indeed many parts of it are Peopled with those that Law or necessity has forced upon it." Finally, in the pre-dawn hours of

Two Faces of Canada

When the Montréal novelist Hugh MacLellan published *Two Solitudes* in 1945, the title gained instant currency as a term to define the historic and linguistic divide between francophone and anglophone Canadians. Neither language, MacLellan noted in his forward, could see the country as anything but dichotomous. "No single word exists, within Canada itself, to designate with satisfaction to both races a native of the country," he wrote. "When those of the French language use the word *Canadien,* they nearly always refer to themselves. They know their English-speaking compatriots as *les Anglais.* English-speaking citizens act on the same principle. They call themselves Canadians; those of the French language are French-Canadians." Whatever advances Montréal has made toward fluent bilingualism, the concept of "two solitudes" still pops up in public discourse—sometimes as an inclusive shorthand, sometimes as an allusion to the melancholy divide in the Canadian soul.

September 13, 1759, Wolfe boldly ordered his armies to scale the cliffs outside the city and assemble on the pastures west of the fortified walls. The French commander, Gen. Louis-Joseph de Montcalm, sent troops out from the city to meet them. At 10 A.M., the two sides engaged. When the last shots were fired around 10:30, Wolfe was dead, but Montcalm was mortally wounded and the French had been destroyed. It was the "half hour that changed the world," as Canadian historians often put it. Québec City surrendered on September 18.

In a desperate attempt to regain Québec, François-Gaston, Duc de Lévis, led an army from Montréal in April 1760 and won a brilliant victory against the British in the western suburb of Sainte-Foy. But he could not breach Québec's walls and was forced to withdraw when British reinforcements arrived in early May. The Chevalier de Lévis, as François-Gaston was known, returned to his Montréal garrison, but with three British armies converging on the city, he was forced to surrender on September 8, 1760. The 1763 Treaty of Paris officially turned over New France to Britain. Voltaire quipped, "I much prefer peace over Canada and I believe that France could be happy without Québec."

Whether the Québecois would be happy without France remained to be seen.

(following pages) This 1688 map highlights French claims to Canada and Louisiana.

CANADA, ou

NOU-

Lac des Poux

Lac des Assiniboüels

Lac DES CHRISTINAUX

NATIONS SOUS LE NOM FR

D'Outa

Lac Alepimigon

Stoux SILEUR des NATIONS

LAC DE BUADE

OU-

LAC SUPERIEUR

LACS

LAC DES ILINOIS

Lac HURO

LES PANI-MAHA

MASCOUTENS

CON-TREÉ

OHIO ou BELLE RIVIERE

DE LA LOUI-

PAYS ET ISLES DES A CANCEA

FLORIDE

CICACHA

SI A- N A E

CAROLINE

Tacura Natche

Kansa Oromi

CAP DE LA FLORIDE

GOLFE DE MEXIQUE

■ BRITISH CONSOLIDATION: 1760–1867

As the hub of the North American fur trade, Montréal proved a magnet for merchants and would-be traders from the British Isles. By 1774, control of the fur trade had passed to Scots immigrants. Ironically, in the same year, the Québec Act granted the original settlers freedom of worship and the right to use the French language—a concession designed to cement Québecois loyalty to the British crown.

During the American Revolution, the Continental Army invaded Québec and held Montréal across the winter of 1775–76. But even the superior military tactics of Gen. Benedict Arnold could not breach the fortifications of Québec City, and the Americans withdrew to fight on their own territory. When another Treaty of Paris gave the United States its sovereignty, the British turned their attention to reorganizing the governance of their remaining colonies. In 1791, the Constitutional Act carved out New Brunswick from the continental portion of Nova Scotia and divided Québec into Upper Canada (later Ontario) and Lower Canada (the modern Québec). Each was governed by an executive council and a legislative council with the advice of an elected assembly.

French immigration ended in 1760, and newcomers to Lower Canada were mostly immigrants from the British Isles or Loyalists fleeing the American Revolution. By 1830, the majority of Montrealers spoke English as a first language. The establishment of the Bank of Montréal in 1817—the first Canadian bank—marked the city's economic dominance of the Canadian colonies, and the Lachine Canal, which opened in the 1820s, made Montréal the gateway to interior continental trade. The industry that grew up along the canal also made the city the industrial leader of Canada.

But wealth and power were unevenly distributed. Descendants of the settlers of Upper and Lower Canada felt shut out from opportunity, and in 1837–38 the self-anointed "Sons of Liberty" rose up in the Patriots' Rebellion. Although the rebellion is often cited by supporters of Québec sovereignty as the first "national affirmation," the Patriots included anglophones and francophones alike. British reaction was swift. Authorities took fourteen hundred rebels prisoner, executing twelve and exiling fifty-eight more to Australia.

Sent out from London to figure out what went wrong, the Lord High Commissioner of British North America, Lord Durham, blamed the French. His 1839 report found "two nations warring in the bosom of a single state," and his roadmap to harmony proposed merging Upper and Lower Canada and stamping out the French language. An unapologetic francophobe, Durham wrote, "There can hardly be conceived a nationality more destitute of all that can invigorate and elevate a people than that which is exhibited by the descendants of the French in Lower Canada, owing to their retaining their peculiar language and manners. They are a people with no history and no literature." In 1840, the British Parliament created United Canada, establishing the capital (temporarily) at Montréal.

At mid-century, Montréal was transformed. When the Great Fire of 1852 destroyed twelve hundred buildings, reconstruction gave the city a Victorian demeanor. Over the next decade, industry boomed and the city became the hub of the new national railroads as well as the country's leading port. While immigrants from Ireland and other parts of the British Isles had streamed into Montréal in the first half of the century, after 1850 increasing numbers of rural French Canadians abandoned the farms to work in Montréal's factories. By 1866, francophones were again a majority.

Montréal built its Métro mass transit system swiftly by burying lines beneath existing streets.

Montréal's most famous jazz pianist, Oscar Peterson, was born in 1925 and began performing professionally at the age of 17. The city's first jazz star to gain international acclaim, he is shown here performing at Jazz at the Philharmonic in New York's Carnegie Hall, circa 1952.

■ CANADA'S MONTRÉAL: 1867–1960

The Canadian Confederation in 1867 worked to the advantage of Québec province in general and Montréal in particular. French was recognized as one of the two official national languages, and schools and hospitals in Québec province remained in the hands of the Catholic Church. Montréal continued to boom, even as the rest of the new country underwent hard times. The need for ever greater numbers of workers encouraged new residential construction, especially on the Plateau and in Hochelaga and Maisonneuve. Between 1883 and 1918, the city annexed thirty-one adjoining villages and neighborhoods.

Immigration continued as tens of thousands of southern Italians flooded into Montréal at the end of the nineteenth century. During the first three decades of the twentieth century, more than 120,000 people arrived from Europe, more than half of them Eastern European Jews. These new Canadians, by and large, preferred English over French, and francophone intellectuals worried about the future. In 1913, Henri Bourassa, founder of the newspaper *Le Devoir,* gave a speech insisting that the "conservation of the language is absolutely necessary for the conservation of the race, its genius, its character, and its temperament."

World War I brought the linguistic and cultural divide into sharper relief. Regarding the war as Britain's fight, francophones rioted against conscription; most anglophones, however, supported the war effort. Québec also set itself apart on another major issue: temperance. When Prohibition swept the anglophone provinces as well as the United States, Québec remained resolutely wet. It had a salutary effect on the entertainment business—jazz, for example, flourished in Montréal—but also attracted organized crime from the United States. Sprawling, brawling, bawdy Montréal became North America's good-time city, even in the midst of the Great Depression. In 1936, the travel journalist Austin F. Cross wrote that Montréal is "a 24-hour town, with more life on its main street at four in the morning than most cities have at four in the afternoon. Montréal has a permanent case of whoopee."

World War II drove another wedge between Québec and Canada, as conscription proved even less popular in the province than during World War I. Camillien Houde, mayor of Montréal, counseled French Canadians to dodge the draft and found himself in an internment camp as a national enemy until 1944. Upon his release, he was promptly reelected by the francophone majority. The war highlighted the gap between francophone and anglophone, leading the historian

Montrealers turn out on Victoria Square on May 24, 1917, to oppose the draft. The issue of military conscription divided anglophones and francophones in Canada during both world wars.

Jean Drapeau celebrates his victory as a reform candidate for mayor in 1954.

Stephen Leacock to observe in 1944, "Each race sees too well the faults, too dimly the merits, of the other. The English think that many of the French are priest-ridden; the French think that many of the English are badly in need of a priest."

While many Montrealers opposed the war, the city's industrial base made it the center of the defense industries, which lifted the city out of the Depression. The economic boom continued after the war, as Montréal enjoyed virtually full employment. Italian, Greek, and Portuguese immigration helped swell the population past one million in 1951, and public prosecutors Jean Drapeau and Pacifique Plante took on the corruption, gambling, and prostitution that had become rampant under Houde's regime. (In the late 1940s, authorities had estimated that illegal gambling alone was earning organized crime $100 million a year at a time when the city of Montréal was only collecting $60 million in tax revenues.) In 1954, Drapeau announced himself as a mayoral candidate just eighteen days before the election—and swept Houde out of office on a pledge to clean up the city. Although voters banished Drapeau in 1957, he was returned to power in 1960, and for the next twenty-six years he presided over the transformation of a large provincial city into a world cultural capital.

Charles de Gaulle's "Vive le Québec libre!" speech on July 24, 1967, galvanized nationalism.

■ THE QUIET REVOLUTION AND AFTERMATH: 1960–PRESENT

Drapeau's administration remade the city, starting construction on the Métro system in late 1962 just as the first modern skyscraper, Place Ville-Marie, also broke ground. In 1964, Montréal successfully bid to host the 1967 World's Fair, which would celebrate the Canadian centenary. Construction moved into high gear and by the time Expo '67 opened, Montréal had established an underground urban transit system, had revitalized its old city, and had built a river island complex to showcase its arrival as a world-class destination. Moreover, despite the rapid growth of Toronto, Montréal remained the economic hub of Canada: home to two transcontinental railroads, the national airline, the largest telephone company, and two of the country's biggest banks. When Charles de Gaulle showed up for the party, he stood on the balcony of City Hall and declared, *"Vive le Québec libre!"*

The French president's pronouncement of "Long live a free Québec!" reflected strong sentiments in the province. In June 1960, the Québecois had elected a Liberal government headed by Jean Lesage on the promise of modernization. His reforms were so sweeping that the press called his transformation of education, economy, and culture the Quiet Revolution. Schools, health care, and social services—all the province of the Catholic Church since the 1630s—were secularized. New pride in French language and culture blossomed into a cultural renaissance. Québecois sentiment that the province was exploited by anglophone Canadians and Americans began to build toward a movement for political independence.

Premier Lesage was already thinking like a head of state rather than a provincial official, having established Québec's own pension plan, investment fund, and a state-owned hydroelectric facility. Yet some Québecois felt he was moving too timidly. In 1963, the radical separatist Front de Liberation du Québec, or FLQ, began a series of bombings and bank robberies, ostensibly in the name of independence. In 1970, they kidnapped the British trade commissioner, James R. Cross, and Québec's labor minister, Pierre Laporte. Pierre Elliott Trudeau, Canada's prime minister and a native Montrealer, invoked the War Measures Act to send troops into Montréal and detain more than 450 political activists, intellectuals, artists, and avowed Québec nationalists. Two months later, Cross was released when his kidnappers were allowed to fly to Cuba. Laporte was found to have been assassinated, however, and three FLQ members went to jail. The October Crisis was over.

But separatist sentiment was only swelling. The Liberal government enacted the first of the language laws in the mid-1970s, mandating French in some workplaces, specifying equal treatment for French and English on signs, and requiring immigrant children to attend French schools. When the Parti Québecois, headed by Réné Lévèsque, came to power in 1976, his administration made French the preferred—and often the only—language of commerce, signage, and public services. English speakers started packing. The anglophone population in Montréal declined from 789,000 in 1971 to 586,000 in 1996, and the departing English speakers took their companies with them, mostly to Toronto.

Yet in the run-up to the 1976 provincial elections, Montrealers were less focused on getting out of Canada than on proclaiming themselves citizens of the world. During the summer Olympics, Drapeau got another chance to show off his splendid city, whose space-station–like Olympic complex presaged Montréal's utter embrace of architectural modernism in the decade to come. As Québec toyed with becoming another country, Montréal was beginning to look like another world.

More than a quarter-century later, Montréal has become a bilingual city. Virtually everyone under the age of thirty-five moves from one language to another without thinking about it. And the older population is working hard to learn the less-familiar tongue, because bilingualism pays—an average of $8,000 more per year. The issue of Québec separating from Canada has come to a referendum in 1980, 1985, and 1994. Each time the vote has been more closely split—coming down to a mere six-tenths of a percent difference in 1994, as confirmed separatists blamed Montréal's voters for thwarting Québec's bid for sovereignty. The Montrealers, on the other hand, seem focused on a metropolitan rather than a national agenda.

Montréal has become increasingly cosmopolitan since 1976, with most of its immigration drawn from former French colonies in North and West Africa, Southeast Asia, the Middle East, and the Caribbean. Yet it has also held true to the visions enunciated by the late Jean Drapeau, slowly transforming the way the urban landscape functions. The Métro system has been expanded; the Underground City has been dug to include twenty miles of passageways lined with shopping and entertainment; the Old Port has been reborn; the industrial wasteland of the Lachine Canal has been transformed into a green parkland; and new World Trade and Convention centers have been built. The work continues—some street or square is always under construction—but that is the price of rushing headlong into the future. During the festivals that light up the streets all summer, and even in the middle of winter, you can almost see the Montrealers dancing toward a destiny all their own: the city of Mary, the royal mountain, the metropolis of the possible.

OLD MONTRÉAL

At quarter to eleven on Sunday morning, the organist climbs into the choir loft of Notre-Dame basilica, turns on the bellows, pulls out the stops, and begins to play. The high notes of the short pipes rise heavenward; the low notes of the long pipes rumble at a frequency more felt than heard. Worshippers file into wooden pews and clatter their kneelers into place. Votive candles flicker around the periphery, and sunlight streams through the ceiling's four rose windows. Bells chime at precisely eleven, and the celebrants parade past the congregation and mount the steps to the altar. The Mass begins.

By noon the Host has been consecrated, elevated, and consumed in the ritual that has bound French Montréal since the first missionary settlers arrived in 1642. The swirling lines of the elevated pulpit, the carved figures at the ends of every pew, the gold leaf fleurs-de-lis on the walls all attest to a faith inseparable from the history of the French-Canadian people. Stained glass windows record seminal events of Montréal's early years. *"Je me souviens,"* Basilique de Notre-Dame de Montréal seems to say. "I remember." Just outside the church doors, Old Montréal cannot forget.

By accidents of history and geography, the area known as Vieux Montréal remains a discrete 90-acre sector of the city, effectively separated from Centre-Ville (the downtown business district) by a natural gully and an unnatural highway. The outlines differ little from the walled fortifications that were removed nearly two centuries ago, and the streets still follow the plan laid out in 1672. Those stone-paved routes echo not only with the clopping hooves of horses drawing tourist carriages, but also with reminders of the commerce, bustle, and messy daily lives of nearly four centuries of Montrealers.

■ POINTE-À-CALLIÈRE AND PLACE D'YOUVILLE

When Paul de Chomedy, Sieur de Maisonneuve, landed on the island in 1642, he selected a small point of land where a stream drained into the St. Lawrence River as the most defensible site for settlement. It wasn't a difficult choice; Samuel de Champlain had called the spot "one of the finest on this river" when he established

Early-twentieth-century office buildings give Old Montréal's western edge a modern feel.

SETTLING IN AT VILLE-MARIE

At first everyone was under canvas, as in Europe in the army, later they worked hard by cutting stakes and in other ways to surround the place and to safeguard themselves against the surprises and affronts to be feared from the Iroquois. This kind of hasty fortification was the easier because M. de Champlain, who had come here formerly to trade, had had many trees cut down for firewood and as protections against the ambushes which might have been made against him in the short time he was here. Further, this post was very advantageously situated since it was enclosed between the River St. Lawrence and a little stream which flows into it, and was bordered by a very pretty meadow called to-day the Common; whilst on the other side, protected neither by the river nor the stream there was marshy and inaccessible ground since drained, out of which has been made the demesne of the seigneury. The advantages of the place were thus obvious. Further, there were in the meadow of which we have spoken, so many birds of different warblings and colours that they helped to make our Frenchmen feel at home in this uncivilised country.

—François Dollier de Casson, *A History of Montréal, 1640–72,*
published in French 1868, in English translation 1928

a trading post here in 1611. Maisonneuve's company erected a wooden fort, and the narrow strip of riverfront became the first settlement of Ville-Marie de Montréal.

All evidence of the wooden fort has rotted away over the centuries, but the foundations of later stone buildings form the main exhibits of the **Pointe-à-Callière** museum of archaeology and history. With four trapezoidal floors fanning off a cylindrical tower, the archaeology museum's 1992 Éperon building is a postmodern landmark that rises from the foundations of the 1695 "château" of Louis-Hector de Callière, second governor of Montréal, and three succeeding generations of buildings. More than a decade of excavations produced a trove of artifacts indicating how people inhabited this site from about A.D. 1350, when native peoples camped here on annual trading expeditions, until the twentieth century. Picking your way through the underground displays is a little like wandering through the catacombs in the silent-movie version of *Phantom of the Opera;* a dry riverbed long ago vaulted over for use as a sewer now serves as a corridor.

The tower's top-level belvedere offers a sweeping view of Old Montréal and the expanded city, which exploded out onto the island in the mid-nineteenth century. It almost seems that you could reach out and touch the great silver dome of Marché Bonsecours, the towers of Notre-Dame basilica, and the former firehouse that houses the social history museum, Centre d'Histoire. *350 Place Royale; 514-872-9150.*

Walking from the Pointe-à-Callière museum to the Centre d'Histoire through the small strip park of **Place de la Grande-Paix,** you pass a peculiar juxtaposition of memorial sculptures. The simple granite obelisk generally known as "the founders' monument" notes the dates of Champlain's first visit to the site (May 28, 1611) and of Maisonneuve's orders to build the fortifications (May 17, 1642). This 1893 monument records forty-six of the original settlers and colonists, and acknowledges "many others whose names are unknown." A granite pathway, representing

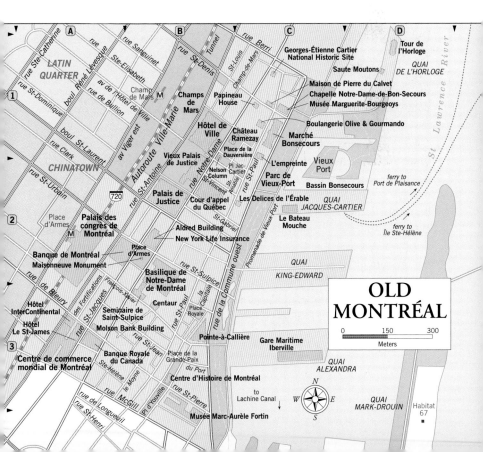

the former bed of the Saint-Pierre stream, leads to the modern metal sculpture, *l'Oeuvre,* that is intended to symbolize the origins of the Roman Catholic Church in North America. The cross and squashed globe look a bit like a hubcap.

The facade of the Flemish-style former fire station at the head of Place d'Youville has a peculiar humor, looking every bit as foppish as a soldier in uniform wearing a periwig. The museum within its early-twentieth-century walls, the **Centre d'Histoire de Montréal,** delivers a lively account of Montréal history. Period maps, photographs, and drawings provide a graphic overview of the growth of the city. Videotaped interviews with contemporary Montrealers hint at what it's like to live here and show intense loyalties to neighborhoods. "Right around my corner was a whole world," reminisces an older resident of Petit Bourgogne, or Little Burgundy. "People come from all over the city to eat," says a chic young denizen of the Plateau. *335 Place d'Youville; 514-872-3207.*

The museum fronts on the square that was the nineteenth-century civic center, **Place d'Youville,** named for the founder of the Congrégation des Soeurs de Charité, known as the Grey Nuns. Rue Saint-Pierre south of Place d'Youville reflects some of the aspirations of Montréal in the early days of Confederation, when it was the richest city in Canada. Extended across the square to the mouth of the Lachine Canal in the 1870s, rue Saint-Pierre was soon lined with massive beaux arts buildings that served as warehouses and factories for a self-satisfied city flexing its economic muscle.

One of those fine old buildings holds the **Musée Marc-Aurèle Fortin,** devoted to the maverick Québec artist (1888–1970) whose unique style of landscape painting synthesized expressionism and postimpressionism. Many of his works contain strongly outlined figures, an effect he accomplished by painting over canvas or board first prepared with black or gray paint. Critical acclaim for the most part eluded Fortin, and when he died thousands of unsold paintings were reportedly destroyed. A revival of interest in figurative art has rehabilitated his reputation, and the museum displays a significant number of surviving works. On a few summer Sundays, rue Saint-Pierre is closed to traffic and transformed into a enormous studio en plein air as artists set up their easels to imagine landscapes à la Fortin. *1118 rue Saint-Pierre; 514-845-6108.*

■ PLACE JACQUES-CARTIER AND RUE SAINT-PAUL

Like a court jester leavening the ponderous affairs of state, Place Jacques-Cartier is a burst of color against the gray limestone backdrop of Old Montréal. Originally the domain of an eighteenth-century governor, the large open tract became available for development when the fire of 1803 leveled the château and ruined the gardens. Developers sprang to build new stone hotels and shops around the periphery, and the city kept the center open as a market. It remained as such until the 1960s, when it was repaved with stone and transformed into a mostly pedestrian area designed to serve tourism. In anticipation of the Expo '67 world's fair, the city began to license outdoor cafés.

Only the Nelson Column hints that this 1894 market was held on Place Jacques-Cartier.

Ice cream, coffee, and pastry are essential in the Montréal diet.

When viewed from the river at night, the oldest city buildings vanish beneath the business district's towers.

The area's tourism aspirations succeeded, perhaps even beyond the grandiose dreams of then-mayor Jean Drapeau. Virtually every building on the square holds a restaurant with an outdoor terrace for a front-row view of the peripatetic musicians, magicians, balloon-twisters, and mimes. Get a hair wrap or a temporary tattoo, sit for a caricaturist attuned to your least flattering feature, or get your face painted. During warm weather, Place Jacques-Cartier is a nonstop outdoor fair.

In 1809, Montréal businessmen displayed their loyalty to the British empire by raising the ten-meter-high **Nelson Column** at the head of Place Jacques-Cartier. The long-winded inscription on the west side of the column's base is virtually a journalistic account of Nelson's victory at Trafalgar, which established British naval dominance over the combined French and Spanish fleets.

Posterity has shown somewhat less awe. A fiberglass replica has replaced the original statue of Nelson, which had to be spirited into storage in 1981 after several attacks by vandals. In one of the more primitive forms of entertainment on Place Jacques-Cartier, an aging gentleman ties a tin can to the iron grate protecting the column. From various points on rue Notre-Dame, dodging traffic all the while, he proceeds to whack a hockey puck into the can and periodically takes up a collection so that onlookers may show their appreciation of his scoring skills.

Few of the lanes that once led off Place Jacques-Cartier remain, though **rue Saint-Amable** on the square's west side persists as a busy gallery of street artists and photographers. Cutting across Place Jacques-Cartier is the handsome **rue Saint-Paul,** a route so venerable it predates the 1672 street design. Named in honor of Paul de Chomedy, Sieur de Maisonneuve, it evolved as the de facto center of commerce in the earliest days of the colony because it stood high and dry above the spring floods. Merchants built their receiving docks and warehouse entries by the river but extended the buildings uphill to create shop entrances on rue Saint-Paul.

The blocks immediately west of Place Jacques-Cartier constitute a classic tourist zone, where eager buyers encounter equally eager purveyors of food, trinkets, and souvenirs. Amid the shops vending T-shirts that say "Good girls go to heaven, bad girls go to Montréal" are a number of good restaurants and a sprinkling of twenty-first-century boutique hotels. **Les Delices de l'Érable** (84 rue Saint-Paul est; 514-765-3456) specializes in maple products such as maple syrup mousse and truffles filled with maple syrup ganache. Once you cross boulevard Saint-Laurent, the hucksterism of rue Saint-Paul subsides as souvenir shops give way to art galleries, designer clothing boutiques, and small cafés, coffee shops, and bakeries—including **Boulangerie Olive & Gourmando** (351 rue Saint-Paul ouest; 514-350-1083), baker of exquisite breads and croissants.

The silvery dome of Marché Bonsecours is a landmark in Old Montréal.

Without abandoning its mercantile ways, rue Saint-Paul assumes more decorum east of Place Jacques-Cartier. The small crafts gallery **L'empreinte** (272 rue Saint-Paul est; 514-861-4427) represents more than 70 Québec craftspeople who create everything from knitted clothing to art glass to jewelry, puppets, and salad bowls. Probably the best single place to shop on rue Saint-Paul is **Marché Bonsecours** (350 rue Saint-Paul est;

514-872-7730), immediately recognizable by its hundred-foot-high silver dome. Constructed in grand neoclassical style between 1844 and 1847, the building has been a public market, concert hall, the House of Parliament for United Canada, and, from 1852 to 1878, Montréal's city hall. Until the 1950s, Bonsecours was the primary fresh food market of the city, but today it's an upscale shopping center, with several boutiques located on the rue Saint-Paul level. **Boutique Diffusion Griff 3000** (514-398-0761) is devoted to pret-a-porter from Québec couturiers. The **Galerie de l'Institut de Design de Montréal** (514-866-1255, ext. 21) focuses on cutting-edge contemporary design in consumer products, and the **Conseil des métiers d'art du Québec** (514-878-2787) champions fine arts in crafts media by Québec artists through a series of changing exhibitions.

"If the love of Mary is engraved in your heart, as you pass by don't forget to say an *Ave Maria*" reads the inscription over the door of **Chapelle Notre-Dame-de-Bon-Secours,** near the east end of rue Saint-Paul. The first chapel on this site was erected in 1657 under the direction of Marguerite Bourgeoys, who had it rebuilt in stone in 1675. That church burned in 1754, but its 1771 replacement still stands and is known as "the sailors' chapel." For generations, mariners have paused beneath the reassuring closeness of its single barrel vault to pray for a safe voyage; no doubt they take heart from the ship models suspended from the ceiling, ex-votos of thanksgiving for perils survived.

A dramatic tower was added to the chapel in 1893 and topped with a six-meter-high statue of open-armed Mary, Star of the Sea, flanked by two herald angels. As viewed from the Old Port, the Virgin is such a dominating presence that she is known as "Our Lady of the Harbour"—dubbed so by Leonard Cohen in the pop song "Suzanne." The view from the angels' shoulders lures many people to visit the **Musée Marguerite-Bourgeoys,** dedicated to the founder of the Congrégation de Notre-Dame, who came to be called "the mother of the colony." Bourgeoys was canonized by the Roman Catholic Church in 1982 and led such a fascinating life that visitors shouldn't need the enticement of the belvedere to visit the museum. From her arrival in 1653, when she began teaching young women to read, until her death in 1700 surrounded by the sisters of her order, she organized the educational system, shepherded and safeguarded the young women sent from France to marry and populate the colony, sent teachers to native villages, and made seven voyages across the Atlantic Ocean—all in an era in which few women ever left their

Singer Céline Dion was married in the Basilique de Notre-Dame de Montréal.

MAISON SAINT-GABRIEL

When Marguerite Bourgeoys founded the Congrégation de Notre-Dame, she had no idea where support for her sisters would come from, only that God would provide. When she purchased the rural farmhouse of François Le Ber in 1668, she dubbed the property on Pointe Saint-Charles "La Providence." Now surrounded by post-industrial suburbs, it remains the home of the Congrégation. Since 1966 the nuns have operated the farmhouse as a museum of seventeenth-century life, with an emphasis on the order's self-sufficiency and its role as protector of the *filles du roy*—the young women given dowries by the king and sent to New France to marry. The girls had little idea at first of how to survive in a wilderness colony, but a stint with the Congrégation provided them the necessary skills. As Sister Emilia Chicoine wrote in her 1986 biography of Bourgeoys, "To prepare varied meals from unvarying ingredients—bread, bacon, peas, eels, corn, pumpkin; pumpkin, corn, eels, peas, bacon, bread—required a good dose of ingenuity." The rooms and furnishings of the farmhouse museum have an austere beauty, and tours in French and English give extensive details about the daily life of the order and of its charges. Among the most poignant artifacts is a *coffre d'esperance*, or hope chest, made of cedar and filled with embroidered linens. *2146 Place Dublin, Pointe-Saint-Charles; 514-935-8136. Open April–late December.*

homes. During extensive renovations in the 1990s, archaeological excavations unearthed the foundations of the first stone chapel as well as a rich array of artifacts. *400 rue Saint-Paul est; 514-282-8670.*

Directly across rue Saint-Paul from the chapel and museum is the low, rough stone **Maison de Pierre du Calvet.** A sign on the building proclaims that it was built in 1725 and is the oldest private house in the city open for public accommodation (it houses an excellent inn). Other sources insist that the house was not constructed until 1771—which might not matter to a casual visitor but makes all the difference to a French Canadian, for whom a thick black line is drawn between everything pre-1760 (the French regime) or post-1760 (after the British conquest). Popular tradition holds that young women sent to the colony by the king would come to this building to meet potential suitors in a respectable environment. Arguments over the age and "authenticity" of the house are probably moot, as the building represents a labyrinth of eras and construction techniques. The best way to get a peek is to book a room or reserve for dinner or weekend brunch in the restaurant. *405 rue de Bonsecours; 514-282-1725.*

■ RUE DE LA COMMUNE AND VIEUX PORT

Montréal winters can be long and severe, and in the colony's early days, settlers spent the season penned up inside the palisades. But when the snow began to melt and a March sun hinted at the possibility of spring, it was a tradition for Montrealers to leave the walls and stroll the riverbank. Once the grass greened up, the livestock would be turned out there to pasture, and later still, the fur traders would drag their freight canoes onto shore to buy, sell, and celebrate outside the walls. The strip of greenery between the walls and the shore was the common, and the harbor pathway eventually became **rue de la Commune,** the thoroughfare between Old Montréal and the Old Port.

When Montréal tore down its fortifications in the early nineteenth century, the footings of the walls served as the foundations for a new generation of warehouses and factories, resulting in one of the few curving routes in the grid of Old Montréal streets. By the mid-twentieth century, manufacturing and shipping had moved from the cramped quarters of Old Montréal eastward to the neighborhoods of Hochelaga

The handsome buildings of the Old Port stand like so many soldiers at attention.

A grain elevator towers over the Old Port.

and Maisonneuve. When the Lachine Canal closed in 1970, Montréal's Vieux Port seemed moribund.

But the former common still had potential, and the city moved to clean up the district and convert the ancient pasture into a green park that stretches two-and-one-half kilometers along the river. The **Parc de Vieux-Port** opened on June 23, 1981, one day before Saint-Jean-Baptiste Day: the unofficial beginning of summer in Québec. Those seventeenth-century pioneers would be astounded to see how the Vieux Port teems today with joggers, walkers, roller bladers, cyclists, and scooter riders. The occasional Great Lakes freighter still passes on the outer harbor, cruise ships and yachts call at the piers, and ferries and sightseeing boats skitter around the inner harbor like waterbugs.

The revival of the waterfront brought about a similar renaissance for rue de la Commune. The sturdy warehouses proved ideal for restaurants where diners at outdoor tables drink in the ambience of the new waterfront and for boutique hotel rooms with both ancient stone walls and high-speed Internet.

Quai de l'Horloge defines the eastern edge of the Vieux Port. Most of the wharf is devoted to a huge parking lot, but it is also home to the high-tech sightseeing-boat tour company, **Saute Moutons** (514-284-9607), which designed the shallow-draft, jet-powered boats it uses to splash around in the Lachine Rapids.

The **Tour de l'Horloge**, or Clock Tower, sits on the far end of the pier and marks the entrance to the inner harbor. This memorial to the sailors lost in World War I was completed in 1922. Panels and photos along the 135 winding steps to the works relate the history of the port. Among the milestones: John Molson inaugurated the first steamboat service between Montréal and Québec in 1809; the last timber raft floated through the harbor in 1911; and in 1964, a merchant vessel reached the port in January, inaugurating year-round shipping. Another 56 steps lead to a lookout with views of the Jacques Cartier bridge, the Molson breweries, and the roller coaster and Ferris wheel of La Ronde amusement park on Île Sainte-Hélène. *514-496-7678. Tower open May–October.*

Bassin Bonsecours, between Quai de l'Horloge and Quai Jacques-Cartier, is filled with pedal-boaters in the summer and gliding ice skaters in the winter. Crafts and antiques shows are often set up on the broad expanse of Quai Jacques-Cartier, which also serves as the departure point for ferries to Parc Jean-Drapeau and the south-shore suburb of Longueil. The Parisian-style excursion boat **Le Bateau Mouche** (514-849-9952) also docks at Jacques-Cartier. The glass-enclosed boat draws less than two feet of water, enabling it to cruise parts of the river too shallow for other craft.

By contrast, the deep-water cruise ships that ply the St. Lawrence River and the North Atlantic Coast call at the **Gare Maritime Iberville** at Quai Alexandra. They tower over the docks, nearly as tall as the derelict grain elevators nearby. Keep their dimensions in mind as you walk to the Lachine Canal's Lock No. 1 at the west end of the port. The cruise ships dwarf the lock, graphically illustrating why the canal went out of business.

Skaters take to the ice at Bassin Bonsecours, where pedal-boaters frolic in summer. (following pages) A shady bicycle path runs along the river's edge.

■ CHAMPS DE MARS AND RUE NOTRE-DAME EST

Old Montréal crept from the riverbank up the slope of the Coteau Saint-Louis, a ridge that rises to a narrow plateau and then drops off to the broad gully where rue Saint-Antoine and the Autoroute 720 are now located. The plateau marked the northern limits of the old city fortifications; footings of the 1744 bastions, which were taken down between 1804 and 1817, were discovered during construction excavations in 1965.

The British military used the public promenade of **Champs de Mars** at the head of Place Jacques-Cartier as a parade ground. Henry David Thoreau watched "a large body of soldiers being drilled" when he visited Montréal in 1850. "They made on me the impression, not of many individuals," he wrote in *A Yankee in Canada,* "but of one vast centipede of a man." Throughout the nineteenth century, Champs de Mars served as the city's central gathering point for everything from public executions and mob rallies to political stem-winders, but was paved over as a parking lot in 1913. Following restoration of the fortifications, it reopened as a public park in 1992. During the summer, French Marine reenactors from Musée Stewart at Fort Île-Sainte-Hélène demonstrate eighteenth-century musket drills on Champs de Mars.

The grand Second Empire–style gray stone structure with green copper roof that towers above Champs de Mars is the city hall, or **Hôtel de Ville,** which faces rue Notre-Dame. The three lower levels, with their pavilions, columns, and formal window arcades, date from the 1878 building, which was gutted by fire in 1922. Left with only a fine formal shell, the city rebuilt, adding another story, the high copper roof, and the lantern cupola in 1926. Even if you have no business to transact, take a look at the soaring interior, decorated with imported marble and travertine. During his official visit to Montréal in 1967—on which he deliberately skipped the Canadian national capital of Ottawa—French President Charles de Gaulle made his famous "Vive le Québec libre!" speech from the balcony, touching on a sore spot in provincial-federal relations with an apparent exhortation to secession. *275 rue Notre-Dame est; 514-972-3355.*

De Gaulle's enthusiasm might have been explained by the splendor around him. Although the capital of Québec province lies in Québec City, not Montréal, the Hôtel de Ville and its surrounding court buildings certainly create the impression of an official seat of government. The **Vieux Palais de Justice** (155 rue Notre-Dame est), inspired by London's main post office, is a model of somber classicism.

The 1856 courthouse was replaced in 1925 by what is now the **Cour d'appel du Québec** (100 rue Notre-Dame est), where local architect Ernest Cormier married art deco decoration to neoclassical pomp. The seventeen-story **Palais de Justice** (1 rue Notre-Dame est), a modernist structure that postdates de Gaulle's visit, now handles all criminal and civil cases. These edifices appear their most majestic at night, when the landmark buildings of Old Montréal are bathed in dramatic illumination.

Directly across from the Hôtel de Ville, the small **Place de la Dauversière** is a popular gathering spot for exhausted tourists who'd rather not pay to sit at a café in Place Jacques-Cartier. A bronze countenance of Jean Drapeau presides over the park, a modest homage to the man who transformed Montréal from a scrappy river town into a world-class city during his reigns as mayor—from 1954 to 1957 and 1960 to 1986.

Rue Notre-Dame est has also been the home of many powerful politicians. Next door to the park, **Château Ramezay** was constructed in 1705 for the governor of Montréal, Claude de Ramezay. But even a governor couldn't muster the fortune necessary to maintain the exquisite château, and this one went broke trying. In

The Hôtel de Ville, Montréal's city hall, sits at the head of Place Jacques-Cartier.

Display rooms at Château Ramezay interpret domestic life in Montréal over the centuries.

1745, the building was sold to La Compagnie des Indies, which doubled the size of the property and used it as a key site in its far-flung network of trading posts. The most elegant French-regime mansion still standing in the city, the building housed the command of rebel American troops when they occupied Montréal in the winter of 1775–76. Since 1895, the château has been a history museum, telling Montréal's tale from 1535 to about 1905 with more than 30,000 artifacts. Although the museum is open all year, the gardens in back are at their best in the summer. Though they do not replicate Governor Ramezay's spread, they are arrayed in a formal French style of the eighteenth century, with discrete sections of vegetables, fruit trees, and ornamental plants and flowers. It's easy to imagine how idyllic the city must have been in 1731, when Montréal boasted 186 gardens. The summer café overlooking the gardens has a menu by celebrated local chef Claude Postel. *280 rue Notre-Dame est; 514-861-3708.*

The **Papineau House,** on the corner of rue Bonsecours and rue Notre-Dame, is one of the few houses in Old Montréal with a wooden facade, although it is incised and painted to look like stone—perhaps in deference to the proclamations of 1721 and 1727 requiring all new construction within the city walls to be made of fireproof materials. The house was built in 1785 and was the birthplace, eleven years later, of the lawyer and politician Louis-Joseph Papineau, leader of the French-Canadian nationalism movement until the Patriots' Rebellion of 1837. When the journalist Eric McLean bought and restored the building in 1961, he set off a wave of historic preservation in Old Montréal that continues to the present. Now owned by the government of Canada, the building is a candidate to become a national historic site, but it is currently not open to the public.

A block east on rue Notre-Dame, the former home of one of the "fathers of Confederation" has been transformed by Parks Canada into the **Georges-Étienne Cartier National Historic Site of Canada.** Constructed in 1837 as a classic Old Montréal side-by-side duplex, the east side commemorates Cartier's political life and achievements: abolishing the French system of land ownership by absentee lords, reforming the educational system, and establishing a new civil code for Québec inspired by the Napoleonic Code. As head of the Conservative Party, he shared leadership of the United Province of Canada with Liberal Party chief John A. Macdonald for most of the decade from 1857 until Confederation in 1867, and served as minister of militia and defense in the first cabinet of the newly defined country.

The west side of the house depicts the lifestyle of the nineteenth-century Montréal bourgeoisie. The drawing room with blue velvet curtains contains a table set for tea; the grand parlor is laid out for a dinner party. Recorded commentaries in each room make it seem as if a gossipy servant is whispering in your ear. "He hardly ever comes in here, even when he is at home," reveals the chambermaid in Madame Cartier's gold-brocaded boudoir. *458 rue Notre-Dame est; 514-283-2282.*

■ PLACE D'ARMES

Nowhere in Old Montréal do history and myth so intermingle as on **Place d'Armes,** a few blocks west along rue Notre-Dame from Champs de Mars. Four centuries of architecture surround the square and the flags of Québec, Canada, and Montréal fly overhead. The first bank organized in Canada, the Banque de Montréal, dominates the north side, and the Basilique de Notre-Dame de Montréal, the south. Caught between the powers of money and faith is a tribute to city founder Maisonneuve. The debacle behind the fund-raising for the **Maisonneuve Monument** is given in detail by the garrulous Montréal journalist

Alan Hustak in his self-described "opinionated" walking-tour guide, *Exploring Old Montreal.* When plans were announced in 1884, France had just donated the Statue of Liberty to New York and Montréal officials presumed that France would pony up along the same lines for their city, given that Maisonneuve was both born and buried in France. But apparently no one ever asked the French government, which ultimately sent a draft for 500 francs—a bit more than ninety-five Canadian dollars. The plans were scaled back.

The monument wasn't ready for the city's 250th anniversary celebration in 1892, but when it was unveiled in 1895, it was studded with symbolism. Four statues project from the corners of the base: Jeanne Mance, who founded the hospitals; fur trader Charles LeMoyne; an unidentified Iroquois brave; and the colony's military leader, Lambert Closse. The dog beside Closse is Pilotte, a beloved figure of city lore who allegedly patrolled the streets every morning, sniffing for traces of the hostile Iroquois. If she discovered any signs, she would run yapping back to the fort to alert the colonists. According to legend, she trained her pups in the same vigilance, making the dogs integral to the survival of the colony. Alas, the dogs could not save Closse, who died in battle with the Iroquois outside the fort in 1662.

Driven by faith and missionary zeal, Maisonneuve was not a man to be deterred by fear of the native people. The west side of the monument records his declaration, "I am determined to go even if every tree on the island turns into an Iroquois." A plaque across from Place d'Armes, on rue Saint-Jacques, memorializes the founder's personal victory over an Iroquois brave in man-to-man combat on the square. In a dramatic demonstration of clashing technologies, the Iroquois reportedly came at Maisonneuve with a knife. The Frenchman drew his pistol and shot him dead.

The oldest building on Place d'Armes is the **Seminaire de Saint-Sulpice,** the original seminary of the Sulpicians. Its central portion was constructed in 1685, and the wings were erected in the first decades of the eighteenth century. The clock face dates from 1701, though the works are far more modern. Having bought the entire island of Montréal from the French crown in 1663 for 100,000 *livres,* the Sulpician order ran Montréal as their feudal fiefdom. When the British took over Québec, the crafty Sulpicians negotiated the right for the populace to continue practicing the Roman Catholic faith. They fared less well within the Byzantine

A statue honoring Montréal co-founder Paul de Chomedy, Sieur de Maisonneuve, dominates Place d'Armes.

SANCTUARY

The five-thirty mass at Notre Dame had just ended as Myra stepped through the wooden doors, the faithful long gone, with the exception of a few desperate souls who stayed late to petition the Lord in solitude. The janitor had turned off the main lights, and the basilica was lit by hundreds of small candles, each one representing private agony, a fervent hope. Though she stopped going to mass ages ago, annoyed by the puerile sermons, she sometimes slips into a church after hours. An empty church is an ideal place to think or just sit with an empty mind and breathe in the vastness. The building is magnificent.

Tonight she wanders along the side pews, past a statue of St-Joseph, the model father, and a faintly disturbing painting of Ste-Marguerite Bourgeoys sitting beside lusty-eyed native children. She kneels to light a candle at the shrine of St-Jude, patron saint of hopeless causes, closes her eyes and feels her speeding heart grow calm. There need not be a God to make this landmark a sacred place. There need only be people gathered together in search of something, a feeling they've lost or suspect they have missed.

—Marianne Ackerman, *Jump,* 2001

world of church politics. They lost much of their power to the Jesuits when the Archdiocese of Québec created a Jesuit-controlled Diocese of Montréal in 1823. The building is now one of the order's residences and is not open to the public, but it's worth taking a look at the outside. *116 rue Notre-Dame ouest.*

The Sulpician fathers did make one last in-your-face gesture to their rivals, replacing their modest house of worship with the glorious **Basilique de Notre-Dame de Montréal,** which opened as the largest church in North America. When the New York City architect James O'Donnell was approached to design Notre-Dame, he wrote to the Sulpicians, "You should keep in mind that you are not erecting a temporary building but rather a monument that will bring glory to yourselves, to your assembly, and to your country."

O'Donnell based his Gothic Revival design on London's Westminster Abbey and St.-Martin-in-the-Fields, but brought modern engineering mathematics to the task of creating what was, at the time, one of the largest vaulted roofs in the world. Construction began in 1824, and though the two towers were not completed until

1839, O'Donnell was apparently satisfied with the structure when it was inaugurated in 1829. He converted to Catholicism and was buried in the crypt in 1830. Church-goers, however, found the bare stone interior too "Protestant," and the church engaged Victor Bourgeau in 1845 to overhaul the decoration, a task that occupied him on and off until his death in 1888. Whatever the perceived shortcomings of the decor, visitors were definitely wowed, and the basilica was among the top two or three tourist attractions in Canada at the end of the nineteenth century.

Other places in Canada rack up more impressive numbers these days, but in the "city of 100 spires," as Montréal is often called, the basilica stands alone as the home church for the entire populace. On Saturdays and Sundays, the faithful come to Mass, and frequent concerts showcase the rich tones of the 1891 Casavant organ, with its seven thousand pipes. The vast nave is where the major rituals are played out, such as the wedding of musical superstar Céline Dion and the funerals of hockey great Maurice Richard and former prime minister Pierre Elliott Trudeau. (At Trudeau's funeral, former president Jimmy Carter and Premier Fidel Castro shared a pew and laid the groundwork for Carter's later visit to Havana.)

But most marriages—as well as christenings, funerals, and weekday Masses—take place in the more intimate Chapelle Sacré-Coeur behind the main altar. The chapel is in such demand that wedding dates must be reserved eighteen months in advance. Montrealers joke that once the bride has made a reservation, she may change the groom but not the date. *110 rue Notre-Dame ouest; 514-842-2925.*

No other building on Place d'Armes can rival Notre-Dame for sheer grandeur, but a few try. The **Banque de Montréal,** founded in 1817 and the oldest bank in Canada, erected a monumental neoclassical building in 1847, and the interior was decorated in 1905 in a sumptuous Italian Renaissance style from designs by New York architect Stanford White. Its vaulted ceilings, marble statuary, veined marble walls, and gold-plated capitals on thirty-two towering Corinthian columns make it as much a temple as the basilica it faces across the square. *119 rue Saint-Jacques ouest; 514-877-6810.*

The east side of the square features two landmarks. The red sandstone **New York Life Insurance** building, constructed 1887–1888, was the city's first skyscraper. No one seems to know when the clock stopped at 1:53. The graceful 1931 **Aldred Building** seems much less imposing than you'd expect from a twenty-three-story

(following pages) Le Mondial SAQ fireworks competition at La Ronde.

structure, thanks to progressive setbacks that let sunshine into the square. Viewed from Pointe-à-Callière, the steps of the art deco Aldred perfectly echo the crenellations in the roof of Notre-Dame. The final structure on Place d'Armes is a run-of-the-mill black glass skyscraper completed in 1967—a missed architectural opportunity for such a significant site.

■ Rue Saint-Jacques and Old Business District

You might find the business district west of Place d'Armes hauntingly familiar. Moviemakers regularly cast the Victorian architecture of these blocks as nineteenth-century London or New York. It's not uncommon to stumble on a film crew shooting on rue Saint-Jacques or rue François-Xavier, where the old stock exchange now houses the city's premier English-language theatrical stage, the **Centaur** (453 rue François-Xavier; 514-288-3161). For touches of antiquity, the crews film the sidewalks of rue Sainte-Hélène, the only street in the city with gaslights, albeit faux antiques.

The French laid their claim at Pointe-à-Callière, but by the mid-nineteenth century the British proclaimed their financial might. This west end of Old Montréal was the first section of the city to undergo "urban renewal." Between 1820 and 1840, the French-regime buildings began to be replaced by four- and five-story structures in the Chicago style, with small factories on the upper levels and wholesale showrooms at street level. By 1880, most evidence of the French regime had vanished. Meanwhile, the Lachine Canal and the railroads had made Montréal the link between interior North America and the Atlantic seaboard, and Montréal was burgeoning as a manufacturing and import-export center.

Lined with banks and brokerages, rue Saint-Jacques (known as Saint James Street to the English-speaking moneymen) was once the Wall Street of Canada. The flight of commerce and banking to Toronto during the surge of Québec nationalism in the 1960s and 1970s, however, left many of the buildings along rue Saint-Jacques as mere token headquarters. Still, aficionados of architectural detail will find exuberant stone carvings and beautiful brass work on almost every building. A family crest of carved Ohio sandstone surmounts the entrance of the **Molson Bank Building** (288 rue Saint-Jacques ouest). The Molsons may be best known for beer—their ale has been a smash hit since the family founder, John Molson, sold the first pints for five cents each in 1786—but the family made additional fortunes in steamships, railways, and banking. Indeed, John Molson

GHOSTS OF THE ANCIEN RÉGIME

Even the self-confident Victorian factories and warehouses that displaced the French domains cannot erase the past. Shades of the old Norman farmhouse architecture persist as images frozen into later walls. The parking lot on rue François-Xavier at the end of rue Saint-Sacrament is perhaps the best place to commune with the spirits. Embedded in brick is the sharp profile of an eighteenth-century gray stone house, unmistakable in its high and narrow proportions and its steeply pitched roofline. All that's missing is the tin roof itself, which would have had a bellcast curve to shed snow and ice off the broad-hipped eaves. Amateur historians can date the age of these stone structures by how the stone was cut. The rougher the edges and more irregular the size, the earlier it was quarried.

pioneered currency exchange by purchasing banknotes at a discount in Montréal and shipping them to Québec on his steamships to exchange them for hard currency, which he would then bring back to Montréal to buy more banknotes. In 1817 he founded his own bank to handle such exchanges and to fund other businesses. In 1866, his heirs built this handsome structure as a monument to their wealth.

The crown jewel of the street is the twenty-three-story **Banque Royale du Canada,** which was the tallest building in the British Empire when it was erected in 1928. The building is open around the clock, so you can visit anytime to see the soaring arches and vaulted ceiling, the marble mosaic floor, and the coats of arms of the six provinces that existed at the time the bank was built. It may actually outdo the Banque de Montréal for sheer opulence. *360 rue Saint-Jacques; 514-874-2959.*

Catercorner to the sumptuous bank is another former bank building: the graceful 1870 structure that now houses the boutique **Hôtel Le St-James** (355 rue Saint-Jacques ouest; 514-841-3111). The hotel is but the southeast corner of a vast block redeveloped in the late twentieth century as the **Centre de commerce mondial de Montréal** (393 rue Saint-Jacques ouest; 514-849-1999), or World Trade Centre of Montréal. The complex embraces several other venerable facades as well as the modern **Hôtel InterContinental** (360 rue Saint-Antoine ouest; 514-987-9900). Even former streets are subsumed by the center. A glass arcade glorifies an erstwhile alley; on its floor, lines trace the limits of the original city walls.

LACHINE CANAL
AND RAPIDS

Forty-five people scream with one voice as a ten-foot wave crashes over the boat in what the captain has warned will be a "brain wash." Frothing and bubbling, the green wall of water smacks onto the open deck as passengers spit and spout and gasp for air. Moments later they each raise a hand, fingers extended in the universal "victory" sign. The boat tosses and turns like a sneaker in a washing machine, shipping water over the side as the engines roar and sputter and roar again and the boat shakes free of a whirlpool into the comparatively tranquil suction of a chute between two rocks.

"Jamais je ne vis un torrent d'eau déborder avec une telle impétuosité," wrote Samuel de Champlain in 1603. "Never did I see such a wildly raging torrent of water." The great explorer was echoing the words of his predecessor, Jacques Cartier, who described the Lachine Rapids in 1535 as *"le sault d'eau le plus impétueux qu'il est possible de veoir"*—"the wildest rapids you can see anywhere." Little could either imagine that by the dawn of the twenty-first century, a wild ride on the rapids in a jet-powered boat would become one of Montréal's most popular tourist attractions.

This is a ride on history, for the rapids explain why Montréal is where it is. Essentially a waterfall in the midst of the St. Lawrence River just west of the port of Montréal, the Lachine Rapids are Class V whitewater studded with huge rocky ledges and laced with whirlpools. Intrepid fur traders would brave the currents to carry their cargoes downriver, then portage their canoes upriver to head back into the continental interior. But larger vessels, which might have sailed all the way from Europe and 1,000 miles up the St. Lawrence, could not pass. That made the harbor at Pointe-à-Callière the westernmost anchorage for oceangoing ships. Recognizing this strategic location, Champlain chose the spot to establish his fur-trading post in 1611, and Maisonneuve followed suit in siting Ville-Marie. Montréal quickly assumed economic dominance as the transfer station between the small craft of the upper-river system and the shipping vessels of the European trade.

The Lachine Canal finally bypassed the rapids in the first quarter of the nineteenth century, just as the fur trade ebbed in Montréal. By permitting ships to step

A Saute-Moutons jet boat splashes through the tumultuous Lachine Rapids.

through the forty-three-foot difference in river levels between Montréal and Lachine, the canal opened up shipping on the upper St. Lawrence, and through other canals and locks, the entire Great Lakes. Wheat and timber flowed through Montréal, making the city one of the great shipping ports of the world.

■ LACHINE CANAL

Almost from the beginnings of Montréal, visionaries dreamed of building a canal to bypass the Lachine Rapids. The first father superior of the Sulpicians floated the idea in 1670, and his successor, the former soldier and engineer François Dollier de Casson, actually put canal excavators to work in 1689. A man ahead of his time, de Casson reasoned that the canal not only would ease upriver shipping, but also could provide waterpower to Montréal's mills. An Iroquois attack halted the venture; another attempt in 1700 dissolved when de Casson died and the contractor went bankrupt. But economic competition from the Erie Canal project—and the accompanying fear that New York might dominate the Great Lakes trade—finally spurred completion of the Lachine Canal. Unable to finance the scheme, Montréal merchants turned it over to the Province of Lower Canada (later, Québec) in 1821. Construction proceeded in a race with Erie and both canals opened in 1825. Running approximately fourteen kilometers between the port of Montréal and Lac Saint-Louis, the Lachine Canal revolutionized trade on the river, though it would have to be twice enlarged to handle bigger ships.

True to de Casson's prediction, the waterpower generated along the canal proved a boon to industry. Even as Montréal expanded its role as a shipping point for grain, lumber, and other materials from the interior, it was growing into an industrial powerhouse with the greatest concentration of heavy industry in the country. Shipyards; flour and sugar mills; and silk, paper, and steel mills were just some of the more than eight hundred concerns that operated along the canal over the years, giving Montréal the moniker "Smoky Valley." Working-class neighborhoods grew up beside the factories—particularly French-Canadian Saint-Henri on the north side of the canal and heavily Irish Pointe-Saint-Charles on the south.

At the peak of usage, just before the stock-market crash of 1929, approximately fifteen thousand ships a year—an average of more than forty per day—passed through the Lachine Canal. The opening of the St. Lawrence Seaway in 1959

Five placid locks enable boats to safely bypass the Lachine Rapids.

The Lost World of Saint-Henri

It was a quarter of contrasts, like no other, thought Emmanuel. Here the eye fell on a thick cluster of roofs under a rain of soot; there a tree grew out of the cement sidewalk like a miracle. Farther off a fountain rippled in a sleepy square. On one side it was pretentious and middle-class, with its three-story buildings and spiral staircases, but over there a small house in the native style gallantly clung to its rustic airs and graces, with a barrel hoop over the gate in the guise of a trellis.

Over yonder freighters, tankers, tugboats, flatboats, and Great Lakes barges went sailing by, carrying wares from the four corners of the earth: huge Norwegian pines, Ceylon tea, the spices of India and nuts from Brazil. But on Convent Street, when the church bells rang for vespers and the nuns passed two by two behind a grille, Saint-Henri might have been any small provincial town.

During the day it knew a life of relentless toil. In the evening it had its village life, when folks gathered on their doorsteps or brought their chairs to the sidewalk and exchanged gossip from door to door.

Saint-Henri: an antheap with the soul of a village!

—Gabrielle Roy, *The Tin Flute,* 1947

spelled the end for the Lachine, whose locks were too small to accommodate immense oceangoing freighters and container ships. Closed in 1970, the canal was largely abandoned and even partially filled with dirt excavated in an expansion of the Métro system.

In 1978, a bicycle path opened along the canal banks, and a bicycle remains one of the best ways to see the historic canal and the handsome old buildings of the industrial corridor. The path begins at the intersection of rues McGill and de la Commune, at the west end of Montréal's Old Port, where the first two of five canal locks account for twenty-five of the total forty-three-foot difference in water levels between Montréal and Lachine.

Following a five-year restoration project, the canal reopened in 2002 to recreational vessels that can putter around at a no-wake maximum speed of ten kilometers per hour. A small boating center has developed just south of **Atwater Market,** a 1933 public market that has enjoyed the same kind of gentrification as the working-class neighborhoods along the canal. Tables that used to overflow with beets, turnips, potatoes, and onions now also hold chervil, endive, chile peppers, and star fruit. Specialty boutiques include seven butcher shops (one of which sells only sausages), a fish market, several bakers, and a cheese specialist. A gourmet can start the day here with a baguette split and grilled and smeared with a few slices of house pâtés or terrines. Atwater Market lies due south of the Lionel-Groulx Métro station. *138 avenue Atwater; 514-937-7754.*

On the Pointe-Saint-Charles side of the pedestrian bridge south of the market, **Ruban Bleu** (beneath Atwater bridge; 514-938-4448) rents electric boats, kayaks, and pedal boats that let you explore the canal on your own. On the north side, you can buy a ticket for **L'Éclusier** (mid-May to mid-October, corner of avenue Atwater and rue Saint-Ambroise; 514-846-0428), a biodiesel-powered Amsterdam-style canal boat that goes west as far as the Saint-Paul lock and then east to Bassin Peel near the Old Port. The craft passes twice through the Saint-Gabriel lock, where the cruise boat is raised or lowered eight feet when twenty-ton pine gates on one end or the other are opened to let the lock fill or empty. The process takes only ten minutes, but because the lock can accommodate up to twenty-five small craft, you might wait as long as a half hour as all the boats jockey into place.

On the east side of the Saint-Gabriel lock, the **Redpath** sugar refinery buildings arc across the canal's whole timeline. In 1854, the refinery was the largest industrial structure in Montréal—no small achievement given that its founder, John Redpath, had worked as a mason on the construction of the canal a generation earlier. The

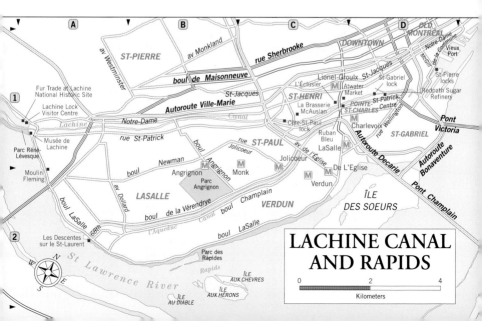

In the 1870s, the Lachine Canal was expanded to accommodate canaliers, *special freight vessels that could handle loads up to 2,000 tons.*

A bicycle path now follows the length of the Lachine Canal.

striking redbrick complex, consisting mostly of buildings constructed after 1890, closed in 1980 when the company moved to Toronto. Today the buildings are being converted to residential and commercial lofts and condominiums.

From the boat docks, the bike path continues west for flat pedaling interrupted only by the occasional need to cross an arched bridge over the canal. You might want to pause for refreshment at the canal-side café of **La Brasserie McAuslan** (4850 rue Saint-Ambroise, No. 100; 514-939-3060), which crafts St-Ambroise and Griffon beers in a former textile factory. As you pedal west, you'll pass two more locks—Saint-Paul and Saint-Pierre—as well as the old Lasalle Coke Crane, used to unload barges carrying coal and coke to fuel the factories. Representing the interdependence of industry and shipping, the crane has become an unofficial symbol of the canal and is being restored by Parks Canada.

At the western end of the canal, the formerly independent town of Lachine has been a leafy, prosperous arrondissement of Montréal since a 2002 merger that incorporated all the communities on the island into the City of Montréal. The **Lachine Lock Visitor Service Centre** has a permanent exhibition on the history of the canal and the industries that sprang up on its banks. Perhaps because this

QUÉBEC BREWS

Although Louis Prud'homme declared his profession as "brewer" in the 1642 census of Montréal, beermakers had a hard time of it in Québec until after the British conquest. Sensing a demand among the new English, Scots, and Irish immigrants to Montréal, young John Molson of Lancastershire brewed his first ales in 1786. He wrote to a friend in London, "My beer has been universally well-liked beyond my most sanguine expectations." **Molson,** which still occupies the same site on the St. Lawrence River, shares dominance of the Canadian beer market with **LaBatt,** which has an ultramodern brewery of its own in LaSalle.

Canadians are famed for their lusty appreciation of beer, consuming sixty-eight and one-half liters per capita in 2002. The Québecois, however, were ten liters ahead of the national average. Perhaps the availability of some great local artisanal brews accounts for the difference.

The English-style ales of **McAuslan Breweries** (4850 rue Saint-Ambroise, No. 100; 514-939-3060), first available in 1989, have set the standard for microbreweries in the region. The coppery-gold St-Ambroise Pale Ale is the flagship drink, though the chocolate, licorice, and roasted-coffee malt overtones of St-Ambroise Noire have gained a strong following among dark-beer drinkers. The company's Griffon Extra-Blonde and Griffon Rousse affect a lighter style with stronger caramel overtones.

Three of Quebec's best microbreweries banded together as **Les Brasseurs RJ** (5585 rue de la Roche; 514-274-4941). One of the three partners, Les Brasseurs GMT, pioneered Montréal microbrews with Belle Guelle (now sold as Belle Guelle Originale), a golden lager that balances malt sugars and bitter hops. Another RJ member, Brasserie Le Cheval Blanc, produces Belgian-style ales bottled on the lees (yeast and other fermentation sediment), giving them a longer shelf life. Both the Blanche de Cheval, a straw-colored brew, and the Ambrée du Cheval Blanc, with a deeper amber color, are characterized by a distinctive spiciness and citrus bite. Fans of fruit beers seek out Folie Douce from Les Brasseurs de l'Anse, the third RJ partner, which still brews in the northern Québec region of Saguenay. This acidic ale is steeped with wild blueberries from Lac Saint-Jean.

The beers of **Brasserie Le Chaudron** (5710 rue Garnier; 514-276-0744) are widely sold on tap at bars and restaurants throughout the city, but are also available at a few stores. The original golden (Coeur d'Or) and amber (Cobra) are notable for their cereal flavors, but the company has made its name with "extreme" brews: the Calumet double-smoked porter, a black beer with a creamy head and strongly smoky malts, and Chanvre Rouge, a nicely balanced red with strong malt tones and distinct overtones of hemp (the herb is prominently displayed on the label).

end of the canal has been less subject to the pressures of development, you can still see vestiges of the three phases of its evolution. When the canal opened in 1825, it was a shallow and narrow route that could handle small boats that carried a maximum load of forty tons. It was enlarged twice—to accommodate five-hundred-ton steamboats and then to handle two-thousand-ton *canaliers*. Ultimately, the behemoth post–World War II Great Lakes freighters were too big for the canal, and it closed to commercial traffic. *500 chemin des Iroquois; 514-364-4490.*

■ LACHINE VILLAGE

In the half century before the canal opened, Lachine flourished as the departure point for fur traders heading upriver into the interior. Just beyond the last lock of the canal, the **Fur Trade at Lachine National Historic Site** brings that era vividly to life. Historical remove often gives the most arduous and dangerous endeavors an aura of romance and adventure. The men of the Northwest fur trade are often remembered as mythic characters who penetrated the frozen heart of the continent to live and trade with the native peoples. The museum does nothing to diminish the accomplishments of the traders—indeed, you're likely to leave more in awe of them than ever—but manages to bring the myths down to a palpable, sometimes gritty reality. The rough, gray stone museum building was constructed in 1803 as a fur warehouse. Pelts would arrive in Lachine in late fall and would be stored here through the winter until ice was out of the St. Lawrence River and the furs could be ferried downriver to Montréal in large canoes.

This warehouse served the North West Company, founded in Montréal in 1779 by an intrepid group of mostly Scots businessmen and adventurers. With its rival, the Hudson's Bay Company, the North West Company dominated the fur industry, which had fueled the northern economy since Champlain established the first French fur-trading post at Québec City in 1608. Europe had an insatiable appetite for the thick, silky furs that animals grow to survive the bitter winters of the Canadian interior. Most prized of all were beaver pelts, because the soft fur was best for felting to make a variety of hats. An amusing display shows how hat shapes and forms changed from place to place and century to century, though the demand for beaver remained constant. The least valuable furs still had coarse outer guard hairs that had to be removed before felting. Pelts that native trappers had worn for a winter with the furry side against their bodies were the most desirable because the friction had removed the guard hairs, and human body oils had softened the furs.

Exhibits at the Musée de Lachine relate domestic life at the western tip of the island of Montréal.

While outlining the mechanics of the trade in detail, the museum excels at conveying the life of the many voyageurs whose hard and nasty work profited the small number of Scottish "bourgeois," as the company partners termed themselves. *1255 boulevard Saint-Joseph, Lachine; 514-637-7433. Open April–November. The arrondissement of Lachine maintains a parking lot adjacent to the fur-trade museum. Bus 195 west from Angrignon Métro serves Lachine.*

The voyageurs were often the youngest sons of large French-Canadian families who did not stand to inherit the family land and had little taste for the life of a farmer. Sometimes recruited in bars, they tended to be a rough-and-ready lot capable of paddling a canoe for sixteen to eighteen hours a day at forty to sixty strokes a minute, singing all the while to keep a rhythm going. Because space in the canoes was at a premium, there were strict physical requirements for the job. A voyageur could not stand taller than five feet, seven inches or weigh more than 140 pounds. Ideally, he would have short legs and broad, muscular shoulders. In the course of a season, he might earn a little less than $100—which was still two or three times the cash income of a farmer.

At the end of the eighteenth century and beginning of the nineteenth, most of the furs came from the network of rivers and streams that connect Lake Athabaska (in what is now northern Alberta and Saskatchewan) to Lake Superior. But the 2,800-mile journey by canoe between Montréal and Lake Athabaska was impossible in a single season. So the North West Company established a midpoint post called Great Portage, later Fort William, at what is now Thunder Bay, Ontario. One team of voyageurs, called "winterers," would stay in the Northwest, trading with the native peoples. In the spring they would set off to Great Portage with their eight-meter-long birch bark canoes laden with furs. Other brigades of voyageurs would set out from Lachine in the spring with larger, eleven-meter-long canoes laden with trade goods, such as pots and pans, guns and knives, liquor and tobacco. They would drop off their cargo at Great Portage, pack up the furs, and paddle back to Lachine by fall.

The magnitude of these fur shipments is hard to imagine. Skins of beaver, fox, otter, martin, muskrat, raccoon, and mink were transported on round stretchers. About thirty furs would be packed in a bale wrapped with jute. Each canoe held sixty bales—a load of four tons that had to be carried on the voyageurs' backs during long portages. The voyageurs traveled with ten canoes in a brigade, and ten brigades would travel together. Each convoy carried approximately 180,000 furs.

During the early nineteenth century, the North West Company dominated its Hudson's Bay Company rival, moving nearly three-quarters of the Canadian fur trade along the St. Lawrence River and through Montréal. But when the two companies merged in 1821, the combined near-monopoly transferred most of the trade to the more direct Hudson's Bay route. Only about five percent of the furs continued to flow through Montréal. Almost seamlessly, the shipping industry shifted to timber and grain.

Across a small bridge from the national historic site, the **Musée de Lachine** includes the oldest building in Montréal of which all four walls are still intact. This point of land at the southwestern end of the island of Montréal was first granted to Robert Cavelier de LaSalle in 1667 and was named Lachine for the explorer's belief that he would find a route to China a short distance upstream. (In his *History of Montréal*, de Casson notes, with tongue firmly in cheek, "We must begin this year with this famous transmigration of China which took place to these parts, by giving its name during this winter to the part of our shore in so permanent a fashion

The Des Berges bike and skate path traces the shoreline between Lachine and the Old Port.

that it has remained ever since.") By 1669, LaSalle had sold the land. He never reached China, but he did manage to claim the Mississippi Valley for France in 1682, including the area that would become New Orleans in 1718.

At Lachine, merchants Jacques LeBer and Charles LeMoyne erected a fur-trading post; their stone warehouse today displays locally made furniture and farm implements of the seventeenth and eighteenth centuries. Glass-covered openings on the floor show the foundations, and display cases hold some of the thirty-two thousand artifacts unearthed during three years of archaeological excavations on the site. Supervised excavations continue each fall as part of the museum's educational programs. In striking contrast to the antiquity of the former warehouse, another building on the site hosts changing exhibitions of contemporary art, and fifty large abstract sculptures dot the grounds of surrounding Parc Réné-Lévesque. *1 chemin du Musée, Lachine; 514-634-3471. Open April–December.*

■ THE RAPIDS

Instead of returning to the Old Port by the Lachine Canal bike path, you can follow the twenty-two-kilometer **Des Berges bike path** as it traces the shoreline of the St. Lawrence River, passing the infamous rapids along the way.

As you head south from the Musée de Lachine, the unmistakable sails of **Moulin Fleming** mark the only surviving English-style windmill in the province. Demonstrations are given on weekend afternoons from May through August. *9675 boulevard LaSalle, LaSalle; 514-367-6387.*

At the intersection of boulevard LaSalle and 68th Avenue, a marina with a substantial parking lot functions as the staging base for **Les Descentes sur le St-Laurent,** a company best known for its whitewater raft trips through the Lachine Rapids. The whole excursion, including safety lessons and suiting up, takes about two-and-one-quarter hours, of which the half hour actually trying to paddle through the rapids can seem either interminable or fleeting, depending on your adrenaline level. The company also conducts jet-boat tours on the rapids, albeit in smaller vessels than those used by rival tour company Saute Moutons, which embarks from the Old Port. *8912 boulevard LaSalle, LaSalle; 514-767-2230. Bus 110 from Angrignon Métro stops next to the marina. Les Descentes also operates a shuttle from the Infotouriste Centre on Dorchester Square.*

There's no need to get soaked to see the rapids. The delightful **Parc des Rapides,** a green strip that parallels boulevard LaSalle between 3rd and 31st Avenues, gets

Lachine village's outdoor sculpture garden of more than fifty works covers an island four kilometers long in Parc Réné-Lévesque.

you close enough to feel the spray. Along this stretch, the St. Lawrence River drops nearly forty feet in about a mile. Islands in the middle of the river squeeze the flow, creating complex currents that delight both kamikaze kayakers and mathematicians specializing in fluid dynamics. From shore, the wild waters look less tumultuous than they really are—until you see a boat or raft dwarfed by the waves. The brute force of the rapids has been on the minds of Montrealers from the earliest days of settlement, so it's not surprising that the first hydroelectric plant in Greater Montréal was built here in 1897.

The churning currents make the rapids one of the largest ice-free bodies of water in southern Québec during the winter, so the islands and waters off the park are set aside as a migratory bird sanctuary named for the largest of the rocky isles, l'Île aux Herons. More than two hundred species of migratory birds have been spotted here at various seasons. Several thousand ducks, from mallards to mergansers and wood ducks, winter over in these waters. In the summer, the sanctuary hosts the largest colony of herons in Québec—all just a ten-kilometer ride from the bustle of the Old Port. *514-367-6351. Bus 58 from Métro de L'Église.*

PARC JEAN-DRAPEAU

Even obscure political figures have subway stops named for them in Montréal, so it was the least the city could do when it renamed its mid-river island park for Jean Drapeau a month after his death in August 1999. The former mayor had ruled the city like a Theban king for nearly thirty years, lifting it to international prominence, his admirers say—and simultaneously saddling it with long-term debt, his detractors add. But at least in the abstract, the islands are his handiwork, as is so much of Montréal.

The watershed event in Montréal's modern history was Expo '67, and Drapeau saw to it that a proper stage was built for the city's debut on the world scene. Twenty-eight million tons of soil dug to make room for the new Métro tunnels went into the harbor to roughly double the size of Île Sainte-Hélène and to create its companion, Île Notre-Dame. The year 1967 marked the centennial of Canada's Confederation and 325 years since Montréal's founding. But "Man and His World," as Expo '67 was officially named, looked forward rather than back. Dramatic, futuristic buildings dotted the islands and signaled a city on the move.

The fair attracted more than forty-five million visitors. For a bright and shining moment, Montréal—a city where French Canadians had only just come into their own—was the epicenter of the era's international euphoria. But the real success of such events is best judged by the legacies left to their host cities, and by that standard, Expo '67 excelled. Montrealers take to the bike paths, gardens, and shores of the islands, now home to Parc Jean-Drapeau, to gorge themselves on the pleasures of a brief, sweet, intense summer, and they return in the winter to skate and to ski the undulating landscape. Fireworks burst, roulette wheels tick, and muskets fire. Dragon-boat racers dig their paddles deep, and Formula One drivers hit the hairpin turns of the racetrack with a sliding cloud of dust and blue exhaust. It's easy to imagine Drapeau, observing the panorama from an elevated perch, nodding his head with approval. "*Bien*," says the little man with big ideas. "OK."

■ ÎLE SAINTE-HÉLÈNE

Samuel de Champlain was cursed with the explorer's penchant to put a name on every mote of land. Surveying the small archipelago between the island of Montréal and the south shore of the St. Lawrence in 1611, he indulged in an

Majorettes at Expo '67.
(following pages) The Tour la Nuit is part of Montréal's annual Bike Fest.

uncharacteristic burst of sentimentality and named the largest of the rocks after his young wife, Hélène Boulle, whom he had left behind in France a year earlier. A century later, the island served as the baronial summer home of a local seigneur, and in 1760, Chevalier François-Gaston de Lévis chose Île Sainte-Hélène to make a last stand against the British forces. Receiving orders from France to surrender his troops, he first burned his colors to protest the treatment his comrades had received at British hands. Summer escape, fortified encampment, and lightly used city park—Île Sainte-Hélène was just the ticket when Montréal suddenly needed a lot of open space for Expo '67. Because it can be reached by road, Métro, ferry, and bicycle bridge, Île Saint-Hélène now serves as the gateway to the two-island park. A circumferential road, rue Tour-de-l'Isle, approximates the original shores of the island. Strolling and hiking paths, some of which date from the nineteenth century, cross the central wooded uplands.

Expo '67 gave Montrealers a taste of the future.

One of the signature structures of Expo '67, the former **American Pavilion,** is just outside the Métro station. Long after the world has forgotten "Creative America," the exhibition it once housed, the geodesic dome designed by R. Buckminster Fuller's "Cambridge Seven" team of Harvard and M.I.T. architects and designers stands as either the largest sculpture or the most stunning building in Parc Jean-Drapeau, depending on your view. Erected in part by Mohawk ironworkers, the dome was covered with pivoting hexagonal acrylic panels that opened and closed according to weather and light levels. In *Wizard of the Dome,* Sidney Rosen shows his appreciation of Fuller's revolutionary design work: "At night, interior lighting turned the dome into a beautiful, glowing sphere, a modern Taj Mahal that was the most magnificent spot in the entire fairgrounds." But the plastic perished years ago in a fire, leaving the elegantly articulated frame of the dome to nest on the landscape like a behemoth steel dandelion about to shed its seeds. The struts create a lacy play of light and shadow on the core building, which consists of platforms hung from a central shaft—essentially a steel-and-glass tree house.

Even without its skin, the dome structure continues to upstage its occupant: currently **Environment Canada's Biosphère.** The science center, built within the

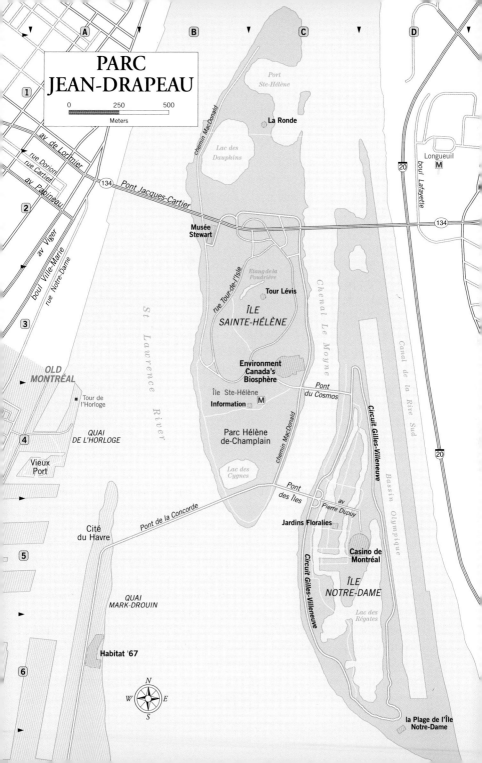

dome, focuses its earnest ecological exhibits on the St. Lawrence River and Great Lakes. Displays on the lower level explain how dams, locks, and canals work, and hands-on models make the principles more palpable than any verbal explanation. In fact, the Biosphère sidesteps bilingualism by forgoing words in favor of sound and images whenever possible. The six-screen, surround-sound multimedia show presents a rousing picture of the river—from cavorting beluga whales to loggers guiding a timber raft through rapids, from idyllic salt meadows to hulking ships pulling into port. Water rushes, birds twitter, foghorns bleat, and hardly a word— in either French or English—is uttered. The observation decks on the fourth and fifth levels are the perfect vantage to see how the city rises from the river up its namesake hill. *160 rue Tour-de-l'Isle; 514-283-5000.*

The proximity of Île Sainte-Hélène to the city made it a natural choice for a fort, which, like so many structures in Parc Jean-Drapeau, has found a second use—in this case, as a history museum. The scenic route to the old fortress follows the south side of the island along the path behind the Biosphère, and passes a dungeonlike water tower on the highest point of land. Built in 1936, the **Tour Lévis** was named for the last standing French commander during the British conquest. A walking path departs from the pavement to traverse the hollow next to a lovely small pond with an unlikely name, Etang de la Poudrière—Powder Keg Pond. The path continues up the opposite hill to the fort.

The British fortified Île Sainte-Hélène between 1820 and 1824 to safeguard Montréal and the western supply routes on the St. Lawrence River from potential American aggressors. They had good reason. With the United States still bruised by the War of 1812, President James Monroe was already rattling the American saber over "foreign intervention." In 1823, his Monroe Doctrine declared the length and breadth of the American continents a U.S. sphere of influence. But the only shots ever fired at the fort were in training exercises and drills. Fort de l'Île Sainte-Hélène was converted to a hospital during the cholera epidemic of the 1830s and became a military prison in 1848. In 1870, the British authorities bade adieu and turned the island over to the city, although the fort remained under control of Canadian military forces until 1946.

Judging by the kilt-wearing, bagpipe-playing highland regiment and the Scottish meat pies at the snack bar, you would think the Brits never left. But the Scots of the Olde 78th Fraser Highlanders are window dressing of the **Musée Stewart,** as are their blue-jacketed counterparts, La Compagnie Franche de la Marine. In the summer, the faux soldiers perform eighteenth-century military

Many of the events of la Fête des Neiges take place on Île Notre-Dame.

drills and show children rudimentary marching and drill patterns—the marines with the francophone kids, the highlanders with the anglophones.

The fort saw other military uses before the Stewart Museum was installed in the former arsenal in 1970. The core of the museum consists of the personal collections of David Macdonald Stewart (1920–84), a Canadian history buff and president of Macdonald Tobacco, the family business he sold in 1973 before establishing a foundation for historic preservation. The museum's holdings have been augmented over the years, but Stewart's own penchant for reaching across the centuries to identify with historic personages comes through in the displays. Deft signage connecting the artifacts to their owners opens a window on the human side of Canada's history. It is one thing to see generic trade goods that the Jesuit priests carried into the wilderness, and quite another to behold the modest pewter plate and spoon that Père Jacques Marquette took on his explorations of the Mississippi River. *20 rue Tour-de-l'Isle; 514-283-5000.*

Looming high above the Stewart Museum, the Pont Jacques-Cartier touches down on the former east end of Île Sainte-Hélène as it spans the St. Lawrence from Montréal to the south shore. Additional fill was laid around the base of the bridge pilings to connect Saint-Hélène to the adjacent Île la Ronde, now home to the amusement park La Ronde. With Walt Disney's personal advice, **La Ronde** was

Habitat '67

Of all the structures erected for Expo '67, only Habitat continues to perform its original function. Envisioned as an exhibit on the future of housing, the complex of stacked modular cubes on the jetty, Cité du Havre, remains one of the most coveted private addresses in the city. As a 22-year-old McGill University architecture student in 1960, Moshe Safdie penned a thesis on modular construction that would grow into plans for Habitat just four years later. He eschewed the conventional construction technique of supporting slab flooring on posts, instead stacking staggered eight-box clusters up to twelve stories high. The completed complex bears a striking resemblance to indigenous cliff-face villages of the Middle East and the American Southwest. In his reflections on the project, *Beyond Habitat,* Safdie suggests that among the many influences on his design, the strongest was his childhood imaginings of the Hanging Gardens of Babylon. "For me, they were the Garden of Eden and I had many fantasies about them. The fact that no one knew how they looked, that they were a mystery, that there were no drawings of them whatsoever, made them all the more attractive to me." Although Habitat is visible from the Pont de la Concorde, which links it to Île Sainte-Hélène, and from the Old Port, the bicycle path that passes the complex provides more intimate views—especially when the occupants haven't pulled their curtains.

constructed as a futuristic amusement park for Expo '67, setting such classics as a Ferris wheel and a carousel next to the "Gyrotron," which was supposed to simulate a trip to outer space followed by a trip to the planetary core. (The ride was a bust because the required speeds were too fast to be safe.) Now a member of the Six Flags family, La Ronde seems to come up with a new mechanical sensation each season to add to its sprawling set of more than thirty rides. The park has become best known for the pyrotechnics of the annual World Fireworks Festival, which runs from mid-June through late July. On festival nights, the Jacques-Cartier bridge is closed to vehicles and Montrealers crowd the span for the best free view of the show. The bridge can be accessed from either the Hochelaga shore or from the ramps off rue Tour-de-l'Isle within Parc Jean-Drapeau. Even when the bridge is open to vehicles, fearless pedestrians can cross on the vertigo-inducing sidewalks. *22 chemin Macdonald; 514-397-2000. Open mid-May through late October.*

La Ronde amusement park was constructed for Expo '67.

■ ÎLE NOTRE-DAME

Île Notre-Dame owes more to human ingenuity than to the gentle artistry of nature. The long, narrow island was conjured out of thin air (or more exactly, out of millions of tons of backfill) as a display ground for Expo '67. Unconstrained by preexisting geography, designers shaped and reshaped the island for another thirteen years, eventually creating lush gardens and a network of canals.

From Île Sainte-Hélène, the Pont du Cosmos near the Biosphère and the Pont des Îles, located southwest of the Métro station, provide access to Île Notre-Dame for walkers, cyclists, and skaters. The Cosmos Bridge enters the island on the edge of the racetrack named for one of Québec's great drivers. Built in 1978 for Formula One racing, **Circuit Gilles-Villeneuve** hosts the Grand Prix du Canada in June and the Molson Indy in August. Outside of the race weeks, an estimated 500,000 in-line skaters and cyclists take to the track each year; competitive cyclists, especially, favor the pavement for race training. The peripheral road around the track swings wide on the south side to follow the edge of the **Bassin Olympique,** a lake added as a

(above) Alexander Calder's stabile Man 1 *was set in place during Expo '67.*
(left) La Ronde is a swirl of light and color.

In the summer, Île Notre-Dame is the site of horticultural spectacles.

venue for water sports in the 1976 Olympics. Rowing and paddling competitions (such as the Rowing Canada Cup and the dragon-boat races) take place here during the summer. During la Fête des Neiges, the city's chief winter festival, skaters can glide along the surface when it's not being used for iceboat races.

The Pont des Îles is perhaps the better choice for strolling through the many gardens, and for accessing the separate paths dedicated to either pedestrians or cyclists and skaters. Visitors on foot and on wheels share the same paths in the lush **Jardins Floralies,** the legacy of a 1980 horticultural exhibition. Given more than two decades to mature, the gardens today appeal to both hard-core plant lovers, who study the well-marked horticultural specimens, and to casual visitors who simply want to stop to smell the roses or drop a line into the canals to fish for perch and carp. Integral to the garden design, the canals link up with other bodies of water on Île Notre-Dame. Pedal boats are available for rent.

Two palatial Expo '67 pavilions have metamorphosed into the **Casino de Montréal,** located between the Floralies gardens and the manmade lake in the heart of Île Notre-Dame. From the gardens, the former French Pavilion, designed by Jean Faugeron, looks like a gleaming, futuristic aluminum stadium; by night, it glows like a floodlit diamond in a marquise setting. After the fair closed, it served as an exposition hall before being converted into a casino in 1993. The casino drew more than double its projected clientele in its first year and expanded in 1995 by annexing the adjacent Québec Pavilion. This truncated glass pyramid was itself a groundbreaking structure that wedded glass-and-steel-box construction to the squat shapes of Brutalism. Its mirrored surface was a radical innovation in the mid-1960s; it made the pavilion virtually disappear by day and glow like St. Elmo's fire at night. When it was joined to the casino, the original black-mirror glass was replaced with a bronze-gold glass, perhaps suggesting the proverbial pot at the end of the rainbow.

The casino began operating around the clock in 1997. It attracts an average of eighteen thousand people a day to its 120 gaming tables and more than three thousand slot machines. Like American gaming centers, the five-floor Casino de Montréal has a cabaret performance hall with marquee performers, but most of the facility is modeled on European rather than American casinos. That translates into a lower return on the slots and at least the rudiments of a dress code—though the tolerance for Bermuda shorts, denims, and running shoes would make a European croupier cringe. The gourmet restaurant, Nuances, does demand "business attire," as befits an establishment often cited among the top restaurants in Canada. Admission to the casino buildings is restricted to those age eighteen and older. *1 avenue de Casino, Île Notre-Dame; 514-392-2746.*

If a few hours of dribbling away your inheritance at the craps tables makes you want to jump in the lake, there's one right behind the casino. Parts of the shore are richly landscaped with bog-loving plants, but this is no swamp. The lake's water comes from the St. Lawrence River through a high-tech filtration system that removes pollutants and makes it safe for swimming. During the brief burst of summer heat—from late June to late August—**la Plage de l'Île Notre-Dame** (514-872-6120) opens on the southern end of the lake, to the great relief of those Montrealers who are not so well-heeled as to have a summer place outside the city. The beach's sports pavilion rents canoes, kayaks, and pedal boats, but the most popular craft is the windsurfer, since the shallow, protected lake is almost the perfect place to learn the sport.

M O N T   R O Y A L
A N D   E N V I R O N S

Frederick Law Olmsted had a point about Mont Royal when he wrote to the Montréal city fathers in 1881 that it was "a mountain barely worthy of the name. You would call it a hill if it stood a few miles further away from the broad, flat, river valley." But the landscape architect also applauded their determination to turn the hill into a park, since "it would be wasteful to try to make anything else than a mountain of it."

The hill is a bit of continental dyspepsia, a bubble of magma from the earth's core that swelled almost to the surface during the tectonic disruptions that opened the Atlantic Ocean. The magma gradually crystallized, reaching the surface 125 million years later when glaciers scraped off the limestone crust. This combination of gray limestone and extruding crags of hard black rock makes the mountain look more rugged and formidable than a hill this size has any right to be.

The prominent landmark caught the eye of Jacques Cartier. The Iroquois of Hochelaga led him to the 230-plus-meter summit on October 2, 1535, where the Frenchman pronounced the hill Mont Royal. Cartier records that the Iroquois were growing crops on the mountain slopes—archaeological evidence suggests tobacco, beans, squash, corn, and sunflowers—and in 1675, the Sulpicians cut a path to the western slope to establish orchards and vineyards. But for the first few centuries, most inhabitants of the island saw the mountain more as obstacle than opportunity. Even today, the two roads around the hill—chemin de la Côte-des-Neiges on the west and chemin de la Côte Sainte-Catherine on the east—follow trails established as canoe portages to north-island fur-trading posts.

The ten-square-kilometer mountain itself remained largely unsettled until the late eighteenth century and the early nineteenth, when the rocky woodlands were divided into estates held by wealthy families. They saw the mountain for what it was—a retreat where one might enjoy unobstructed views and look down upon the activity below.

Crowds gather in the summer around the Georges-Étienne Cartier monument.

■ PARC MONT-ROYAL

The existence of Parc Mont-Royal is owed to a Mont Royal landholder known to posterity only by his surname, Lamothe. During the bitter winter of 1862–63, he cut all his trees for firewood. Horrified by the scarred landscape of stumps, Lamothe's merchant-prince neighbors pushed the city council to set aside Mont Royal's slopes as parkland. Ultimately, the city expropriated fourteen percent of the mountain's surface at a cost of one million dollars, and Frederick Law Olmsted, by then much sought after because of his contributions to New York City's Central Park, was engaged to make something of it. Parc Mont-Royal officially opened in 1876.

Olmsted's plans were never fully implemented, and the park has acquired some decidedly non-Olmstedian features over the generations, but the **chemin Olmsted** (the Olmsted path) remains the centerpiece. The landscape architect identified the natural features and designed a set of meandering footpaths to link them in a cohesive narrative. An auto road cuts through the northern side of the park (voie Camillien-Houde/chemin Remembrance), but the designer's original trail is the better way to experience the nuances of the environment.

Parc Mont-Royal becomes a snowy wonderland in the winter.

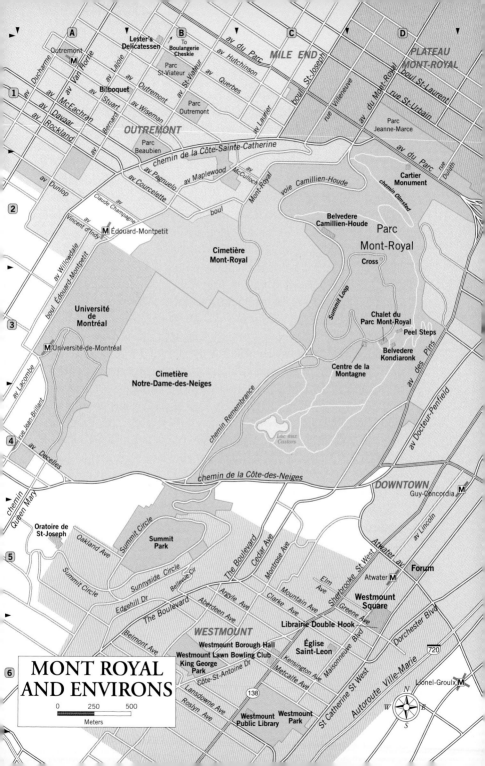

MONT ROYAL
AND ENVIRONS

0   250   500
Meters

Chemin Olmsted begins off avenue du Parc at the **Cartier monument,** which does not honor explorer Jacques, but rather nation-builder Georges-Étienne Cartier, one of the fathers of Confederation. The forty-meter-high conglomeration is topped with a winged Glory and guarded by four bronze lions. Two quotations by Cartier are carved into the stone base. The English reads, "We are different races, not for strife, but to work together for the common welfare," while the French asserts, *"Le Canada doit être un pays de liberté et toutes les libertés doivent être protegées par la loi."* ("Canada should be a country of liberty, and all liberties should be protected by the law.") Nationalists periodically deface "Canada" and spray "Québec" in its place. As the McGill University intellectual Witold Rybczynski once quipped, "spray paint has replaced civilized discourse."

Olmsted's broad dirt path begins to the right of the monument and wends gradually uphill into the wooded flat that makes the rocky outcrops above seem higher and craggier. Walkers, cyclists and runners all share the trail, many accompanied by their various huskies and retrievers. The route loops west and in about two kilometers reaches the **Peel Steps,** which mark the northern end of Lamothe's historic clear-cut. The Olmsted path continues in a gentle looping rise, passing one of the original pumping stations for the reservoirs buried on the mountain on its way to Lac aux Castors and the chalet. But the 205 stairs of the Peel Steps trim two kilometers from the route, zigzagging sixty meters up the face of a cliff. Fitness freaks literally run up and down, but the steps are wide enough to accommodate runners and strollers alike. Taken fast or slow, they give direct access to one of the most striking views in the park.

Constructed in 1908, **Belvedere Kondiaronk** received its current name in 1998. Because the new name was Algonquian, not French, the Commission de Toponymie du Québec had to mull it over for four years before officially honoring Kondiaronk—the Tionnontates Huron chief who brokered a 1701 peace among the French, Hurons, and Iroquois to end a century of warfare. Brass markers along the arc of the retaining wall pinpoint distant structures, from the harbor bridges to the downtown cathedral. But specific landmarks are ultimately less striking than the composite splendor—this is the best vantage in the city on Montréal's vitreous skyscraper forest.

The belvedere forms an extended front porch for the **Chalet du Parc Mont-Royal,** a Depression-era public-works project. Hikers and cross-country skiers treat the chalet as a grand rest stop, but its elegant vaulted hall, where carved stone squirrels perch in the crotches of exposed timbers, is also a popular concert venue.

A street performer serenades summer crowds in Parc Mont-Royal.
(following pages) Skaters twirl on the park's Lac aux Castors.

The frescoes were commissioned from young and then-unknown artists, including Paul-Émile Borduas and Marc-Aurèle Fortin, who became two of the leading Québecois artists of their generation. Children like to search for fossilized worm tracks and coral formations in the rough Westmount limestone on the outside walls. *514-872-3911.*

From the back of the chalet, the **Summit Loop** winds about two kilometers around the summit of Mont Royal. Hardy Montrealers take the walk even between November and April, when seven bird-feeding stations are set along the route for the fifty or so species that winter on the mountain. Against a snowy backdrop, a flash of red cap betrays the downy woodpecker, a blur of blue-slate the nervous nuthatch.

The most prominent feature of the loop is the **Cross,** a Montréal landmark since 1924. The illuminated, thirty-meter-high skeletal metal structure commemorates a cross erected lower on the mountain by Maisonneuve in January 1643 to give thanks that Ville-Marie had been spared from floods—and, not coincidentally, to put the French stamp on the mountain. Since 1992, fiber optics have replaced the original incandescent bulbs. At night, the cross is visible for 60 kilometers across the St. Lawrence River plain.

The trail skirts the summit, which is topped with a communications tower. A small side path leads up to **Belvedere Camillien-Houde** on the auto road voie Camillien-Houde. The views are as sweeping as those at Kondiaronk, but the parking lot is better known for dashboard romance than its view of the cross. Houde would have shrugged. Montréal's mayor off and on from 1928 to 1954, he is reputed to have said, "As long as we keep a balance between the praying and the sinning, we'll never sink into wickedness."

A few hundred meters west of where the loop trail returns to the chalet is the blocky, rubble-stone Maison Smith—Montréal's last nineteenth-century farmhouse. Built in 1858 for one of the sixteen landowners who sold their spreads to the city to create the park, it's now home to the **Centre de la Montagne,** where you can get information on guided walks and purchase walking tour books. The building's free exhibits highlight natural history (from how to interpret the rocks to how to identify poison ivy), human history (the evolution of Olmsted's plan), and the ecosystem of the boreal forest. *514-843-8240. Open early May–early November.*

For eight weeks in the summer of 1964, a dozen sculptors lived in Maison Smith as part of the **North American Symposium**, an international sculpture event. They created abstract works, mostly in marble and granite, on the meadow west of the house while the public watched the process. One sculpture had to be removed (vandals kept getting stuck inside it), but the others now form a rolling garden of modernist lawn art. The sculptures have become so much a part of the landscape that they serve as picnic spots, impromptu soccer goals, and places for friends to rendezvous.

West of the meadow, the erstwhile marshes of Olmsted's park plan were transformed into **Lac aux Castors** (Beaver Lake), named for the ancient beaver lodges uncovered when the lake was excavated as part of a 1937–38 federal jobs scheme. Olmsted would have hated such a recreational center, but Montrealers love it. In the summer, children fly kites on the slope above the lake, teenagers tour the shallow waters in rental pedal boats, and families queue up for ice-cream cones at the landmark glass-and-steel pavilion. Come winter, the kite-flying slope becomes a slide for tubing; the surrounding lanes, a network for cross-country skiing. One lobe of the lake is cleared and groomed for ice-skating, and hot food and drinks are served on the upper level of the pavilion; skates and skis can be rented on the lower level. *514-872-6559. Bus 11 serves the park. There are parking lots off voie Camillien-Houde adjacent to Maison Smith and Lac aux Castors.*

■ Mont Royal Slopes

The institutional presence on the slopes of Mont Royal—there are about a hundred hospitals, religious orders, and educational institutions—suggests the wisdom of setting aside parkland while there was still land to set aside. Two million people per year visit the religious shrine **Oratoire de Saint-Joseph,** many of them ascending the 283 steps to the basilica on their knees. Built between 1924 and 1955, the massive church can accommodate ten thousand standing for Mass. The ninety-seven-meter-high dome is the second tallest in the world, exceeded only by St. Peter's in Rome. Yet the site had humble origins as a small chapel built in 1904 by Frère André—born Alfred Bessette in Saint-Grégoire, Québec, in 1845. The monk was said to have the power of healing through prayers for the intercession of Saint Joseph, and as word spread, the chapel became a pilgrimage site. A million people are reported to have turned out for André's funeral procession in January 1937. He was beatified by Rome in 1982. The shrine includes extensive grounds, a small museum, André's tomb, the original chapel, and stations of the cross in the surrounding woods. *3800 chemin Queen-Mary, at chemin de la Côte-des-Neiges. 514-733-8211.*

Oratoire de Saint-Joseph boasts the largest dome of any church in Montréal.

The **Université de Montréal** sprawls across a ridge on the northwest slope of Mont Royal. Formerly a branch of the Québec-based Université de Laval, the now-independent francophone university enrolls more than fifty thousand students. Ernest Cormier planned and designed the campus in an art deco style. The main building was completed in 1943 and subsequent additions have followed Cormier's use of yellow brick. *2900 boulevard Édouard-Montpetit; 514-343-6111.*

Cemeteries cover the sweeping inter-peak valley between Mont Royal peak and Outremont peak. On the west, **Cimetière Notre-Dame-des-Neiges** (Our Lady of the Snows) was established in 1855 as the city's main Roman Catholic cemetery. Its formal row-on-row layout of more than a million graves gives the burial ground an austere formality. By contrast, the adjacent 165-acre **Cimetière Mont-Royal,** established in 1852, is a vast garden with lush plantings and rambling trails. While it's tempting to suggest that the "two solitudes" persist even in death, Mont Royal Cemetery makes it clear that the purported duality is actually a multitude. You can pick up a map at the main entrance on chemin de la Fôret to search for the graves of six victims of the *Titanic* disaster, seek out the Molson brewers' mausoleum, or pay respects to author Mordecai Richler, but you can also stand in one spot and read Montréal's ethnic diversity from the stones: Fiala, Proudfoot, Ferguson, Biermayer, Pancalo, Dzyndzyrysty, Dikaranian, Kalvaitis, Dickie, Akulic, Shepherd, Boassaly, Geracimo, Bishara, Griffith, Banos, Opychany, Voss, Toole . . .

■ WESTMOUNT AND OUTREMONT

The communities of Westmount and Outremont grew up in the late nineteenth and early twentieth centuries below Mont Royal's secondary peaks of the same names. By tradition, the two cities—now reduced to Montréal arrondissements—were the homes respectively of the English-speaking and French-speaking elites. The primarily residential neighborhoods loom large in Montréal lore as symbols of the linguistic and cultural divide. The classic Westmounter would be a lawn-bowling Anglo-Scot plutocrat with a taste for single-malt Scotch and kidney pie whose only French might be what he whispers to the maid when his wife isn't listening. The comparably caricatured Outremontais would be a pince-nez-wearing, *Le Devoir*–reading lawyer or publisher who champions the modern, secular state while wishing he could pack his daughters off to convent school until they turn thirty.

A great cheese shop is a neighborhood necessity, and Fromagerie Outremont fills the bill.

Both Westmount and Outremont still have their wealthy sections—in both cases, on the heights around the summits—but they also have districts of more modest means below the hills. And the former suburbs are not uniformly monolingual. Many Westmount residents speak French as a first language, and an equally large number of Outremont residents speak English, Yiddish, or Hebrew as a primary tongue. Nonetheless, both arrondissements have histories of privilege and still tend to attract certain communities—anglophone businesspeople to Westmount, francophone artists and intellectuals to Outremont.

■ OUTREMONT

One of Outremont's most famous native sons, the former Canadian prime minister Pierre Elliott Trudeau, embodies many of the contrasts, contradictions, and aspirations of Outremont. He was born to a Québecois francophone father and Scots-French anglophone mother in a part of town near the railroad tracks just two blocks from immigrant Mile End. By the time Pierre was thirteen, the Trudeau family had become wealthy enough to rocket up the social ladder to a home on avenue McCulloch on the Outremont heights.

Formal plantings and gracious landscaping make Parc Bernard a tranquil oasis.

Speaking of Montréal

Over the years, I have often been asked how, in a bilingual family like mine, we handled the problem of what language to speak at home. My answer is: it was the most natural thing in the world. I never felt that there *was* any problem. My father spoke to us in French, and my mother spoke in either language, depending on the subject and on how she felt at the time. My Trudeau grandmother, uncles, aunts, and cousins always spoke French; my Elliott grandfather spoke English with my mother, but switched to French to talk with my father. Did that create any difficulties for us children? Very few and minor ones. In elementary school at Académie Querbes, for example, I was transferred to the French side in fourth grade after having studied in English for the first three years. Was it a difficult transition? Hardly.... You might say that, long before it was formally invented, I benefited from "total immersion."

—Pierre Elliott Trudeau, *Memoirs,* 1993

You can almost determine social class in Outremont with an altimeter. The arrivistes live above eighty-five meters elevation, and the higher they dwell, the farther they have arrived. The southern and western portions of Outremont—those closest to the mountain—are the most desirable. Chemin de la Côte Sainte-Catherine, haughty avenue Maplewood, and haute bourgeois boulevard Mont-Royal follow the elevated ridgeline of upper Outremont. Homes mimic the lines of Loire Valley châteaux, and their manicured front yards often give way to precipitous drop-offs on the rear.

And then there is Outremont below the hill—prosperously middle class around Parc Outremont and Parc Beaubien, decidedly working class closer to the avenue Hutchinson border with Mile End. Outremont's Hasidic community lives on the streets of the arrondissement's eastern side. About six thousand strong, the Hasidim—easily recognized by their distinctive dress and hair—bring a social complexity to leaven the social complacency of middle-class Outremont.

Two commercial streets are tinged by the worlds of upper and lower Outremont. **Avenue Laurier** west of Hutchinson is known for its fine *pâtisseries,* its upscale home decor shops, and a sprinkling of classic French restaurants filled at midday with Outremont ladies who lunch. The boutiques stock goods from

Avenue Bernard serves as Outremont's principal shopping street.

Provence, spoken English is an afterthought, and you can stand at the bar in a Belgian chocolate shop to enjoy a cognac or an *allongé* (a double-size, half-strength espresso) with your truffle.

On the northern end of Outremont, heading away from the mountain and toward the railroad tracks, **avenue Bernard** serves a more diverse community. Its immigrant past—central European and often Jewish in the first half of the twentieth century—lingers in such landmarks as **Lester's Delicatessen** (1057 avenue Bernard ouest; 514-276-6095), one of the top destinations in Montréal for smoked meat, and **Boulangerie Cheskie** (359 avenue Bernard ouest; 514-271-2253), the *heimishe* (Yiddish for "home-style") bakery frequented by French-Canadians and Hasidim alike for its robust Old World breads. But the rising tide of Canadian prosperity has also lifted the boats of working-class Outremont, and Bernard has sprouted cafés, clothing boutiques, housewares shops, and the ultra-popular ice-cream parlor **Bilboquet** (1311 avenue Bernard ouest; 514-276-0414). It is, as they say, a "neighborhood in transition"—on its way up.

■ WESTMOUNT

Leonard Cohen—master of obscure songs, spare poems, and priapic comedies of manners—is often accused of betraying his class with his bohemian leanings. Although he grew up on the heights of Belmont Avenue, he has described Westmount as "a collection of large stone houses and lush trees arranged on the top of the mountain especially to humiliate the underprivileged."

The grandest of the trophy homes—Highlands castles and cantilevered Hollywood Hills–style slab piles—perch along Sunnyside and Bellevue Circles near the top of Westmount, the shortest of Mont Royal's peaks at 201 meters. The streets get their share of gawkers navigating the hairpin turns. Of course, the interlopers could be heading to **Summit Park,** the densely wooded nature reserve and sanctuary that birders know as one of the best places in eastern Canada for adding warblers to their life lists. Or they might be bound for the overlook on Summit Circle, with limited parking but sweeping views.

A stroll from The Boulevard past Cohen's childhood home on Belmont passes 14-acre **King George Park,** with its baseball diamonds and koi pond. Westmount tilts steeply downhill until it reaches rue Sherbrooke ouest, the principal public thoroughfare of the one-and-one-half-square-mile borough. On the flats, Westmount becomes a merely middle-class district with strong echoes of suburban London and Edinburgh. In 1897, Westmount celebrated Queen Victoria's Diamond Jubilee by launching the first tax-supported public library in the Province of Québec. Opened in 1899, **Westmount Public Library** (4574 Sherbrooke Street West; 514-989-5300) still presents a cheerfully Victorian face to the world, though it has been twice enlarged. Interior details from the original design by Robert Findlay—leaded glass, classical columns—have been scrupulously maintained, even as microfilm machines and Internet access have been installed. Orchids and other tropical plants bloom throughout the year in the attached conservatory.

Twenty-six-acre **Westmount Park** extends south of Sherbrooke behind the library. A rambling park with meandering footpaths, it remained a wild space in central Westmount until 1912, when it was laid out in frank homage to the principles of Frederick Law Olmsted. Subsequent additions have given it three baseball diamonds, several tennis courts, a playing field, a large playground, and widespread formal plantings.

LANDSCAPE FOR DREAMS

[King George Park] nourished all the sleepers in the surrounding houses. It was the green heart. It gave the children dangerous bushes and heroic landscapes so they could imagine bravery. It gave the nurses and maids winding walks so they could imagine beauty. It gave the young merchant-princes leaf-hid necking benches, views of factories so they could imagine power. It gave the retired brokers vignettes of Scottish lanes where loving couples walked, so they could lean on their canes and imagine poetry. It was the best part of everyone's life. Nobody comes into a park for mean purposes except perhaps a sex maniac and who is to say that he isn't thinking of eternal roses as he unzips . . .

—Leonard Cohen, *The Favourite Game,* 1963

The triumphal formality of the borough continues east on Sherbrooke Street from the park with the Tudor Revival **Westmount Borough Hall** (4333 Sherbrooke Street West). Its castellated walls of cut limestone make it look like a wing of the ducal castle in Edinburgh. Behind the political center, where borough councilors repeatedly call for secession from the Ville de Montréal ("de-merger," they call it), the **Westmount Lawn Bowling Club** (401 Kensington Avenue) celebrated its centennial in 2002 in its new clubhouse, an exact replica of the one that was razed in 1995.

It's worth a detour one block south on Clarke Avenue to visit the francophone Catholic church of Westmount, **Église Saint-Leon,** at the corner of Maisonneuve Boulevard. It is perhaps the purest masterpiece by artist Guido Nincheri, who worked in a studio in Maisonneuve for many years. Nincheri frequently collaborated with other artists and architects, but he did it all at Saint-Leon—from the architecture of tan sandstone to the stained glass windows, from the frescoes to the sculptures. *4301-11 Maisonneuve Boulevard West; 514-935-4950.*

Greene Avenue between Sherbrooke and Saint Catherine Streets constitutes a diminutive but chic shopping district that includes an entrance to the upscale underground shopping mall of **Westmount Square.** Receptionists at the mall's Spa at Westmount carefully schedule hair appointments so the wives of rival national politicians do not show up at the same time. **Librairie Double Hook** (1235A Greene Avenue; 514-932-5093), in business since the early 1970s, claims to be the only store in Canada to stock Canadian authors exclusively. The clerks have an almost encyclopedic knowledge of Canadian writing, and their offerings include French-Canadian authors in translation.

Elm Avenue, parallel to Greene, is a veritable gallery of the dominant Westmount architectural hodgepodge that could be called Early Nostalgia. Buoyant with the expansiveness of Montréal's economic golden age, late-nineteenth-century architects indulged a Victorian version of postmodernism by ransacking the British past. With their discordant stone towers, castellated rooflines, neoclassical pediments, and Gothic arches, the homes march along the street like dollhouses in a history museum.

Three black-glass towers at the foot of Elm rise above Westmount Square. Designed by Mies van der Rohe, they look forward rather than back, signaling Montréal's embrace of modernism in the 1960s. But nostalgia virtually overwhelms the old **Forum** (2313 Saint Catherine Street West). Built in 1924 and enlarged several times, it was the longtime home of the Montréal Canadiens, the city's legendary entry in the National Hockey League. At the avenue Atwater entrance, brass plaques in the pavement record twenty-four Stanley Cup victories between the 1915–16 and the 1992–93 seasons along with the motto "*la fierte pour toujours*" (forever proud). The Canadiens last played here in March 1996, and the structure has gone from a venue for athletic drama to a virtual-entertainment emporium, with a multiplex cinema and a humongous bar with electronic simulation games. The developers saved section 210 of the old seats, now a favorite photo op for hockey fans. Look for photographs of Canadiens stars, especially the late Maurice "Rocket" Richard, a hero to the locals for his spirit. The legendary number 9 once said, "I wasn't a good skater. I was just a guy who tried hard—all the time."

Mies van der Rohe's groundbreaking towers.

D O W N T O W N

Montréal's Downtown is really uptown, at least as viewed from the old city. Perhaps the French *centre-ville* is more descriptive, for the tentacles of the Montréal metropolis all extend from this central hub. Much of the city's genius lies in its simultaneous embrace of opposites, and nowhere is this more true than Downtown, where glass-box skyscrapers rise next to gray stone religious buildings, where the latest fashion is hawked just down the street from the oldest profession, and where the rich got richer even as the poor got the barest toehold.

This chapter covers the broad band of mostly modern Montréal between the pedestrian-hostile gulf of Autoroute 720 and the aerobically challenging slopes of Mont Royal. As such, it stretches from the city's ethnic lowlands—still-vibrant Chinatown and the nearly vanished African-American portion of Petit Bourgogne—to the heights of the Golden Square Mile along rue Sherbrooke. Between these extremes stands the busy shopping district of rue Sainte-Catherine, where the leading department stores connect to about two thousand boutiques and restaurants of the Underground City.

■ CHINATOWN

From Old Montréal, boulevard Saint-Laurent, the perennial boulevard of immigrant dreams, enters Chinatown through the ceremonial gate at avenue Viger. When this gate and its companion at Saint-Laurent and boulevard René-Lévesque were installed in 1999, these gifts from Shanghai celebrated the resilience of the Chinese neighborhood, which had managed to survive a half century of development that seemed intent on wiping it out. Chinese characters facing outward on the gate simply announce "Chinatown," while those facing inward declaim the fortune-cookie sentiment "A splendid environment fosters a great people."

The elaborate gates obscure the fact that the neighborhood's real axis is rue de la Gauchetière, which is a pedestrian mall for several blocks. At the west end at rue Jeanne-Mance, a more modest concrete gate welcomes you to Montréal's Chinese world. Immediately inside, the back entrance to the **Palais des congrès de Montréal** (the Montréal Convention Center) asserts the presence of one of the

The Downtown business district cuts loose at night in its numerous clubs and bars.

A gift from Shanghai, this gate provides a formal entrance to Chinatown.

massive projects that has encroached on Chinatown's narrow lanes. Indeed, the Palais des congrès covers the spot that historians cite as the beginning of Montréal's Chinatown: the laundry that Jos Song Long opened in 1877 at the corner of rues Jeanne-Mance and Saint-Antoine.

Chinese settlement in Montréal is a story repeated across the continent. Seeking to escape famine, many young men from South China came to North America to build the railroads. When the coast-to-coast rail lines were completed in the 1880s, few Chinese could afford to return home and instead gravitated to the cities. By 1900, Montréal's Chinese population had reached about nine hundred, of whom only four were women. Today, Montrealers of Chinese descent number about thirty thousand, though most live in outlying arrondissements and come Downtown for shopping and festivals.

Those who have stayed in claustrophobic Chinatown have found ways to cope with the pressures of urban development. The community lost its battle to block construction of the Complexe Guy-Favreau, directly across de la Gauchetière from an entry to Palais des congrès. But it may have won the culture war by colonizing

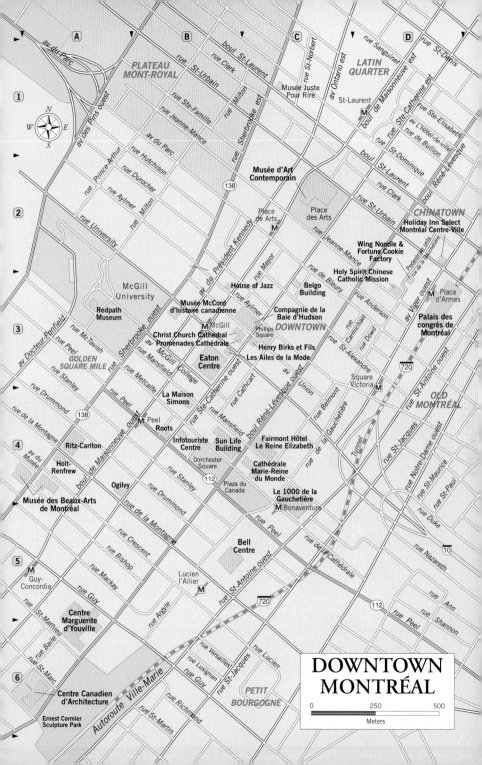

DOWNTOWN MONTRÉAL

the small shopping center within the sprawling Guy-Favreau office building. Community elders claim the benches to play cards, read, and catch up on gossip. Chinatown residents come and go all day, picking up Chinese-language papers at the newsstand or buying bulk ginseng from the dried-goods grocer.

Outside the hush of climate-controlled Guy-Favreau, the restaurants, bakeries, herbalists, and small markets of rue de la Gauchetière are marked by signs where large Chinese characters completely trump small French and English lettering. The sights, sounds, and smells are hardly enough to evoke Hong Kong, or even Vancouver, but Montréal's Chinatown hasn't lost its distinctive character; it has even converted some of the landmarks of the French and British cultures to its own purposes.

The oldest surviving Protestant church building in Montréal, a structure of unadorned gray stone constructed in 1835 for the Secessionist Church of Scotland, has become the **Holy Spirit Chinese Catholic Mission** (205 rue de la Gauchetière ouest). Across de la Gauchetière at the corner of rue Côte, the massive 1826 building

Fruit vendor hawks his wares in Chinatown.

that once housed the first non-denominational school in Montréal is now **Wing Noodle & Fortune Cookie Factory.** The company is Canada's largest manufacturer of Chinese noodles and fortune cookies, and is said to be the only manufacturer of kosher fortune cookies that promise "a new life ahead" in both French and English. While Montréal's Chinese have long had reason to be wary of development, they have been more accepting of the **Holiday Inn Select Montréal Centre-Ville.** The Hong Kong–based developers of the project were rumored to have spent an additional $1 million to alter the entrance to the $40 million hotel so it could conform to the principles of feng shui. Opened in 1991, the hotel often hosts bus tours and conventioneers, and the local community embraces it as the venue of choice for lavish wedding receptions. The bar overlooks a shallow koi pond, and the main restaurant, Chez Chine, is the most elegant dining room in Chinatown. *99 avenue Viger ouest; 514-878-9888.*

■ PLACE DES ARTS

Spectacle is nothing new at Place des Arts, where tens of thousands of people stand cheerfully on the concrete plaza for concerts. But few scenes compare to the event on May 26, 2001, when approximately twenty-five hundred Montrealers stripped off their clothes in the gray dawn and lay down on the pavement to pose for the New York photographer Spencer Tunick.

Empty of its crowds, the stepped plaza north of Chinatown along busy rue Sainte-Catherine between rues Jeanne-Mance and Saint-Urbain can seem sprawling and forbidding, relieved only by a row of fountain jets. But Montréal loves a party, and as soon as rue Sainte-Catherine is blocked off and a stage or projection screen is erected, Place des Arts sheds its austere demeanor. As the principal outdoor venue for the summer performing arts festivals, Place des Arts greets 1.6 million fans for the Festival du Jazz, 750,000 for the FrancoFolies, and more than 400,000 for outdoor movies during the Festival des Films du Monde. Even in February, when temperatures stay resolutely below zero, another 400,000 people carouse at Place des Arts during the Festival Montréal en Lumière. Events in the five halls that bracket the plaza draw another 800,000 to 1 million a year.

Like so many aspects of Montréal infrastructure, Place des Arts was set in motion by Jean Drapeau, who began agitating for a new major concert hall and arts center in 1955. When the Grand Salle opened on September 21, 1963, the Montréal Symphony Orchestra program was resolutely modern: Zubin Mehta conducted Gustav Mahler's First Symphony, and MSO founder Wilfrid Pelletier conducted a world premiere by Jean Papineau-Couture.

Probably no single figure had as profound an effect on classical music in Montréal as Pelletier. Born in the city in 1896, he debuted as a pianist at age 14 in the old Théâtre National, the first French professional theater in North America. Pelletier went on to become the rehearsal pianist for the Montréal Opera Company and for the Metropolitan Orchestra in New York before returning to Montréal in 1934 to found the Société des Concerts Symphonique de Montréal, which became the Montréal Symphony Orchestra in 1953. The Grand Salle at Place des Arts was renamed to honor Pelletier in 1966.

Pelletier's MSO was the first resident company at Place des Arts in 1963, but these days the orchestra shares the halls with touring shows and other resident companies: Compagnie Jean Duceppe (theater), Les Grands Ballets Canadiens, L'Opéra de Montréal, McGill Chamber Orchestra, Orchestre Métropolitain, and the Société Pro-Musica. During the height of the fall and spring seasons, all the larger halls are lit, and plans are being hatched to build a new, larger facility on the site for the MSO.

The **Musée d'Art Contemporain** was built on the rue Jeanne-Mance corner of Place des Arts in 1992. Established to promote contemporary Québecois art, the museum has a permanent collection of about six thousand pieces that includes the most comprehensive compilation of works by Paul-Émile Borduas. The museum takes the "contemporary" aspect of its title seriously—more than three-quarters of the artists represented are still alive and working. Spencer Tunick was commissioned by the museum to create the site-specific performance piece of nude people in public places, and a poster of the event sells briskly in the gift shop. Four galleries are devoted to shows drawn from the permanent collection, four others to temporary exhibitions of art from around the world. The museum also hosts avant-garde performances and multimedia events. *185 rue Sainte-Catherine ouest; 514-847-6212.*

Contemporary art not yet enshrined in a museum can be found nearby at the **Belgo Building** (372 rue Sainte-Catherine ouest). Originally a manufacturing center and showroom for the fur trade, the building now houses more than a dozen small art galleries.

Summer crowds gather on Place des Arts.
(following pages) Performers at the Festival du Jazz de Montréal.

■ BOULEVARD RÉNÉ-LÉVESQUE OUEST

As Montréal's population began to swell in the early nineteenth century, some of the first planned urban expansion took place along the crest of the escarpment that rises from rue Saint-Antoine. The new street at the top of the ridge was named to honor Guy Carleton, Lord Dorchester, the first post-Conquest British governor of Québec. The merchants and moneymen who ran much of Canada from Old Montréal's Saint James Street built their grand homes on what was then called Dorchester Street, and by mid-century the neighborhood had become a focal point for French-Canadian resentment of the British elite.

When the politician Réné-Lévesque died in 1987, the newly resurgent French took the opportunity to launch a cartographic counter-revolution. The street was renamed to honor Lévesque, founder of the Parti Québecois and Québec's prime minister from 1976 to 1985. He had led the province to the brink of separation from Canada and was the architect of the language laws that made French the sole official tongue of the province. The message was loud and clear: *Nous sommes arrivé* (we have arrived).

Ignace Bourget, the bishop of Montréal from 1840 to 1885, had a similar assertion of identity in mind when he decided to build the francophone Roman Catholic **Cathédrale Marie-Reine du Monde** in the heart of anglophone, Protestant Montréal. The cornerstone for Mary Queen of the World was laid in 1870, the dome was completed in 1886, and the cathedral finally opened for worship in 1894. Plans called for a quarter-scale reproduction of St. Peter's in Rome, and that's pretty much what Bourget got. But the details are purely Montréal— from the row of thirteen patron saints of the city parishes across the front to the paintings of local saints and martyrs that enliven the vast interior. *Boulevard Réné-Lévesque ouest and rue Mansfield; 514-866-1661.*

Architects of the cathedral set it back from the street so that it would welcome worshippers up the steps to the doors. Equally large but more modern buildings have ignored street-friendliness, giving pedestrians along the boulevard the feeling of walking in a highway tunnel. The process began, innocuously enough, when the **Fairmont Hôtel Le Reine Elizabeth** opened in 1957 on top of the Gare Centrale, the passenger rail terminal built between 1938 and 1943. As the new gal in town, the Queen Elizabeth became the toast of Montréal society. It was no coincidence that the Beaver Club opened here in 1959 as an avatar of the original association, formed in 1785 by an elite group of fur traders who had spent at least a winter in the Canadian Northwest. The modern club is more strictly social and gastronomic, and the Beaver Club remains one of the grand classic restaurants of the city.

John Lennon and Yoko Ono staged a "bed-in" for peace in Suite 1742 of the Queen Elizabeth in May and June 1969. Gold records and photos of the couple are mounted on the wall, and the room still has the table where Lennon composed "Give Peace a Chance." (It was recorded on the spot.) Lennon biographer Albert Goldman quotes the musician as saying, "In me secret heart, I wanted to write something that would take over 'We Shall Overcome.' " *900 boulevard Réné-Lévesque ouest; 514-861-3511.*

Dominion Square was renamed Dorchester Square in 1988 as a sop to traditionalists who felt Lord Dorchester deserved *something* after ceding his street. The main **Infotouriste Centre** (1001 rue du Square-Dorchester; 514-873-2015) sits at the head of the square, and city tour buses load and unload out front. The square is nearly overrun with memorial statues, including figures of Queen Victoria; the poet Robert Burns; Canada's first prime minister, John A. Macdonald; and its first francophone prime minister, Wilfrid Laurier.

Dorchester Square is a shady respite in the heart of Downtown.

Swinging Montréal

Montréal's best known jazz musician, pianist Oscar Peterson, was born in 1925 at 3021 rue Delisle (near the corner of avenue Atwater) in the predominantly black neighborhood of Petit Bourgogne, or Little Burgundy. With its proximity to the railyards of the Grand Trunk, Canadian Pacific, and Canadian Northern railroads, Little Burgundy was a magnet for American and Caribbean blacks who moved to Montréal in the early years of the twentieth century to work on the trains. Peterson's pianist father was, in fact, a porter with Canadian Pacific Railway. As Prohibition put out the lights in bars and clubs across North America, Montréal was the only large city to ignore temperance, and the clubs of Little Burgundy served as a refuge for many top jazz musicians, both Canadian and American.

The last vestige of this golden age of jazz is the **House of Jazz** (2060 rue Aylmer; 514-842-8656), known until the summer of 2003 as Biddle's Rib House and Jazz Club. Bassist Charlie Biddle came to Montréal with a road band in 1948 and was so taken with the city that he stayed. Selling cars by day, he played jazz by night—at Biddle's for the last twenty-two years of his life. In 1979, he organized a hugely successful three-day jazz festival that led to the founding of the Festival du Jazz de Montréal the following year. Biddle died in 2003 at age 76.

The massive beaux arts **Sun Life Building** (1155 rue Metcalfe) on the east flank of the square took two decades to complete after ground was broken in 1913. It was for many years the largest commercial office building in the British Empire. During World War II, its underground vaults protected the British crown jewels as well as the gold reserves of many European countries. On the day the Parti Québecois came to power in Québec—November 15, 1976—the Sun Life Assurance Company announced it would move its headquarters to Toronto.

The bizarre turns in the streets and ill-planned crosswalks make the area south of Dorchester Square a pedestrian challenge. Nonetheless, if you've ever laced on ice skates, it's worth working your way down to rue de la Gauchetière. On the corner of rue Metcalfe, the fifty-one-story building **Le 1000 de la Gauchetière** rises 205 meters. The office tower holds the year-round **Bell Atrium le 1000** skating rink (514-395-0555), where Montrealers can practice their figure eights and work

Thousands of spectators cheer on musicians at the Festival du Jazz de Montréal.

up speed until the outdoor ponds freeze. The telephone giant also has its name on the **Bell Centre** (1260 rue de la Gauchetière ouest; 514-932-2582), which opened in 1996 as home ice for the Montréal Canadiens hockey team—also known as Les Habitants, or the Habs. Seating more than twenty-one thousand, the indoor stadium also hosts rock and classical music concerts as well as other forms of bread and circuses. Guided tours take you to the rink, the Canadiens' Hall of Fame, television broadcast studios, and—in the off-season only—the Habs' dressing room.

Boulevard Réné-Lévesque continues west into Westmount, where it reverts to the name Dorchester. A few blocks short of the border between arrondissements, the **Centre Marguerite d'Youville** occupies a large and tranquil tract amid the urban hubbub. Marguerite d'Youville founded the Soeurs de Charité, or Sisters of Charity, in Old Montréal in 1738. Dedicated to caring for the sick, poor, and elderly, the order—also known as the Grey Nuns—established schools, hospitals, and orphanages. In 1871, construction began on the sisters' massive stone convent, which also served as a school and hospital. With the secularization of social services during the *revolution tranquille* of the 1960s, the provincial government compelled the order to separate its religious center from its charitable works. Members of the laity had to leave, and the convent's population declined from around 1,000 nuns to about 280 today.

The guided tours of the chapel and crypt begin with a corridor of paintings showing the life of Marguerite d'Youville, from her childhood and First Communion to her death, when she was surrounded by the community that would carry on her mission. It's a quick lesson in the utility of didactic "lives of the saints" paintings.

D'Youville was interred beneath the order's original Old Montréal chapel when she died in 1771, but her body was dug up in 1855. The remains were augmented with wax, covered with a habit, and put on display under glass until 1885, when the case for her canonization was made in Rome. At that point, the body was sealed in a zinc case. Following her beatification in 1959, the case was unsealed. Inside, pushed through cracks, were hundreds of rolled scraps of paper, each asking an intercession by Mother d'Youville. She was canonized in 1990, and her remains are now encased in the main altar of the convent chapel. *1185 rue Saint-Mathieu; 514-932-7724. Open in the afternoon, except Monday.*

Dating from nearly the same period as the convent, the Shaughnessy House on boulevard Réné-Lévesque at rue du Fort is one of the few mansions not destroyed when Dorchester was widened to become a boulevard in the 1950s. Built in 1874 for Baron Thomas Shaughnessy, a railroad magnate, the home now forms a wing of the **Centre Canadien d'Architecture.** The center, founded by the architect and Seagram heiress Phyllis Lambert, is more a study library than a museum per se. It does, however, mount exhibitions, and admission includes the opportunity to glimpse the sumptuous Victorian comforts that Baron Shaughnessy enjoyed. Directly across boulevard René-Lévesque, the **Ernest Cormier Sculpture Park** (honoring Montréal's premiere art deco architect) is filled with fanciful outlines of architectural forms. *1920 rue Baile; 514-939-7026.*

■ RUE SAINTE-CATHERINE

On one inevitably steamy weekend in July, three hundred merchants along rue Sainte-Catherine lug their wares out of their stores and set up along a two-|kilometer stretch in what they claim is Canada's largest *vente trottoir,* or sidewalk sale. Around 350,000 people hit the street to hunt for bargains, listen to musicians, and scoop up free samples. In the spirit of the city's summer festivals, Montrealers manage to transform shopping into family entertainment.

Hijinks and lights of the Festival Montréal en Lumière brighten the long winter nights. (following pages) La Baie anchors Phillips Square on rue Sainte-Catherine.

Running fifteen kilometers west to east across the city, rue Sainte-Catherine has what is often touted as the largest concentration of stores in Canada. The core shopping district is the thirteen-block segment from rue Saint-Mathieu (just west of the Centre Marguerite d'Youville) to Phillips Square (four blocks west of Place des Arts). Small boutiques and coffee shops are interspersed with large department stores, cinemas, and spacious shopping malls.

King Edward VII continues to rule over **Phillips Square** in the person of a pigeon-besmeared statue erected in 1914 "in memory of a much loved sovereign." Peace, abundance, liberty, and the "founding races"—England, Scotland, Ireland, and France—make allegorical appearances on the plinth, reflecting a self-assurance that the square has lost in the ensuing decades.

Yet as drab as it can appear in the wilting heat of summer, Phillips Square was retail Montréal's hub a century ago. In 1891, the city's leading department store, Henry Morgan's, abandoned its base on Saint James Street in Old Montréal and built a new retail emporium on rue Sainte-Catherine. In his 1897 *History of Montréal,* the Reverend J. Douglas Borthwick gushed, "Within is a perfect panorama of almost everything to delight the eyes and it is hard (with a light purse) not to break the commandment. (Thou shalt not covet.)" Morgan's success attracted other businesses, and within a generation, rue Sainte-Catherine had lost all traces of its residential origins. The grand building of Henry Morgan's, further enlarged in 1923, now houses **La Baie**—that is, **Compagnie de la Baie d'Hudson** (585 rue Sainte-Catherine ouest; 514-281-4422), as the Hudson's Bay Company is known in Québec. Founded in 1670 as a fur-trading concession, it's now the largest department store operation in Canada.

Phillips Square acquired even more cachet in 1894, when **Henry Birks et Fils** (1240 Phillips Square; 514-397-2511) also relocated from Saint James Street, where the jewelry business had been founded in 1879. For many generations, Birks was the jeweler of choice for Montréal's elite. The family-owned business was sold in 1993 to an Italian investment firm that wisely retained the Birks name and the trademark blue box with rampant lion.

The neo-Gothic **Christ Church Cathedral** was erected in 1859 for an Anglican congregation that dates back to 1760. It's taken both ingenuity and entrepreneurship to keep the church operating in the midst of such prime retail real estate. The original 1.6-million-kilogram stone central tower was so heavy that it sank unevenly into the ground; it developed such a severe tilt that it had to be removed in 1927. (A replica aluminum steeple was erected in 1940.) In 1987, the church participated in a development project that called for even more unusual engineering. Two levels of retail shops were carved out beneath the church and a thirty-four-story office building was erected behind it. The cathedral was raised on stilts and new foundations were driven into the bedrock to support the entire complex. The mirrored surface of the office tower reflects the gray stone of the church, providing a dual image of old and new Montréal. In addition to regular worship services, the cathedral has an extensive program of choral and organ music programs. *635 rue Sainte-Catherine ouest; 514-843-6577.*

At the same time that many communities in North America were letting their historic shopping districts go to seed while consumers flocked to suburban shopping malls, Montréal invited the malls downtown, installing them in office and retail buildings and scattering them through the subway system. The retail center

Stopping for breakfast after a late night out.

THE OTHER "DOWN" TOWN

When Place Ville-Marie, the cruciform skyscraper designed by I. M. Pei, opened in the heart of downtown in 1962, the tallest structure of the time also signaled the beginning of Montréal's subterranean city. Montrealers were skeptical that anyone would want to shop or even walk around in the new "down" town, but more than four decades later, they can't live without it. About half a million people use the thirty-kilometer underground pedestrian network daily. The tunnels link ten Métro stations, seven hotels, two hundred restaurants, seventeen hundred boutiques, and sixty office buildings—not to mention movie theaters, concert halls, convention complexes, the Bell Centre, two universities and a college, and subway, commuter rail, and bus stations. Montrealers who live in one of more than two thousand apartments connected to the Underground City can pop out to buy a liter of milk on a February day and never have to change out of shirt sleeves and house slippers.

Most of the Underground City parallels the Métro lines. The six-block sector of continuous shopping between La Baie (east of the McGill station) and Les Cours Montréal (west of the Peel station) is perhaps the densest portion of the network. Montréal was ahead of the curve in requiring all construction in the Métro system to include an art component, resulting in such dramatic works as Frédéric Back's mural of the history of music in Place-des-Arts and the dramatically swirling stained glass windows by Marcelle Ferron in Champs-de-Mars. In all, about a hundred works of art are distributed over fifty stations. The Art Nouveau entrance to the Square Victoria station, a gift from the city of Paris, is the only original piece of Hector Guimard's architectural-design work outside the City of Light.

Going up . . . going down—in the Underground.

beneath Christ Church, **Promenades Cathédrale** (625 rue Sainte-Catherine ouest; 514-849-9925), opened in 1988 as an important link between the McGill Métro stop and the subterranean entrance to La Baie and set the template for the retail galleries that connect much of the Underground City parallel to rue Saint-Catherine.

Second in size only to Macy's in New York, Eaton's was Montréal's leading department store from 1925 until it foundered in the 1990s. The immense space between avenue McGill College and rue University has since been divided into the **Eaton Centre** (705 rue Sainte-Catherine ouest; 514-288-3759), a vertical shopping mall of small stores, and the flamboyant **Les Ailes de la Mode** (677 rue Sainte-Catherine ouest; 514-282-4537), a multilevel clothing and housewares emporium that seems devoted to staying au courant, if not always avant-garde. To set itself apart, Les Ailes offers such amenities as a carousel for toddlers, a workshop where consumers can paint their own enamels, and a spa where weary shoppers can grab a massage. Its food vendors include a sushi bar.

One of the more lamented casualties of the economic downturn of the late 1980s and early 1990s was the venerable Simpson's department store. Its space has been split between a Paramount multiplex and IMAX Cinema, and the Québec City–based clothier **La Maison Simons** (977 rue Sainte-Catherine ouest; 514-282-1840), a frequent winner of city polls as best clothing store. A short distance west is Toronto-based outdoor clothing and gear retailer **Roots** (1035 rue Sainte-Catherine ouest; 514-845-7995), best known for outfitting the Canadian Olympic teams.

Farther west still, **Ogilvy** holds on—minus its historic possessive " 's," courtesy of the Québec signage laws—in its 1908 Romanesque Revival building at the corner of rues de la Montagne and Sainte-Catherine. When the Ogilvy family sold the business in 1927, twenty-year-old J. Aird Nesbitt took the helm and guided the store into merchandising legend. In 1950, he launched his most lasting innovation by hiring bagpipe players in tartans and kilts to walk through the store playing during the lunch hour—a practice that continues today. Since 1987, Ogilvy has been an umbrella store for independent boutiques, from staunchly traditional Burberry to younger, more adventurous designers. In his 1897 *History*, the Reverend Borthwick rose to high oratory to sing the store's praises, noting that it was "an ornament to the street and the place where every thing 'Scotch' can be procured.… Everything is very substantial in this establishment from that of the owner himself to the quality of his goods and Daughters of Old Scotia flock there knowing they will get all the Clan Tartans of Caledonia and the best of English goods." *1307 rue Sainte-Catherine ouest, 514-842-7711.*

■ GOLDEN SQUARE MILE

For a self-proclaimed historian, the ever-ebullient Borthwick was overstating a bit when he declared in 1897 that "Sherbrooke Street has always been the aristocratic street of Montréal." But by his day, it was widely touted as the city's answer to New York's Fifth Avenue. The area known as the Golden Square Mile—rue Sherbrooke from rue Aylmer west to chemin de la Côte-des-Neiges—had displaced Dorchester Street in Montréal's social hierarchy. In the late 1870s, Montréal moneymen had won the contract to build the Canadian Pacific Railway, a deal that made Montréal the hub of the country's rail system. Goods and money rode into town on the rails. By the early twentieth century, it was estimated that denizens of the trophy homes along the Golden Square Mile controlled seventy percent of Canada's wealth.

David Ross McCord (1844–1930) was the scion of an Ulster Irish family paradigmatic of the anglophone assumption of power and wealth in post-Conquest Montréal. They arrived in the 1760s and quickly prospered. As McGill University history professor Brian Young has written, "If it moved and it was English, they had their fingers in it," magnifying their original mercantile fortunes through early-nineteenth-century land deals in southwestern Montréal. Heir to the family fortune, David McCord trained for the law but found his true vocation as a collector. Possessing both the fierce nationalism of the Montréal English-speaking business elite and the Victorian penchant for imposing order through exhaustive inventory, he began assembling a private collection of Canadiana in the 1880s. In 1919, he donated his collection of fifteen thousand artifacts to McGill University.

The **Musée McCord d'histoire canadienne** opened in 1922. McCord's private holdings still form the core of the museum's much-expanded collections, now housed in the former Student Union building. McCord salvaged the artifacts of First Nations cultures as emblematic of the heroic origins of Canada, and enshrined the trappings of his own anglophone merchant class as the flower of civilization in the wilderness. Among the museum's holdings are Canadian costumes and decorative arts, portraiture from the late eighteenth and early nineteenth centuries, and artifacts from the tribes of Québec and the fur-trade regions.

"Wintering" is perhaps the most entertaining section of the permanent exhibit "Simply Montréal: Glimpses of a Unique City." It illustrates what Stephen Leacock called, in his 1942 *Montreal: Seaport and City,* the "attitude of Montreal toward its winter, midway between apology and praise and at best something like the defense

SCOTIA PRINCES

The Methuens felt themselves as much an integral part of Montréal as the mountain around which the city was built. They had been wealthy for a sufficient number of generations to pride themselves on never making a display. Instead, they incubated their money, increasing it by compound interest and the growth of the Canadian Pacific Railway. They were all Scotch-Canadians who went to a Presbyterian church every Sunday and contributed regularly to charities and hospitals. They served as governors of schools and universities, sat as trustees on societies founded to promote the arts, joined militia regiments when they left the Royal Military College, and had the haggis piped into them at the Saint Andrew's Day dinner every winter

No Methuen found it possible to feel inferior to the English in any respect whatsoever; rather they considered themselves an extension of the British Isles, more vigorous than the English because their blood was Scotch, more moral because they were Presbyterians. Every branch of the family enjoyed a quiet satisfaction whenever visiting Englishmen entered their homes and remarked in surprise that no one could possibly mistake them for Americans.

—Hugh MacLennan, *Two Solitudes*, 1945

of an old friend gone wrong." Indeed, Montrealers delight in the extremity of the season, which routinely brings at least thirteen snowstorms of more than ten centimeters each. (The city spends more than $50 million Canadian a year in snow removal.) Displays ask visitors to guess such records as largest snowfall in forty-eight hours (two hundred centimeters in 1827) or lowest recorded temperature (–33.9 degrees Celsius in 1933). Examples of sleighs and snowshoes, warm parkas, fur hats, muffs, and multilayered gloves show how Montrealers have learned to cope—and even revel—in the season. Signage in a case of skates and uniforms notes that in Montréal, hockey is "more than a sport—a religion." *690 rue Sherbrooke ouest; 514-398-7100.*

One of those early residents of what became the Golden Square Mile probably welcomed the winter for a more practical reason. James McGill made his money in the fur trade as a member of the North West Company (See "Lachine Canal and Rapids," page 72). In 1813 he bequeathed his fortune and his country estate at the foot of Mont Royal to the Royal Institution for Advancement of Learning to establish the college that has grown into **McGill University**. Since holding its first

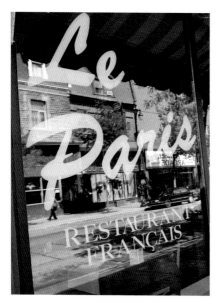

Established in the 1950s, Le Paris serves traditional cuisine bourgeois.

classes in 1829, McGill has become one of the leading English-language universities in Canada. The neoclassical Roddick Memorial Gates across from the end of avenue McGill College mark the main entrance to the low-rise, leafy campus. A small clock inset into the west gate presumably is intended to help students get to class on time. The Welcome Centre is located in Burnside Hall, the first building on the right inside the gates. Guided tours are conducted on most weekdays. *805 rue Sherbrooke ouest; 514-398-6555.*

McGill's **Redpath Museum** looks like a Victorian period piece, with its Romanesque Revival building and unapologetically old-fashioned specimen displays. The museum's core collections go back to the accumulation of rocks, minerals, fossils, birds, and butterflies that Sir William Dawson brought with him to McGill in 1855. At the time, they represented cutting-edge evolutionary science—Charles Darwin would not publish *The Origin of Species* until four years later. In 1857, Dawson became McGill's "principal" and presided over the school's emergence as a world-class university. In 1882 Peter Redpath, a sugar magnate and Golden Square Mile resident, funded the museum to celebrate the twenty-fifth anniversary of Dawson's leadership. The high ceilings permit a first-floor airborne ossuary of sorts, with skeletons of beluga and minke whales hanging in the entry hall along with leatherback turtle and fur-seal skeletons. A stuffed lion and gorilla flank the staircase between floors two and three, with signs requesting, "*S.V.P. Ne Touchez pas le Lion*" and "Please Don't Touch the Lion." The third-floor ethnology exhibits, which include Egyptian mummies, underwent extensive renovation in 2003. *859 Sherbrooke ouest; 514-398-4086.*

Following the steps uphill from the Redpath completes the cut through the McGill campus to **avenue Docteur-Penfield,** where more of the fine manses that gave the neighborhood its reputation survive than on rue Sherbrooke. The section of the street near avenue du Musée is sometimes called "Embassy Row," because foreign consulates occupy many of the old homes.

In the last quarter of the twentieth century, towering office buildings altered the stately quality of rue Sherbrooke, but the streets that rise up to meet it between Peel and Bishop have retained some of the neighborhood's privileged character. The Victorian buildings on Crescent between Sherbrooke and boulevard Maisonneuve are occupied by art galleries, couturiers, luxury boutiques, and a smattering of fine restaurants. The same bank of streets, particularly between Maisonneuve and rue Sainte-Catherine, is known for bars, nightclubs, and outdoor cafés.

With its signature black awning and golden lanterns and its sumptuous marble lobby, the **Ritz-Carlton, Montréal** was a home away from home for generations of Montréal aristocracy after its opening in 1912. In his 1980 novel *Joshua Then and Now,* Mordecai Richler's title character recalled the good old days: "Where once impeccably schooled brokers could conspire over malt whiskies and dishes of

Avenue McGill College is the busy north-south thoroughfare of Downtown.

A gallery in the Musée des Beaux-Arts.

smoked almonds to send a dubious mining stock soaring. Where, after a morning of trying on dresses in neighboring Holt-Renfrew, matrons of good family could meet for a lunch of cold Gaspé salmon and tossed salad in the garden café." Both the Café de Paris and the adjoining dark wood-paneled bar remain popular places for civil midday meetings. The hotel, where Elizabeth Taylor and Richard Burton were married in a guest room in 1964, still finds favor with film and fashion crews. *1228 rue Sherbrooke ouest; 514-842-4212.*

Richler chose the perfect stand-in for the Sherbrooke retail world. The Streamline Moderne building of **Holt-Renfrew** opened in 1937 for the retailer's hundredth anniversary. Holt carries chic pret-a-porter design collections, but the brass bas reliefs of fox, beaver, squirrel, rabbit, and lamb on the rue de la Montagne doors bespeak the retailer's origins as a furrier. *1300 Sherbrooke ouest; 514-842-5111.*

The two buildings of the **Musée des Beaux-Arts de Montréal** not only straddle rue Sherbrooke, they also bridge past and future. Founded in 1860, the Museum of Fine Arts owns a marvelously encyclopedic collection of art through the ages. Most of the permanent holdings are housed in the original beaux arts building on the north side of the street. The Canadian collection is one of the strongest in the country, ranging from eighteenth-century portraits to contemporary art. Some of the most striking work is by the Group of Seven, painters who imbued the Canadian landscape with heroic and mythic qualities. One member, A.Y. Jackson, had close ties to Montréal and a special affinity for the closed horizons of Québec, perfectly captured in *Grey Day, Laurentians* (1930–31).

A subterranean passageway to the Jean-Noël Desmarais Pavilion is like a walk through the tombs—past Japanese, Pre-Columbian, Egyptian, Islamic, Asian, and African art. Galleries devoted to art after 1945 make a smooth transition to the sheer modernism of the new pavilion, which opened in 1991. Montréal's best-known modern artist is Jean-Paul Riopelle, who was born in the city in 1923 but spent much of his mature life in France, where he died in 2002. His abstract expressionist period is neatly summed up by the 1952 painting *Crosswind* and a circa-1950 paint-encrusted easel that resembles his compositions of the period.

Paul-Émile Borduas was born in 1905 in Saint-Hilaire, near Montréal. His 1948 manifesto, *Refus global* (Total rejection), assailed the conformity and narrowness of Québec culture and became a rallying cry for a generation of artists and intellectuals who dreamed of a new modernism in the province. Examples of his work show his evolution from an ashen realism to ever greater abstraction, first abandoning form and finally jettisoning color to work in black and white.

The new pavilion is architect Moshe Safdie's second contribution to the iconographic buildings of Montréal. Less radical than Habitat, it demonstrates the mature architect's postmodernist sense of visual rhythm—comparable to Philip Glass's musical compositions. Safdie repeats elements until they become lulling, then interrupts the sequence by skipping or adding a beat. The mathematical feel of the pavilion is summed up in the half-height, double-depth stairs, which must be taken either in baby steps or in stretching leaps. The museum uses the long and airy corridors and gargantuan galleries primarily for touring exhibitions, many of which make their only North American stop in Montréal. *1379 rue Sherbrooke ouest; 514-285-1600.*

PLATEAU MONT-ROYAL
A N D   E N V I R O N S

The Plateau Mont-Royal is literally the most storied portion of Montréal. The city's two best-known authors—the anglophone Mordecai Richler and the francophone Michel Tremblay—grew up on opposite ends of the neighborhood, and the worlds they describe sound like alternate universes. Encompassing both the immigrant enclaves along "the Main" and the stolidly French-Canadian working-class districts clustered around the parish churches, the Plateau is "the old neighborhood" for Central European Jews, Greeks, Italians, Portuguese, Haitians, West Africans—and for the *pur laine* Québecois, as descendants of the colonists of New France sometimes style themselves.

Although it is one of the city's larger residential areas—extending north and northeast from rue Sherbrooke to the Canadian Pacific Railway tracks, and east from Mont Royal to rue d'Iberville—affordable apartments become scarcer all the time. Pockets of the Plateau Mont-Royal are still gateways for new immigrants, but since the 1960s, the broader neighborhood has metamorphosed into a lively blend of young professionals, students, and artists and other bohemian types.

As long as the weather permits, people laze around the parks, chat with great animation in the outdoor cafés, and call to each other from the balconies of their classic triplexes with outdoor staircases. The physical limits of the Plateau are distinct, but it spills over on its edges. This chapter includes some of those adjacent areas as well: notably Little Italy on the north, and the Latin Quarter and the Village on the south.

■ LATIN QUARTER

Located just east of Place des Arts, the Latin Quarter is defined by the Université de Québec à Montréal (UQÀM), the Berri-UQÀM Métro station, and a concentration of cinemas, film centers, libraries, and performing arts venues on boulevard de Maisonneuve and rue Saint-Denis. It has been a student district since 1878, when the first francophone university in Canada, Québec City's Université Laval, established a Montréal campus. Changing its name to Université de Montréal in 1920, the burgeoning institution built a massive new campus on the slopes of Mont Royal and began moving there in the 1940s. Its departure left a void in the

Enjoying a petit déjeuner *(breakfast) en plein air on the Plateau.*
(following pages) The Latin Quarter vibrates with energy and attitude.

Latin Quarter, filled when the provincial government merged five schools and colleges to establish the francophone Université de Québec à Montréal in 1969.

With nearly forty thousand students, UQÀM sprawls across the district, but its chief administrative building neatly marries past and present. The 1860 facade of the former Cathédral Saint-Jacques, on boulevard de Maisonneuve between rues Berri and Saint-Denis, forms the exoskeleton of a modernist building of linked and stacked glass, brick, and concrete cubes—creating an instant dissolve between the Gothic Revival pieties of the 320-foot spire (Montréal's tallest) and the beehive of scholarship. The airiness of the Saint-Jacques facade disguises the sheer bulk of the complex, which occupies most of the block south to rue Sainte-Catherine. One side of the behemoth structure holds the **Galerie de l'UQÀM,** which focuses on contemporary artists, with an emphasis on work from Québec. *1400 rue Berri; 514-987-8421.*

The preponderance of students keeps the neighborhood young, and during the summer's comedy and film festivals, the Latin Quarter turns into a peripatetic street carnival as tens of thousands of people turn out to catch free performances

Street performers set up on every corner.

and attend screenings. Montréal has a strong busking tradition, and mimes, stilt-walkers, magicians, musicians, and other street performers from around the world seem to set up on every corner. The construction of the **Théâtre Saint-Denis** (1594 rue Saint-Denis; 514-849-4211) between 1908 and 1915 established the neighborhood as an entertainment district, and the twenty-five hundred seats make the theater the second-largest concert hall in the city. Virtually every major performer who toured North America between the world wars played the Saint-Denis. It continues to book stand-up comedians, Québecois singers, and rock bands, and it hosts the "gala" nights of the Just for Laughs/Juste Pour Rire comedy festival.

Comedy is not the only thing Canadians take seriously. The National Film Board of Canada has helped support thousands of feature, documentary, and animated films. The Montreal branch of the **Office National du Film du Canada** has scheduled screenings in a 142-seat theater. The facility also makes films available for nearly instant viewing at fifty individual CineScope stations powered by the automated CinéRobothèque. When you order a film, a robot under a glass roof opens one of 2,340 drawers, removes a videodisc and mounts it in a player—all in about ninety seconds. You can browse the database and watch as many films as you can fit in before closing. The film students are obvious—they're the ones punching the freeze-frame and single-frame advance buttons to scrutinize technique. *1564 rue Saint Denis; 514-496-6887.*

Literally around the corner, the **Cinémathèque québecoise** has more than twenty-five thousand films, television programs, and videos from all over the world, and schedules more than fifteen hundred screenings each year. On Friday nights, the museum shows silent films with live piano accompaniment. *335 boulevard de Maisonneuve est; 514-842-9768.*

Continuous screenings are the cornerstone of the **Musée Juste Pour Rire/Just for Laughs Museum** at the northwest corner of the Latin Quarter. From its name to its programming, the comedy museum is perhaps the most successfully bilingual institution on the island—all the more amazing, considering the verbal subtleties of comedy. A time line that begins with Aristophanes and ends with Mark Twain and Oscar Wilde (with stops in between for the likes of Rabelais, Cervantes, and Honoré Daumier) honors the Immortals of Comedy. "Immortals" of the twentieth and twenty-first centuries get more extended treatment, and you can laugh yourself silly with more than four hours of comedy clips in seven theaters. Who's an "Immortal"? Well, the Québecois are almost French, so Jerry Lewis qualifies. Ditto the Three Stooges, Bob Hope, Red Skelton, Dame Edna, Richard Pryor, Johnny Carson, Peter Sellers, Dario Fo, Mel Brooks, and Larry Gelbart. French-Canadian comics include Claude Meunier (whose television show, *La Petite Vie,* was wildly popular), Yvon Deschamps, Gilles Latulippe, and the loony duo, Dodo et Denise. Francophone comics are subtitled in English, anglophone comics in French. This museum is the perfect rejoinder to a rainy day. *2111 boulevard Saint-Laurent; 514-845-4000.*

The Just for Laughs Festival takes over the Latin Quarter in July.

■ THE VILLAGE

Montréal's primary gay residential district lies east of the Latin Quarter. The Village, as it's called (or the Gay Village, as some residents prefer), centers on rue Sainte-Catherine and the rainbow-emblazoned Beaudry Métro station. The staffers at the **Village Tourism Information Centre** (1260 rue Sainte-Catherine est; 888-595-8110) provide personalized services—with a special emphasis on meeting the needs of gay and lesbian travelers—while officially promoting a Pollyannaish vision of the neighborhood as full of "carefully restored brick homes, shaded backyard gardens, and window boxes brimming over with flowers." There's truth in such clichés, but the Village is both grittier and more vibrant than such descriptions suggest. By day, it's a fairly sedate section of town, notable for its film and video production facilities, for the desultory porno shops on rue Sainte-Catherine, and for the stores selling antiques and mid-twentieth-century modern furniture on rue Amherst. By night, the neon blossoms along rue Sainte-Catherine, boys in dresses and heels arch their backs on street corners, and male couples hit the streets, arm in arm.

Montréal's gay community, self-proclaimed as the largest in Canada, is as addicted to festivals as is the rest of the city. Virtually every weekend in warm weather features a gay-themed event, and at the end of July, **Divers/Cité** fills an entire week with drag cabaret, outdoor screenings of queer cinema, modern dance performances, and hot salsa nights. It all builds up to the Pride Parade, a celebration of human diversity in nearly every imaginable form. More than one million visitors come to Montréal for the party.

The Village was originally the industrial district known as *Faubourg à m'lasse*, or Molasses Suburb, for the strong-smelling molasses tanks of the nearby sugar companies, and many of the decaying factory and warehouse buildings have yet to be gentrified. Nostalgia permeates the **Ecomusée de fier monde** (Ecomuseum of the proud world), which uses striking historical photographs of industrial life to try to recapture the gritty blue-collar sensibilities that dominated the neighborhood only two generations ago. Interpretation is entirely in French, and some of the signage verges on the French-Canadian dialect *joua*—virtually unintelligible even to a speaker of European French. But the museum is included on some discount passes and is worth a visit just to see the interior of the art deco public bath house. *2050 rue Amherst; 514-528-8444.*

The Pride Parade in the Village celebrates diversity …

■ SQUARE SAINT-LOUIS

Square Saint-Louis sits north of rue Sherbrooke off rue Saint-Denis, technically just north of the Latin Quarter. A mid-nineteenth-century reservoir was transformed into a park in 1879—just in time to appeal to the francophone upper middle class. By the end of the century, Square Saint-Louis had become an enclave of artists and authors, including the literary intelligentsia of French Canada at the time.

The houses surrounding the square exude a nostalgia for all things French, but with practical adaptations to the Québec winter. Most are topped by mansard roofs, steeply pitched and bluntly truncated. Bay windows bulge from nearly every facade to gather in the light, and none of the buildings has a main entrance at ground level—one mounts the stairs above the snowbanks to go in the front door. Perhaps more than any other pocket of Montréal, Square Saint-Louis captures the soft-focus life of the haute bourgeoisie from an earlier time. Jan Morris wrote in her book *O Canada,* "I shall remember a room I glimpsed one evening in St-Louis Square, an exhibition, I thought of franco Canada—so snug, so heavy with lamps and pictures, so velvety-looking in the twilight, as though bombazined aunts lived eternally up there, drinking inexhaustible infusions in antimacassared armchairs."

… with makeup and costumes to simply die for.

Although the neighborhood has seen some seedy years, it has fully rebounded. In the middle of the park, a tall, two-level fountain gushes water into a broad pool. Mature trees provide a shady canopy over the benches and flower beds. On a summer evening, people walk their dogs, play guitars and sing, carry on conversations, and eat ice cream. It's not uncommon for a harpist to set up and play for change. All in all, it's a genteel scene.

On the west side, the square connects to pedestrian **rue Prince-Arthur.** In the 1960s, head shops, used clothing stores, and sandalmakers served the counterculture here. When the city converted the street to a pedestrian mall in 1981, inexpensive restaurants proliferated. Today, Greek, Afghan, Italian, Vietnamese, Mexican, and Polish dining spots dominate rue Prince-Arthur, and signs in the windows advise diners *"apportez votre vin,"* or "bring your own wine." The combination of reasonably priced ethnic food and the savings of supplying one's own plonk makes Prince-Arthur a dining destination all year round, but especially in summer, when restaurateurs set up tables along the streets and an army of fire-eaters, jugglers, accordionists, chanteuses, and flamenco dancers amuses diners between courses.

■ THE MAIN

Boulevard Saint-Laurent was the first road to connect the harbor to the hinterlands. It cuts across the island like a line drawn in the sand—dividing east from west, and in popular lore, francophone from anglophone. Every immigrant group from the seventeenth-century French to the twenty-first-century Haitians has landed on its feet along the Main, as it's been alternately known since at least 1825. Most traces of early immigrant life were erased in 1892, when the city broadened the southern part of Saint-Laurent below rue Prince-Arthur to create Montréal's own Champs-Élysées. But north of that grand boulevard, each successive wave of immigration has left evidence of its passing.

Three segments of boulevard Saint-Laurent remain particularly evocative of immigrant life—the flank of Mont Royal between rue Sherbrooke and boulevard Saint-Joseph, covered here, and the districts of Mile End and Little Italy.

From about 1880 until World War I, immigrants streamed into Montréal, balkanizing the Main with ethnic enclaves; eastern European Jews and southern Italians were by far the largest groups. Immigration fell to a trickle between the

Whenever the weather permits, Montrealers live in their outdoor cafés.

ANGEL OF THE COLONY

Jeanne Mance nurtured Montréal from a wilderness mission to a thriving community. One of the cofounders of Ville-Marie in 1642, she was Canada's first lay nurse and the founder, three years later, of the city's first hospital, the Hôtel-Dieu. Her victories over illness and penury are recounted at the **Musée des Hospitalières de le Hôtel-Dieu de Montréal** (201 avenue des Pins; 514-849-2919), which stands in the shadows of the massive 1861 hospital on the southern slope of Mont Royal, a few hundred meters west of the Main.

The small and elegant museum, completed in 1992, tackles several big subjects— the city's founding and growth, the evolution of medicine, and the evolving role of the religious order that provided most of the city's health care into the mid-twentieth century. Ultimately, the lives of the nuns emerge as the most fascinating part of the mix. Nineteenth-century photographs show sisters in the wards or in the pharmacy grinding medicines. A display case holds a plate filled with wedding bands, worn thin from a lifetime of work. At the end of the day, each bride of Christ would retreat to a small cell furnished with a bed, two chairs, a wash basin, commode, table, two devotional books, religious pictures, a crucifix, and a kneeler.

world wars, but picked up dramatically in the late 1940s and continues steadily today. Ethnicity keeps shifting. Many Jewish and Italian families moved to the suburbs after World War II—just as the Greeks, Portuguese, and Hungarians arrived to take their place. By the end of the twentieth century, the children of the immigrants of the 1950s and 1960s were moving on, and the face of Saint-Laurent had taken on a Haitian and West African look. The Main is still a boulevard of immigrant dreams, and a walk up the street can feel like a tour of the globe.

Below avenue des Pins, boulevard Saint-Laurent is essentially a continuation of the Latin Quarter, with youth-oriented shops and **Ex-Centris** (3536 boulevard Saint-Laurent; 514-847-2206), a digital film-editing facility and screening room for auteurist cinema and "new media"—a mecca for avant-gardists. Above des Pins—where the gentrification project of the 1890s halted—Saint-Laurent wears an older, more ethnic face. The long block between des Pins and rue Duluth, for example, is a virtual international food court. Restaurants serve falafel, Vietnamese food, pan-Asian noodle dishes, Thai cuisine, Canadian steak, brick-oven pizza, Portuguese grilled chicken, homemade ice cream, Indian food, sushi, Venezuelan tropical juices, and the obscure cuisine of l'Île Maurice (a dot of land in the Indian Ocean midway between India and Madagascar).

Just north of avenue des Pins, the Main takes a turn for *mittel europa* with a pair of butcher shops turned delicatessens that can send your taste buds into a frenzy. **Charcuterie Hongroise** (3843 boulevard Saint-Laurent; 514-844-6734) has been making its own sausages since 1954, as well as providing the Hungarian community with several varieties of bulk paprika, from sweet to very hot. This is where you go for ham hocks, European noodles, and old-country sauerkraut. Almost next door, **La Vieille Europe Charcuterie et Fromagerie** (3855 boulevard Saint-Laurent; 514-842-5773) has ridden Montréal's gourmet enthusiasms into the twenty-first century. The proprietors roast their own coffee (a whoosh of espresso-tinged smoke accompanies the rush of beans from the roaster) and make specialty sausages, including bison, deer, and Barbary duck.

Food has become the Main's main business. **Moishe's Steakhouse** (3961 boulevard Saint-Laurent; 514-845-1696) has served massive slabs of beef in its swank upstairs dining room since 1938, and in a city where restaurant fashion runs hot and cold, there's *still* often a long wait for a table—even when you have a reservation. By no means kosher, Moishe's commands great loyalty from Jewish families who've been in the suburbs for generations.

There's also a wait at the decidedly more casual **Schwartz's Smoked Meat** (3895 boulevard Saint-Laurent; 514-842-4813). Montréal's famed smoked meat is similar to American pastrami, but with a distinctive spicing and smoking indigenous to the city's eastern European Jewish community. Schwartz's is not the originator of smoked meat (that honor probably goes to the founder of Ben's, Downtown on boulevard de Maisonneuve), but it serves what most Montrealers consider the best. In pouring rain or blowing snow, people line up on the sidewalk for take-out. It's often easier to grab seats in the dining room and order a sandwich. Seating is family style, so be prepared to make new friends. Pastrami fans often order the "fat," which can be very greasy, while most people new to smoked meat order the "lean," which can be dry. Ask for "medium." And don't forget the pickle. The cherry Coke, alas, now comes from a can.

The slice of the Main between avenue Duluth and boulevard Saint-Joseph is a worldly jumble of cultures that you might pass through like stations across the band of a shortwave radio. Import stores advertise specialties from Africa, from

People-watching is elevated to an art on Square Saint-Louis.

MAIN LINE, MONTRÉAL

Mercedes had met Béatrice on the number 52 streetcar that left the little terminus at the corner of Mont-Royal and Fullum, then went down to Atwater and Sainte-Catherine, going by way of Saint-Laurent. It was the longest ride in town and the housewives from the Plateau Mont-Royal took great advantage of it. They would set off in a group on Friday or Saturday, noisy, laughing, tearing open bags of penny candy or chewing enormous wads of gum. As long as the streetcar was going down Mont-Royal, they were in their element, giving each other slaps on the back if they choked, calling out to other women they knew. . . . But when the streetcar turned down Saint-Laurent, heading south, suddenly they'd calm down and sink back into the straw seats: all of them, without exception, owed money to the Jews on Saint-Laurent, especially to the merchants who sold furniture and clothes; and for them, the long street separating rue Mont-Royal from rue Sainte-Catherine was a very sensitive one to cross. . . . They didn't even dare to look outside; they told themselves it was harder to recognize a face seen in profile than straight on. Some, but really just a few, even took out their rosaries.

—Michel Tremblay, *The Fat Woman Next Door Is Pregnant*
(translation by Sheila Fischman), 1978

Latin America, from Portugal. Cinema l'Amour sells XXX videos next to L. Berson & Fils Monuments, where the second language is Hebrew. A mainstay of the neighborhood is the outstanding **S. W. Welch Used & Rare Books** (3878 boulevard Saint-Laurent; 514-848-9358), where the Holstein-marked cat Rosie holds down the front window. Mojo Head Shop stands next to a beauty salon, while a sports bar holds forth adjacent to Les Minots Bistro et atelier du jazz. Beat Record Store sits cheek by jowl with a piercing and tattoo salon.

Bain Schubert (3950 boulevard Saint-Laurent; 514-872-2587) opened in 1929 as one of sixteen public baths built around the city for blue-collar families in cold-water flats. The tan brick art deco building, with a gracefully curved roof, was restored a few years back to serve as a public pool. Two streets east, **Bain Colonial** (3963 rue Coloniale; 514-285-0132) provides a true bath house experience. Built in 1914, it originally catered to eastern Europeans with a tradition of the steam bath, or *shvitz*. Although it once served both men and women, Colonial Bath is now a male preserve, offering Turkish (wet steam), Russian (dry steam), and Finnish (dry sauna) rooms. The Russian sauna, with its three-tiered wooden benches and large oven set into the wall, figures in Mordecai Richler's novel *The Apprenticeship of Duddy Kravitz*. The period ambience makes Colonial a favorite for both gay and straight men.

The nest of narrow streets just east of and parallel to the Main includes rues Saint-Dominique (dismissed as "St. Dump" by Leonard Cohen, who has long owned a house on the 4300 block), Coloniale, and Bullion. The *frango* chicken joints, tile stores, and travel agencies underscore the Portuguese presence in this neighborhood—an ethnicity that only becomes more pronounced as the Main rises up the hill from rue Rachel. At the corner of rue Marie-Anne, **Parc du Portugal,** with benches covered in blue and white tiles, captures the style of a pocket park in Lisbon. The small bandstand is often used for concerts. A steep escarpment rises at boulevard Saint-Joseph; beyond it lies Mile End.

Nightlife along the Main.

■ HEART OF THE PLATEAU

In the mid-nineteenth century, when the Québecois left the countryside to seek work in Montreal's factories, they created a cluster of French-Canadian villages on the farmlands east of the Main and north of rue Sherbrooke. Each had a parish church and school at the center. During the Great Depression, the parishes added a *caisse populaire*, or credit union, to the mix, and looking for a church spire and then scanning the surrounding buildings is still the easiest way to find an automated teller machine in this checkerboard of streets.

The first large-scale suburb in Montreal housed the miners and stonecutters who worked in the limestone quarries that were later filled in to create Sir Wilfrid Laurier Park. Many of the earliest houses were little more than shacks. Three such structures in a row—architectural historians affectionately call them "the three little pigs"—survive on rue Pontiac just north of avenue du Mont-Royal and south of rue de Bienville.

But this working-class district quickly evolved a vernacular architecture peculiar to Montréal—the three-story house with separate entrances (and street numbers)

Residential stairways of traditional Plateau houses make patterns in the snow.

for each level, reached by twisting external iron staircases that left more room for the big families inside. As the houses march down a long street, their stairways establish a visual rhythm; they are a favorite subject of photographers, particularly when the angular light of early morning or late afternoon creates a xylophone of shadows. Traditionally, the owner would live on the first level and control the small patch of lawn or garden out front. The second and third levels—cold in the winter, sweltering in the summer—were rental flats. If you visit in early summer, before all the leases expire on July 1, the buildings will be dotted with signs advertising something like *3½ à louer*, meaning a flat with a bathroom (the half), kitchen, living room, and one bedroom for rent.

While most of the Plateau is residential, it is crossed by two of Montréal's most dynamic commercial streets: rue Saint-Denis and avenue du Mont-Royal.

■ RUE SAINT-DENIS

Possibly the most electric and eclectic street in the city, Saint-Denis is the heart and soul of Montréal nightlife, which, in characteristically French fashion, revolves around the pleasures of eating and drinking. The sidewalk terraces of Saint-Denis are full to bursting in good weather, especially as *tout Montréal* gathers for drinks between 5 P.M. and 7 P.M. to make plans for the evening ahead. Certainly there's no shortage of choices. Rue Saint-Denis was in the vanguard of imaginative fine dining through the 1990s, as chefs rediscovered the delights of such Québec products as salt-meadow lamb from Îles des Madeleines, local foie gras, and salmon from the Gaspé peninsula, heralding a nouvelle Québecois cuisine. In similar fashion, the street's restaurants have been a bellwether in the citywide maturation of ethnic dining from falafel and chow mein to menus that specialize in the cuisine of Galicia, the Bengali coast of India, or the French-Swiss Alps.

Style-setters in the long block between rue Roy and avenue Duluth keep Plateau residents au courant in other ways. **Revenge** (3852 rue Saint-Denis; 514-843-4379) sells both men's and women's wear by designers from across Canada, with an emphasis on Québec talent, including Simon Chang, Jean-Claude Poitras, and Marie Sainte-Pierre. Up the street, **Chapofolie** (3944 rue Saint-Denis; 514-982-0036) augments the look with accessories and a whole lot of hats, including summer and winter berets. **Le Théâtre d'Aujourd'hui** (3900 rue Saint-Denis; 514-282-3900) hews close to its name, producing contemporary French-language plays that carry on the tradition of rue Saint-Denis as a francophone performance area.

Avenue Duluth crosses Saint-Denis at the 4000 block, and a branch of the Société d'Alcools de Québec, or SAQ—the provincial liquor and wine shop—sits at the intersection. Duluth is another of Montréal's destination dining districts, with many bring-your-own-bottle establishments in the stretch between Saint-Denis and rue Saint-Hubert. On most evenings between 6 and 9, half the pedestrians along the street are carrying SAQ bags to their favorite restaurants.

North of Duluth, the boutiques are interspersed with cafés and boîtes, often situated on the ground level of former haute-bourgeois town houses. A sushi bar may sit next to a Parisian bistro, but the clientele ignore the invisible boundaries on the sidewalk, leaning from table to table to trade a joke or light a cigarette. Cultural landmarks include **Champigny** (4380 rue Saint-Denis; 514-844-2587), which claims to be the largest French bookstore in North America; the modest offices of Montréal publisher **Les Editions Boréal** (4447 rue Saint-Denis); and **Théâtre Rideau Vert** (4664 rue Saint-Denis; 514-844-1793). This famed French-language theater, a forum for Québecois playwrights, produced Michel Tremblay's debut, *Les Belles Soeurs,* in 1968. In this comic drama—the first major stage piece in the Québec vernacular—fifteen women at a stamp-licking party discuss their lives.

■ RUE RACHEL

Rue Rachel crosses rue Saint-Denis at the 4200 block. A century ago, Rachel was one of the major commercial thoroughfares of the Plateau, and the gigantic **Église Saint-Jean-Baptiste** (309 rue Rachel est) gave its name to an incorporated town later absorbed into Montréal. Today Rachel is more run-down than most major east-west streets, and the lower property values translate into a hodgepodge of ethnic shops, tattoo parlors, and other bits of youth culture.

Seven blocks east of rue Saint-Denis, **Parc Lafontaine** is the Plateau's leafy playground. An S-curve lake is a favorite ice-skating spot in the winter and serves as a summer backdrop for the outdoor **Théâtre de Verdure.** The gently rolling landscape of mature maples and oaks swallows the many facilities—baseball diamond, soccer fields, playgrounds, even a pit for *pétanque* (a game similar to the Italian bocce). For a sedate stroll, the west side was planted with a geometric regularity that echoes the grovelike parks of Paris.

On the north side of the park, **La Maison des Cyclistes** (1251 rue Rachel est; 514-521-8356, ext. 344) functions as the nerve center of the considerable Montréal cycling community. It houses Café Bicicletta, which proffers snacks and

Strolling by the lake in Parc Lafontaine.
(following pages) Harpists by the kiosk in Square Saint-Louis provide a decidedly Gallic
alternative to the amplified rock or plaintive folk songs of most street musicians.

serious coffee, as well as the provincial cycling association, Vélo Québec, creator of Le Route Vert (a series of cycling trails throughout the province) and organizer of BikeFest, an annual event that brings out a pack of thirty thousand or more bicyclists to tour the streets of Montréal.

■ AVENUE DU MONT-ROYAL

The heart of the heart of the Plateau is the **Mont-Royal Métro station,** just east of the intersection of rue Saint-Denis and avenue du Mont-Royal. When the Métro opened in the 1960s and cut the commute to downtown to mere minutes, this area was set on a course of gentrification. The chic little flower and vegetable market that surrounds the station sets the tone for the current residents.

Just west of Saint-Denis, **La Binerie Mont-Royal** (367 avenue du Mont-Royal est; 514-285-9078) is a holdover from the neighborhood's more blue-collar days and the setting for much of Yves Beauchemin's best-selling novel *Le Matou* (*The*

LES FÈVES

On June 2, 1974, a month after they'd taken over The Beanery, Florent and Slipskin had a gross profit of $5,682.74, the bulk of which, it's true, went toward paying off their loan.... The Beanery served an average of 250 meals a day. In one month, customers devoured 500 gallons of soup, 122 loaves of bread, 80 dozen eggs, 400 pounds of beef stew, 77 veal hearts, 350 pounds of shepherd's pie and the same of meatball stew, 1,837 pounds of pork and beans, 168 tourtières, 150 sugar pies, 600 gallons of coffee and 28 pans of bread pudding.

–Yves Beauchemin, *The Alley Cat* (translation by Sheila Fischman), 1981

Alley Cat). Using recipes that date from 1938, the restaurant serves such Québecois specialties as *fèves au lards* (baked beans), *pâté chinois* (akin to American chop suey), and *ragout de boulettes* (meatballs in gravy).

Other establishments on Mont-Royal west of rue Saint-Denis tend to mimic rue Rachel, with a mix of Goth clothing stores, ethnic eateries, old-fashioned barber shops, and tattoo parlors. But east of the Métro station, the avenue becomes livelier and more well-off, albeit with a distinct sense of whimsy. It is not hard to find, for example, a Chinese herbalist next door to a pizza joint where an Elvis impersonator croons Frank Sinatra songs.

A branch of the upscale bakery-delicatessen **Première Moisson** (860 avenue du Mont-Royal est; 514-523-2751) signals the beginning of the street's gourmet district. But the morning crowds cluster at **l'Avenue du Plateau** (922 avenue du Mont-Royal est; 514-523-8780), where a cook prepares fresh fruit in one window while customers chain-smoke in another. In the afternoons, it's safe to presume *les fumeurs* have adjourned across the street to **Chez Baptiste** (1045 avenue du Mont-Royal est; 514-522-1384), a bar that specializes in local microbrews and weekend jazz jams.

The only smoke rising inside **Saint-Viateur Bagel & Café** (1127 avenue du Mont-Royal est; 514-528-6361) comes from the wood-burning ovens, as a few of the sesame seeds on the hand-rolled bagels get extra toasted. This trendy café is a next-generation spin-off of the old-fashioned Saint-Viateur Bagels in Mile End.

■ MILE END

Named for the Canadian Pacific Railway yards just beyond avenue Bernard, Mile End is a former immigrant neighborhood poised on the edge of gentrification. Montréal's best-known anglophone author and journalist, Mordecai Richler (1931–2001), grew up in Mile End at 5257 rue Saint-Urbain, a building that now wears a modern, renovated face. In *The Street,* he describes "an all but self-contained world made up of five streets, Clark, St. Urbain, Waverley, Esplanade, and Jeanne Mance, bounded by the Main, on one side, and Park Avenue, on the other." The Main separated Richler and his Jewish immigrant neighbors on the west from similarly struggling "pea soups" on the east, as young Richler and his friends called French Canadians. Saint-Urbain's Jewish identity persists, albeit in rather different style from Richler's childhood. A yellow school bus pulls up daily

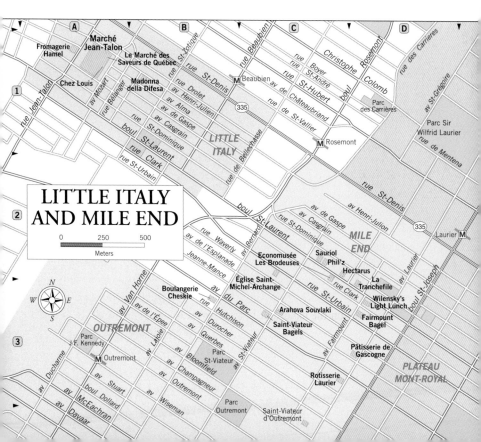

STRIVING

On St. Urbain Street, a head start was all. Our mothers read us stories from *Life* about pimply astigmatic fourteen-year-olds who had already graduated from Harvard or who were confounding the professors at M.I.T. Reading *Tip-Top* comics or listening to *The Green Hornet* on the radio was as good as asking for a whack on the head, sometimes administered with a rolled-up copy of *The Canadian Jewish Eagle*, as if that in itself would be nourishing. We were not supposed to memorise baseball batting averages or dirty limericks. We were expected to improve our Word Power with the *Reader's Digest* and find inspiration in Paul de Kruif's medical biographies. If we didn't make doctors, we were supposed to at least squeeze into dentistry.

—Mordecai Richler, *The Street*, 1969

to disgorge little boys with dangling earlocks at the Hebrew School, established on the 5200 block by the Hasidim in 1955.

Mile End is so mythic that its borders blur. The traditional boundaries extend from boulevard Saint-Joseph on the south to the train tracks on the north, from rue Hutchinson on the west to rue Saint-Denis on the east. The former Mile End City Hall, now a fire station, sits at the corner of Saint-Laurent and avenue Laurier. The contradictions of class, ethnicity, and time are most evident as Laurier marches toward the mountain with a swagger. Hand-crafted chocolates, artisanal cakes, and savory deli salads and quiches make **Pâtisserie de Gascogne** (237 avenue Laurier ouest; 514-490-0235) the very model of upscale indulgence. A block closer to the mountain, a green sloping roof topped with a giant chicken weathervane identifies **Rotisserie Laurier** (381 avenue Laurier ouest; 514-273-3671), where French-Canadians have tucked into plates of roast chicken and mashed potatoes since 1936. Gourmet shops, chocolatiers, kitchen supply stores— Laurier seems dedicated to both the art and substance of eating.

In Mile End, cuisine is culture. One block north of Laurier, avenue Fairmount shows its Jewish roots. Just nine stools line the worn counter at **Wilensky's Light Lunch** (34 avenue Fairmount ouest; 514-271-0247), a place that still serves

A baker slides bagels into a wood-fired oven.

half-sour pickles and remembers how to make an egg cream soda. The Wilensky Special is a grilled salami and bologna sandwich. Hand-lettered verse above the counter advises newbies: "When ordering a special you should know a thing or two. / They are always served with mustard, they are never cut in two. / Don't ask us why, just that this is nothing new. / This is the way it's been done since 1932."

Virtually next door, **Fairmount Bagel** (74 avenue Fairmount ouest; 514-272-0667) claims descent from Montréal's first bagel shop, opened by Isadore Schlafman in 1919 and moved to this location in 1949. The shop was closed for about a decade before Isadore's son Jack reopened it in 1979. Now open around the clock, Fairmount also makes matzo bread and upsets some purists by mixing blueberries, chocolate chips, black olives, and sun-dried tomatoes into its bagels.

The long stretch of boulevard Saint-Laurent between avenues Laurier and Bernard was one of Montréal's three major manufacturing districts in the early twentieth century. Heavy industry concentrated on the Lachine Canal and the Hochelaga-Maisonneuve waterfront, but the Mile End section of the Main was devoted to millinery, clothing, shoes, and brewing. The old industrial buildings are being recycled as fast as the market can absorb them—the sweatshops of yesteryear being transformed into luxury loft condos.

Still other industrial operations have been designated as provincial "economuse-ums"—small manufacturing operations willing to put up explanatory displays and welcome visitors. Appropriately enough, three are clustered on the Main.

The aroma of bindery leather permeates the air at **La Tranchefile** (5251 boulevard Saint-Laurent; 514-270-9313), an artistic bookbinder. A block farther up the street, **Hectarus** (5329 boulevard Saint-Laurent; 514-495-2629) makes glass sinks, basins, shelves, and other objects for the kitchen and bath that could be (and have been) in *Architectural Digest*. Across the street, the **Economusée Les Brodeuses** (5364 boule-vard Saint-Laurent; 514-276-4181) gives a similar educational treatment to the art of hand embroidery. The shop is an excellent source of needlework supplies and also offers classes. One popular local embroidery project is the decoration of berets.

This same stretch of Saint-Laurent is also home to small pottery ateliers, wood-working shops, and a pair of stores that specialize in mid-twentieth-century furni-ture. **Sauriol** (5417 boulevard Saint-Laurent; 514-895-0858) is deeply stocked with Scandinavian design, which was very popular in Montréal in its heyday of the 1950s and 1960s. Almost next door, **Phil'z** (5377 boulevard Saint-Laurent; 514-278-2323) is stronger on kitschy American style, especially heavily chromed furniture.

Mile End feels most like an immigrant neighborhood on rue Saint-Viateur, where many cafés set up tables beneath leafy arbors and the Byzantine mass of **Église Saint-Michel-Archange** presides over all from the corner of rue Saint-Urbain. Aristide Beaugrand-Champagne (1876-1950), a pioneer in the use of reinforced concrete in Montréal and dean of architecture at the École des beaux-arts de Montréal, designed and built St. Michael's in 1914–15. With stained-glass motifs of Irish roses, shamrocks, and a Celtic cross, it's easy to surmise that the original congregation was Irish. But their symbols are overshadowed by the ceiling frescos painted a decade later by Guido Nincheri. Archangel Michael dominates the huge central dome; vignettes around the base show him sending eight fallen angels down to hell. Most members of the parish today are Greek, Italian, and Polish. *5580 rue Saint-Urbain; 514-277-3300.*

The bakery that made the street famous—at least in foodie circles—is **Saint-Viateur Bagels,** which has been in business "only" since 1957. The shop never closes, baking 1,020 dozen bagels a day and selling them a few at a time. The dough—eggs, malt, sugar, flour, water, and yeast—is shaped by rolling out strips by hand and pinching them into rings. These rings are then dipped in a honey-water solution to make the seeds stick, dropped onto long wooden planks, and baked in a wood-fired oven. The owner of Saint-Viateur learned the trade at Fairmount Bagels, and the two shops have a friendly rivalry. Saint-Viateur claims to be the oldest in continuous operation, and a wall of newspaper clippings documents the ongoing war about age and authenticity. The only thing Fairmount and Saint-Viateur agree on is that Montréal bagels are superior to the bigger and heavier bagels made in New York City. *263 rue Saint-Viateur ouest; 514-276-8044.*

Across the street, **Arahova Souvlaki** is perhaps the physically largest reminder that this section of Mile End was principally Greek a generation ago. The restaurant occupies a full city block, flies U.S., Canadian, Québec, and Greek flags from its roof, and draws Greeks back from the north-island suburbs for authentic moussaka in the old neighborhood. *256 rue Saint-Viateur ouest; 514-274-7828.*

■ LITTLE ITALY

Just over the Canadian Pacific Railway tracks, boulevard Saint-Laurent enters Little Italy through a marble gate. Essentially a continuation of Mile End, Little Italy sprang up when early-twentieth-century immigrants moved north to buy open land where they could build houses and plant gardens. Stroll the side streets and you'll see neat little plots with flowers out front and a tomato patch and grape arbor in back. Order a coffee in any of the dozens of cafés and you'll get an espresso.

One of the city's largest fresh markets, **Marché Jean-Talon** (7075 avenue Casgrain; 514-277-1588) opened in Little Italy in 1934. Less gentrified than Marché Atwater, Jean-Talon attracts many of the city's top chefs, who come seeking the perfect fruit or vegetable for the evening meal. The farm market is ringed by boutique dealers of specialty items: **Fromagerie Hamel** (220 rue Jean-Talon est; 514-272-1161) is one of the city's great cheese shops; **Chez Louis** (222 Place du marché-du-nord; 514-277-4670) searches out such exotic produce as French melons and fresh morels; and **Le Marché des Saveurs de Québec** (280 Place du marché-du-nord; 514-271-3811) makes geography its theme, selling top cheeses, beers, wines, ciders, and other food and drink produced entirely in Québec.

The creation of the Italian parish of **Madonna della Difesa** in 1910 provided a spiritual and social anchor for the neighborhood. The church was built from the designs of artist Guido Nincheri, who spent many years painting the wall and ceiling frescos, including a depiction of Mussolini that caused sufficient furor to get the artist thrown into a detainment camp during World War II. Although Montréal's roughly half a million Italian-Canadians are scattered across the island, it often seems like they all want to get married in and buried from the "cathedral of the Italians in Canada." *6800 avenue Henri-Julien; 514-277-6522.*

Growers throughout the Québec countryside sell their produce at Marché Jean-Talon.

HOCHELAGA-MAISONNEUVE

Rising from the St. Lawrence River between the Old Port and the Jacques-Cartier Bridge, the neighborhood of Hochelaga-Maisonneuve stands apart from the rest of the city, a muted mass of workers' housing relieved only by church spires and the Olympic Park, which glows at the crest of the hill. Even from miles away, the Olympic Stadium and Tower stand out above this rolling gray world like a clump of white mushrooms sprung up overnight.

Named for the Iroquois village that Jacques Cartier visited in 1535, Hochelaga was the product of industrial expansion in the 1870s, as textile mills and shoe factories rose along the riverbanks east of the port. When Montréal moved to annex cash-strapped Hochelaga in 1883, several landowners protested and formed their own community of Maisonneuve, with centralized urban planning and enough public works projects to earn the town the sobriquet *le petit Westmount de l'est* (the little Westmount of the east) for its free-spending ways. Despite the economic success of its factories—it was the fifth-largest industrial city in Canada in 1900—Maisonneuve spent its way into insolvency and merged with Montréal after all in 1918.

The Great Depression effectively destroyed the textile mills, shoe factories, and other labor-intensive enterprises of Hochelaga-Maisonneuve. The "jobs schemes" of the era, however, did give the neighborhood one significant amenity: the Botanical Garden, in a corner of Maisonneuve Park. Forty years later, a portion of the open land at the crest of the escarpment behind the former Maisonneuve city hall was transformed into the Olympic Park for the summer games of 1976.

And that's what most visitors to Hochelaga-Maisonneuve come to see—the Botanical Garden, the Olympic Stadium, and the Biodôme, which occupies the former Olympic velodrome. The predominantly francophone residential neighborhood south of this complex is perhaps most notable for a handful of signature public buildings and its dramatically decorated parish churches.

As a point of orientation, broad boulevard Pie-IX (named for Pope Pius IX), the first four-lane road to run north-south across the island, divides Maisonneuve on the east from Hochelaga on the west.

Chinese Lantern Festival at the Jardin Botanique.

■ JARDIN BOTANIQUE DE MONTRÉAL

Starting late in June, you can follow the heady scent of ten thousand rose bushes from the Pie-IX Métro stop to the **Botanical Garden**. This horticultural showcase—among the largest in the world—was launched in 1931 by then-mayor Camillien Houde. When Houde was voted out of office the next year, weeds grew where the garden was planned and the initial greenhouse was turned into a rabbit hutch. When Houde regained office, he was inspired by Université de Montréal botanist Frère Marie-Victorin, who contended that the city's tricentennial should be celebrated with a new botanical garden. "Montréal is Ville-Marie, a woman," Marie-Victorin reasoned in a speech in 1935, "and you certainly can't give her a storm sewer or a police station. It's obvious what you must do! Give her a corsage for her lapel. Fill her arms to overflowing with all the roses and lilies of the field!" In 1936, work began anew. Workers spread rich muck excavated from Lac aux Castors in Parc Mont-Royal and built greenhouses to nurture the collection.

The ten exhibition greenhouses added in 1958 are a particular delight in the winter. The garden of "economic tropical plants" could inspire a shopping trip to the ethnic markets on boulevard Saint-Laurent. A dense canopy of coffee, cacao, cola, cinnamon, cardamom, and allspice trees overhangs vanilla orchids, black pepper bushes, and other gustatory enhancements. Not all the plants produce edible products—stay away from the strychnine and Bushman's poison (used in Australia to kill fish in watering holes). The greenhouses are each controlled to specific climates—tropical heat and humidity for the orchids, subtropical warmth for camellias and begonias, a parching aridness for cacti and succulents. The "Garden of Weedlessness" is actually a container garden, including bonsai more than a century old donated by the Shanghai Botanical Garden, the Chinese government, and the Hong Kong industrialist Wu Yee-Sun. Wu had planned to donate his bonsai to the United States—until the U.S. Department of Agriculture balked at letting the prized specimens into the country in 1980.

Many of the outdoor gardens follow cultural themes—a Japanese garden, a garden of plants used by the eleven First Nations peoples of Québec, and the amazing **Chinese Garden**. A construction crew of one hundred came from China and spent a year laying out and assembling this Shanghai-style garden, complete with tiled paths and traditional sculptures. One of the most popular sections of the Botanical Garden, the pavilions are regularly used for tea ceremonies, Chinese painting demonstrations, and recitals of Chinese music and dance.

Even while making use of the free trolley that tools around the considerable grounds of the Botanical Gardens, it could take the better part of a day to see the outdoor gardens without ever entering the **Arboretum,** established in 1970. This museum of trees is planted with multiple examples of each species hardy enough for the Zone 4 winter. Stroll along the main road heading north, and you'll walk past scented groves of white and red pines before being struck by the woodsy pungency of hemlock and spruce. Black-fringed gray squirrels and impertinent chipmunks romp through the grounds in the fall, stuffing their cheeks with the pea-sized seeds of beeches and scampering off to store big meaty acorns. You can pick up hints for identifying less obvious species by studying examples of bark, leaves, and flowers at the Maison de l'arbe (Tree House), the arboretum's interpretive center. A birders' checklist details more than 190 species that have been spotted in the Botanical Garden and Arboretum. *4101 rue Sherbrooke est; 514-872-1400.*

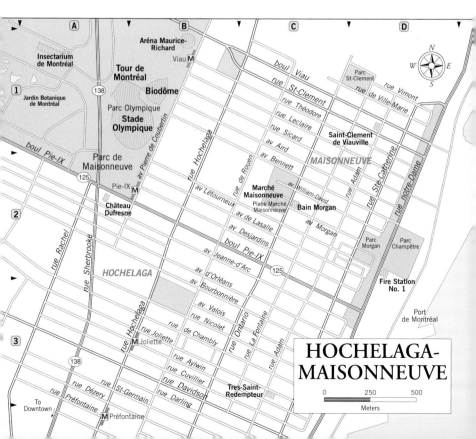

■ Insectarium de Montréal

Set on the rue Sherbrooke lawn of the Botanical Garden, the **Insectarium** is the natural complement to the horticultural site. A cross between insect zoo and natural history museum, the Insectarium tells and shows more than most people might want to know about the world of six-legged creatures. It begins innocuously enough, with an outdoor garden planted to attract bees. Things get more exotic inside, with displays of insects from what the curators call the planet's six "biogeographic" zones.

With specimens ranging from mounted carcasses and carapaces to live creepy-crawlies, it's not surprising that the Insectarium is a favorite stop for prepubescent boys. The Insectarium bends its definition to include arachnids as well as insects, so you can watch the perambulations of a Mexican redknee tarantula and study the fluorescent colors of scorpions under ultraviolet light. Next to the tank filled with giant spotted cockroaches—each around four inches long—are less-than-reassuring signs that explain not only that the cockroach is the oldest winged insect, having appeared 250 million years ago, but also that there are thirty-five hundred known species.

Not all the creatures induce queasiness. A display devoted to butterflies emphasizes their beauty: the blue and black swallowtails from tropical Africa, for example, and the "ghost of the night," the gigantic mottled gray Noctuid as big as your hand. *4581 rue Sherbrooke est; 514-872-1400.*

■ Biodôme

Montréal's other "zoo" is also indoors. The **Biodôme**, however, is less a zoo than a museum of four environments, each with its own weather, flora, and fauna. Inside the bicycle-race facility built for the 1976 Olympics, the Biodôme, which opened in 1992, squats in the shadow of the Olympic Stadium and Tower like a giant albino horseshoe crab, a self-contained ark that resembles a spaceship sent out to carry Earth's lifeforms to distant planets.

The pathway through the facility begins in the heat and humidity of the **Tropical Forest,** where trees tower over the path and a lazy, shallow stream runs through. True to its model, the tropical forest is a noisy place, with the sound of water, the occasional rude squawks and screeches of the scarlet and military macaws, and the excited piping of small children exclaiming over the golden marmosets as their parents admire the scarlet ibis and pink roseate spoonbills feeding in the shallows.

Not all the insects are in display cases at the Insectarium.

The **Laurentian Forest** is a more temperate world that collapses the density of the trees and animals found just a few miles from the city limits. Reluctant porcupines try to stay out of sight on a riverbank lined with paper birches, and a bobcat paces back and forth behind a well-concealed fence as ducks paddle and splash around the beaver lodge. In the spirit of reality television, a "beaver-cam" even shows what the giant rodents are up to inside. The pathway leads to a lower level where glass windows on the pond reveal the underside of the beaver lodge and schools of fish common to the nearby forest streams and lakes—longnose suckers, brook and lake trout, and lake whitefish.

The segue to the **St. Lawrence River** is almost seamless, for many of the same species of shrubs and trees line the shores, but as the trail progresses, the river seems ever closer to its mouth. The brackish water smells of salt in the final rock-lined pool, where giant sturgeon up to two meters long patrol the depths. Terns and gulls fly overhead and eider and merganser ducks try to avoid the darting murres, which seem to fly through the water like stubby-winged avian bullets.

Many exotic birds, including the scarlet ibis, inhabit the Tropical Forest environment of the Biodôme.

The murres paddle around the **Polar World,** too, but they're upstaged by impossibly cute puffins. Visitors tend to ignore both birds because an adjacent enclosure that looks like an ice floe is populated with comic Antarctic penguins, toddling and hopping over the ice and rocks, sliding and slipping, diving into the icy water. *4777 avenue Pierre-de-Coubertin; 514-868-3000.*

■ STADE OLYMPIQUE ET TOUR DE MONTRÉAL

In 1969, still flush with the success of Expo '67, mayor Jean Drapeau proposed Montréal as the host city for the XXI Olympiad, to be held in 1976. It remains a controversial decision even today. At the close of the twentieth century, the city still owed more than a quarter of a million dollars on the **Olympic Stadium**—a sum being chipped away at by a tobacco surtax. Moreover, the Montréal Olympic planners ruffled a lot of feathers and affronted Québecois pride by selecting the French architect Roger Tallibert to design the signature stadium. He unveiled the plans for the futuristic, exoskeletal structure in 1972, and the foundation was poured in 1974. The games took place, per Olympic tradition, under open skies. Not until 1985, when construction began on the **Tower of Montréal** and the stadium's retractable roof, did the engineering weaknesses of Tallibert's plan become apparent. The retractable roof of Kevlar fabric was installed in time for the home opener of the Montréal Expos, the National League baseball team, in April 1987, but despite modifications, the roof has never been completely waterproof.

The tower dangles over the stadium like a fishing pole over a trout pond. It has the distinction of being the world's tallest inclined tower (it leans thirty degrees), with the observatory standing 170 meters above the ground. A funicular rail carries glassed gondolas up and down the length in less than two minutes, and the views from the top are worth the trip. The panorama from the southwest windows is the most interesting, for it shows the roof of the stadium and reveals the geometric pattern of the Olympic plaza in the near ground. At a distance, you can see the Ferris wheel that identifies La Ronde amusement park in one direction and the high-capped dome of Oratoire Saint-Joseph in the other. The bridges between Montréal and the southern shore line up like fallen jackstraws, and the silver cupola of Marché Bonsecours gleams amid the matte gray stone of Old Montréal.

(following pages) The observation deck on the Tour de Montréal.

The crowd cheers a 1957 goal by Maurice "Rocket" Richard.

The "Big Owe," as the stadium is often called, is Montréal's largest venue—almost empty for Montréal Expos games, nearly full for massive rock concerts. When no events are scheduled, half-hour guided tours take place. From the perspective of the Montrealers, however, the best legacy of the 1976 games may be Le Centre Sportif, whose vast Olympic pools are still well used. Small children do cannonballs off the competition diving boards and seniors in rubber bathing caps swim laps in the race lanes. *4141 avenue Pierre-de-Coubertin. Stadium and tower: 514-252-4737; Centre Sportif: 514-252-4622. Stadium closed Jan.–mid-Feb.; Centre Sportif closed Christmas Day–New Year's Day.*

Although separate from the Olympic complex, the adjacent **Aréna Maurice-Richard,** opened in 1962, prefigures the Olympic Stadium with its flying-saucer architecture. Former home ice of the Montréal Rocket hockey team (in the Major Junior Hockey League), it was named for Maurice "Rocket" Richard, star of the Montréal Canadiens from 1942 to 1960. Outside, a bronze statue of Richard leans at a sharp angle as he prepares to shoot for the net. The lobby is devoted to a museum of his accomplishments, mentioning such milestones as his National Hockey League record of fifty goals in fifty games in 1945, and his five hundredth career goal in 1957. *2800 rue Viau; 514-251-9930.*

■ CHÂTEAU DUFRESNE

The Château Dufresne is overshadowed by the structures of Olympic Park across boulevard Pie-IX. But it too was radical for its time: the first private home in Montréal built with a reinforced steel frame. Begun in 1915 and completed in 1918 at a cost of more than $1 million, it is possibly the most sumptuous duplex mansion in the city. Civil engineer Marius Dufresne designed the building with the Parisian architect Jules Renard. Marius lived on one side, while his brother Oscar, who ran the family shoe manufacturing business, occupied the other. The brothers' wealth was the legacy of their mother, Victoire du Sault Dufresne, who started making shoes in her summer kitchen in the city of Trois Rivières.

The château was supposedly inspired by the Petit Trianon palace at Versailles, and the brothers certainly aspired to French regal grandeur. In 1920, they befriended Guido Nincheri and let him set up a stained-glass studio in one of the buildings they owned in exchange for taking on the decoration of their homes.

Oscar's side of the house is the more lavish. It is covered with examples of Nincheri's paintings, mostly executed on canvas that was then fastened to the walls, a technique called *marouflage*. In executing the cycle of the seasons in the salon, Nincheri took on such mythic subjects as the court of Aphrodite, Victorian picturesque scenes such as Venice's Grand Canal, and charming but unsubtle modern symbolism—as in a depiction of a modern-dress bride and groom above six baby carriages circling flowering trees. The artist pulled out the stops for his clients; risqué ceiling frescoes that had been painted over when the building was used as a religious school are still being discovered. Nincheri mixed and matched expensive marbles, put up carved and coffered ceilings,

The marvelous gates of Château Dufresne.

Visions of the Divine

Sometimes called the "Michelangelo of Montréal" for his mastery of traditional fresco, Guido Nincheri practically defined the imagery of heaven and earth for Roman Catholic churches in eastern Canada. From his arrival in Montréal in 1914 until his internment as an alleged fascist sympathizer during World War II, Nincheri left his mark on nearly a hundred churches, with paintings, stained glass, and sculpture.

Born in 1885 in Prato, Tuscany, Nincheri found himself stranded in Boston when the outbreak of World War I interrupted a trip to Argentina. Six months later, he made his way to Montréal, where new churches were springing up rapidly. The Florentine-trained artist quickly won a commission to paint frescos in **Saint-Viateur d'Outremont** (183 rue Bloomfield). He also made the preliminary drawings of the church's stained-glass windows for artisan Henri Perdriau, who taught him how to work with leaded glass.

Nincheri's big breakthrough came in 1918, when he was asked to submit plans and make a bid for the construction of Madonna della Difesa in Little Italy, a building that has come to be called the "cathedral of the Italians in Canada." Because he was not a member of the architects' guild, he partnered with Roch Montbriand, but the structure, the stained glass, and the extraordinary frescos are principally by Nincheri. The work progressed over nearly two decades, and after meeting the Dufresne brothers, Nincheri was able to open his own stained glass studio in 1921.

In the years that it took to complete Madonna della Difesa, Nincheri worked on fifteen other churches in Montréal, including two in Hochelaga-Maisonneuve: **Saint-Clement de Viauville** (4903 rue Adam) and **Tres-Saint-Redempteur** (3530 rue Adam). But the artist's masterpieces are the three churches where he handled nearly the entire process of construction and decoration: **Saint-Léon de Westmount** (4301-11 boulevard Maisonneuve ouest), the Byzantine **Église Saint-Michel-Archange** (5580 rue Saint-Urbain), and **Madonna della Difesa** (6800 avenue Henri-Julien). The Italian church proved his undoing. In 1933, he acceded to the parish's request to paint a mural showing Benito Mussolini and Pope Pius XI signing the Lateran Pact of 1929, which created the Vatican City State.

The depiction came back to haunt him when World War II broke out and Nincheri was interned for three months as a enemy alien. On his release, he moved to Providence, Rhode Island, where he died in March 1973 at age eighty-seven.

and installed stained glass, fluted columns, and the occasional decorative sculpture. He treated the Dufresne brothers as his Medicis.

The decoration is more restrained on the side of the house occupied by Marius, but his family furnishings—spanning art nouveau to art deco—offer a fascinating peek at the lifestyle of the rich, if not exactly famous. *2929 rue Jeanne-d'Arc; 514-256-4636.*

■ MAISONNEUVE

The industrialists who conceived of Maisonneuve built it as a model of the industrial city of the future. They laid out spacious streets and avenues, lining most of them with dense but "modern" workers' housing while reserving the finest for the homes of owners and managers. The entire city was provided with municipal water, gas, and electricity. Grand beaux arts public buildings—a soaring city hall, gleaming public baths, and a large public market—surrounded the intersection of avenue Morgan and rue Ontario. Even the parish churches were ambitious structures with sumptuous decor. But when World War I sent real estate values plummeting and industry into a tailspin, Maisonneuve's prosperity evaporated and the neighborhood went into a decline only recently reversed.

The handsome public buildings now are being restored, and soaring real estate values in the rest of Montréal have spelled the beginning of gentrification in Maisonneuve. Three of the neighborhood's grandest public buildings were designed by Marius Dufresne. The **former Marché Maisonneuve** (4375 rue Ontario est), an imposing structure that now serves as the neighborhood cultural and sports center, is considered his crowning architectural achievement. Dufresne faced the building with cut limestone on all four sides so it would make a good impression on train passengers as they whizzed by on the Montréal-Québec route. In its heyday, the market specialized in the sale of livestock and contained about twenty stalls and several grocery stores.

The market closed in the 1960s from lack of use, but a smaller, less architecturally ambitious market opened on its east side in 1995. Now one of the city's major farm markets, surpassed only by the Atwater and Jean-Talon markets, the new **Marché Maisonneuve** (4445 rue Ontario est; 514-937-7754) has some upscale gourmet delis that hint at the neighborhood's resurrection. The **Place Marché Maisonneuve** functions as a community gathering point for neighborhood festivals and concerts.

Across rue Ontario from the market stands **Bain Morgan** (1975 avenue Morgan). Its Greek Revival portico, beaux arts lines, and tiled pool suggest a noble aspiration beyond simply providing for "hygiene and cleanliness among the working population." Renovated in the summer of 2003, it functions as a community gymnasium and swimming pool.

The garden boulevard of avenue Morgan was the showpiece of Maisonneuve. With its grand houses and former Granada Cinema (now the Théâtre Denise-Pelletier), it presents a vivid picture of bourgeois aspiration in the early years of the twentieth century. Yet you need only step a few blocks away from its four-block length to enter the working-class neighborhoods of housing chronicled in francophone literature. The typical three-level homes have outdoor staircases and balconies that families treat as their living rooms for as many months as they can. Even as other parts of Montréal become more diverse, Hochelaga-Maisonneuve remains ninety percent old-stock French-Canadian.

The foot of avenue Morgan features a lovely green park on the former estate of James Morgan, founder of the department store now occupied by La Baie. At the rue Notre-Dame side of the park stands the most controversial of the buildings Marius Dufresne designed for Maisonneuve. Departing from the French beaux arts style, Dufresne modeled the 1915 **Fire Station No. 1** (4300 rue Notre-Dame) on Frank Lloyd Wright's 1904 Unity Temple in the Chicago suburbs. Despite being equipped with both horse-drawn and automotive fire trucks, the building drew the scorn of the architecture critic at the newspaper *Le Devoir,* who decried the style as "Egyptian."

The green lawns of Parc Champêtre, next to the station, overlook the St. Lawrence River. Just downstream from La Ronde, it is an excellent, if little-known, spot to watch the summer fireworks competition.

Sometimes held at the Stade Olympique, sometimes at the Palais des congrès, Bal en Blanc heralds spring with a techno dance festival.

QUÉBEC CITY

On a July day, the sun seems close enough to scorch the wooden planks of the Dufferin Terrace, but the crowds are undeterred. Tour buses are lined up on rue du Fort, engines idling to keep the air-conditioning on. Vacationers clump around the larger-than-life statue of Samuel de Champlain, craning their necks to see over each other as a pair of acrobatic clowns cavort with a unicycle, honk their noses, and occasionally drop their pants to expose polka-dot underwear. As the crowd swells, agile youngsters and grimly determined photographers grab the shiny toes of an angel at the statue's base to pull themselves up to a better vantage.

According to the long-winded inscription, the bronze was cast in Paris and "erected by subscription of the citizens of Québec, governments of Québec and Ontario and the municipal council of Québec in 1898, in the 62nd year of the reign of her majesty Queen Victoria." Few if any of the visitors stop to read it all. One of the clowns has singled out a slender young woman, who smiles nervously as he pulls her into the central ring and mimes that she is to climb onto his back. Reluctantly, she does as he indicates. Moments later, she is riding his shoulders as he pedals the unicycle. He raises his hands triumphantly. She holds on for dear life. The crowd cheers.

The inscription continues: "Champlain was born in Brovage in Saint-Onge around 1567. He served in the French army under King Henri IV, explored the West Indies from 1599 to 1601 and Acadia from 1604 to 1607. In 1608 he founded Québec. He went on to discover 'the Region of the Great Lakes' and led expeditions against the Iroquois between 1609 and 1615. He was successively lieutenant governor and then governor of New France. He died in Québec on Christmas Day 1635."

And now his statue is a landmark—the place your bus group will assemble at precisely four-fifteen-and-don't-be-late. It's been four centuries since he first set foot on the sandbars below Cap-aux-Diamants, and nearly as long since he ordered the first wooden fortress built. Thousands of miles from France, he carved a foothold in the wilderness, and his little fur-trading post soon governed an empire that stretched from Louisbourg to Louisiana. Québec he called it, after the Algonquian word for "the river narrows." The French adventure in North America began and ended here.

Since Victorian times, the Dufferin Terrace has been Québec City's favorite promenade.

■ FORTIFICATIONS

Charles Dickens called Québec "this Gibraltar of America." From a distance, it presents the visage of a castle on a hill, the redoubt of a medieval lord. Almost every early settlement in North America had a fort or palisade, but Québec wrapped itself in a stone fortress and never tore it down. The great gray walls that ring the old city are its monument to an embattled past, and one reason why UNESCO named Québec a World Heritage Site in 1985.

The fortifications stretch four and six-tenths kilometers to girdle Vieux (Old) Québec. They were built for soldiers, but today they're covered with civilians. Above the old parade ground (now Parc de l'Esplanade) families scamper along the ramparts between two of the ancient gates, gazing down the grassy embankment of the park and across to the formal gardens of Parliament Hill. Some of the children play at being soldiers, imagining the invading hordes on the spreading plains beyond. On the opposite side of the city, the walls on rue des Remparts are notched with cannon emplacements. The sun heats the black iron of the stoppered cannons until, by midafternoon, they feel as if they'd just fired on some interloper in the harbor.

Sketch from Samuel de Champlain's journal shows his defeat of the Iroquois at Lake Champlain.

DISTANT WALLS

The fortifications of Cape Diamond are omni-present. They preside, they frown over the river and surrounding country. You travel ten, twenty, thirty miles amid the hills on either side, and then, when you have long since forgotten them, perchance slept on them by the way, at a turn of the road or of your body, there they are still, with their geometry against the sky. The child that is born and brought up thirty miles distant, and has never travelled to the city, reads his country's history, sees the level lines of the citadel amid the cloud-built citadels in the western horizon, and is told that that is Quebec. No wonder if Jacques Cartier's pilot exclaimed in Norman French, *Quebec!*— "What a beak!"— when he saw this cape, as some suppose. Every modern traveler involuntarily uses a similar expression.

— Henry David Thoreau, *A Yankee in Canada*, 1850

The three remaining historic gates to the city—Porte Saint-Louis, Porte Kent, and Porte Saint-Jean—all lie on the west, providing a ceremonial transition into Vieux Québec from the modern world. Within the embrace of the high walls, the city seems close, secure, almost snug—protected from the Indians, from hostile troops, from modernity itself. New France shrugs off two and a half centuries of British rule. The spirit of the ancien régime echoes off every rubblestone wall, every painted wooden shutter.

Québec was a natural for fortification: a high escarpment that controlled a narrowing of the river. When Champlain founded his fur-trading post in 1608, he erected only a minimal defense. Experience with the Iroquois taught him better, however, and in 1620 he began building Fort Saint-Louis atop the escarpment so that he could bombard the enemy below. But a small English fleet ousted Champlain and company in 1629. After 1632, the founder returned and rebuilt the fort to bristle with artillery. The main portion of the settlement moved from the riverbanks to the escarpment. As the religious orders began to expand in 1639 with the arrival of two orders of nuns to complement the missionary priests, a new Québec—the upper city—began to rise around Fort Saint-Louis.

Exhibitions at the **Fortifications Interpretation Centre** (100 rue Saint-Louis; 418-648-7016; open May–Oct.) at the Saint-Louis gate trace the development of the walls in response to threats both real and perceived. In 1689, France and

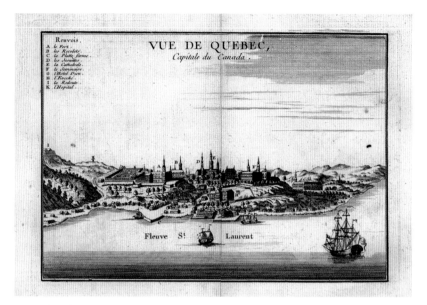

View of Québec in 1755.

England went to war in the first of many conflicts that would not conclude until the defeat of Napoleon. A year later, an English flotilla was dispatched from Boston to take Québec. Secure in his wooden palisade linking stone redoubts, the governor of New France, Louis du Buade, Comte de Frontenac, rebuffed demands that Québec surrender, saying that his only reply would come from the mouths of his cannon. The French count was as good as his word, and the invaders were sent packing. The close call set off a fifty-year spate of building that would forever envelop Québec in the comforting gray stone of its defensive walls.

The St. Lawrence River and the steep embankment of Cap-aux-Diamants presented a formidable obstacle to invasion. It took only a wall on that side of the city to discourage an enemy from scaling the cliffs. The west and southwest edges of the city, on the other hand, opened onto rolling countryside. Bastioned ramparts were needed to protect the flanks. Frontenac started building at the edge of the Plains of Abraham in 1690, constructing an *enceinte*—eleven redoubts linked by a palisade. Thirty years later, the master engineer of the French regime, Gaspard-Joseph Chaussegros de Léry, finished unifying Québec's fortifications. By the end of the 1720s, the walls constituted a suit of stone armor.

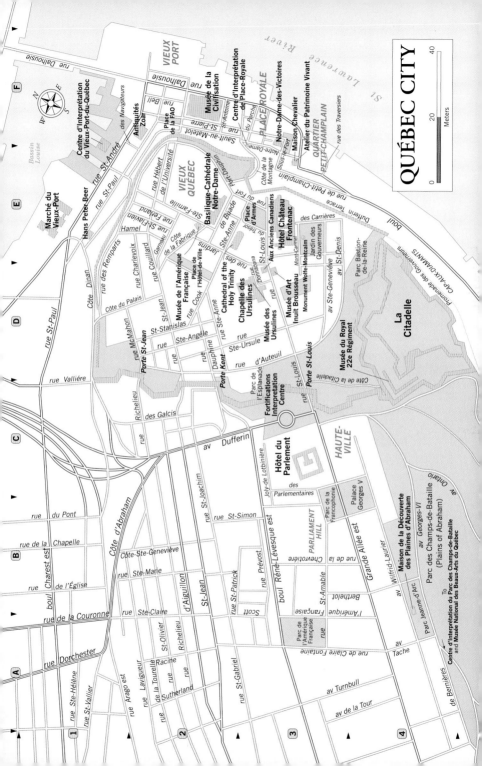

QUÉBEC CITY

Meters

0   20   40

VIEUX PORT

rue Dalhousie

Dalhousie

rue Dalhousie

Centre d'Interprétation
du Vieux-Port-du-Québec

Marché du
Vieux-Port

Hans Peter-Beer

rue St-André

des Navigateurs

Antiquités
Zoar

rue St-Paul

Place
de la FAO

Bell

rue

Musée de la
Civilisation

Centre d'Interprétation
de Place-Royale

PLACE-ROYALE

du Porche

St-Antoine

Sault-au-Matelot

St-Pierre

Notre-Dame

Notre-Dame-des-Victoires

Maison Chevalier

Atelier du Patrimoine Vivant

**QUARTIER
PETIT-CHAMPLAIN**

rue de Petit-Champlain

rue des Traversiers

St. Laurence River

---

rue Dalhousie

Bassin
Louise

rue Hébert

de l'Université

VIEUX QUÉBEC

rue St-Paul

rue Ferland

rue St-Flavien

Hamel

rue Charlevoix

rue Couillard

Garneau

Côte
de la Fabrique

Basilique-Cathédrale
Notre-Dame

Ste-Famille

Ste-Anne

de Buade

Place
d'Armes

**Hôtel Château
Frontenac**

Côte de la
Montagne

Sous-le-Fort

du Trésor

des Carrières

Dufferin Terrace

boul

CAP-AUX-DIAMANTS

Promenade des Gouverneurs

Côte Dinan

rue des Remparts

Côte du Palais

rue St-Jean

Musée de l'Amérique
Française

Place de
l'Hôtel-de-Ville

rue Cook

Jardins des
Jésuites

Cathedral of the
Holy Trinity

Chapelle des
Ursulines

Musée d'Art
Inuit Brousseau

Aux Anciens Canadiens

Jardin des
Gouverneurs

Mont-Carmel

Monument Wolfe-Montcalm

av St-Denis

Parc Bastion-
de-la-Reine

**La
Citadelle**

---

rue St-Paul

Côte d'Abraham

rue McMahon

rue St-Stanislas

rue Ste-Angèle

Dauphine

Porte Kent

rue Ste-Anne

rue Ste-Ursule

rue d'Auteuil

Musée des
Ursulines

rue St-Louis

Porte St-Louis

St-Louis

Côte de la Citadelle

**Musée du Royal
22e Régiment**

av Ste-Geneviève

Mont-Carmel

Dominaire

Porte St-Jean

rue Vallière

Richelieu

des Galcis

av Dufferin

Parc de
l'Esplanade

**Fortifications
Interpretation
Centre**

**Hôtel du
Parlement**

des
Parlementaires

Joly-de-Lotbinière

**HAUTE-
VILLE**

**PARLIAMENT
HILL**

Parc de la
Francophonie

Palace
Georges V

---

rue du Pont

rue de la Chapelle

rue de l'Église

boul Charest est

Côte-Ste-Geneviève

rue Ste-Marie

rue St-Joachim

rue St-Simon

boul René-Lévesque est

rue St-Patrick

rue Prévost

Chevrotière

rue de la

av Georges-VI

**Maison de la Découverte
des Plaines d'Abraham**

**Parc des Champs-de-Bataille
(Plains of Abraham)**

av Wilfrid-Laurier

Grande Allée est

av Georges-VI

av Ontario

To
Centre d'Interprétation du Parc des Champs-de-Bataille
and Musée National des Beaux-Arts du Québec

---

rue Dorchester

rue Ste-Hélène

rue St-Vallier

rue Arago est

Lavigueur

de la Tourelle

Racine

rue de la Couronne

rue Ste-Claire

d'Aiguillon

St-Jean

Richelieu

St-Olivier

Scott

l'Amérique Française

St-Amable

Berthelot

Parc de
l'Amérique
Française

rue de Claire-Fontaine

av Tache

av
Parc Jeanne-d'Arc

de Bernières

---

av Ste-Hélène

de la Tourelle

Racine

Sutherland

rue St-Gabriel

av Turnbull

av de la Tour

A   B   C   D   E   F

1   2   3   4

N
W   E
S

Ironically, when Gén. Louis-Joseph de Montcalm was defending Québec in 1759, he chose to take his armies outside the safety of the walls and meet Gen. James Wolfe on the Plains of Abraham. His gallant gesture lost New France forever. The following year, when the Chevalier de Lévis laid siege to Québec in a last-ditch effort to save the French colony, the British remained inside until reinforcements arrived. Britain made Québec its military nerve center for North America, attracting an invasion from the south during the American Revolution. In 1775–76, British soldiers again took refuge behind the walls and picked off the troops of Gens. Richard Montgomery and Benedict Arnold until reinforcements arrived.

Worried about the upstart Americans, the British rebuilt and strengthened the ramparts between 1786 and 1812. During the War of 1812, they erected four Martello towers (circular blockhouses) to fend off a U.S. attack that never came.

■ LA CITADELLE

In 1820 Lt. Col. Elias Walker Durnford was put in charge of building a citadel for the permanent garrison stationed at Québec. He drew on the plans devised in 1727 by French engineer Chaussegros de Léry to create a four-sided enclosure that envelops thirty-seven acres on the heights above the Plains of Abraham. It took a decade to complete the ramparts and another twenty years to finish the interior buildings.

The Citadel is still an active military base, the home of the francophone Royal 22e Régiment since 1920. Although the Royal 22nd is an active force—participating most recently in Bosnian peacekeeping under the United Nations—members of the regiment also provide crowd-pleasing military fanfare with the Changing of the Guard and Retreat of the Guard ceremonies daily during the summer. Putting a cheerful face on the grim business of war is hardly new. When Henry David Thoreau visited in 1850, he wrote of the Citadel in *A Yankee in Canada* that it was "a ruin kept in remarkably good repair. There are some eight hundred or thousand men there to exhibit it." He further observed, "One regiment goes bare-legged to increase the attraction. If you wish to study the muscles of the leg about the knee, repair to Quebec."

Once the Changing of the Guard ends, many visitors elect to see the entire fortress on a guided tour, offered from April through October. The spiel rattles through detailed histories of almost every building within the Citadel, including the 1693 redoubt built by Frontenac. Among the most chilling structures is the

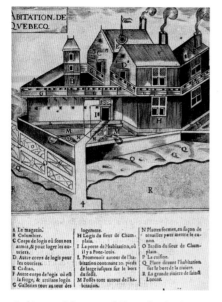

Architectural drawing of Champlain's 1613 Québec fort.

shooting gallery—a narrow stone building with slits in the walls where infantrymen could mow down any invaders who penetrated the citadel. In the center of the compound stands another building with slit windows: the fort, built in 1842 as a refuge for British soldiers in case the local French population rebelled, as it had in the Eastern Townships in 1837–38.

The overview of Québec from the King's Bastion reveals why this high ground had to remain in friendly hands. A nine-ton cannon cast in 1860—the soldiers call it "Rachel"—controls the port but could as easily fire on the city. The lookout provides a famous postcard view of the **Château Frontenac** rising among the squat older buildings. The Prince of Wales Bastion occupies the highest point above the river (120 meters) at the head of the Promenade des Gouverneurs, a kilometer-long staircase down to the Dufferin Terrace. Sighting along the big Frasier gun, even tankers on the river look like toys. This 1872 artillery piece required an entire fifty-pound barrel of gunpowder to fire a single shot.

In 1950, the **Musée du Royal 22e Régiment** was established in the oldest powder magazine, which dates from 1750. The museum displays uniforms, weapons, and medals of British and French armies from the eighteenth to the twentieth century. Its dollhouse-sized historic dioramas dramatize turning points in Québec military history, such as the Chevalier de Lévis burning his regimental colors on September 8, 1760, rather than surrendering them to the British at Montréal. *Côte de la Citadelle; 418-694-2815. Tours April–Oct. Changing of the Guard June 24–first weekend in Sept.*

(following pages) Racers get set at the Carnaval de Québec.

■ PLACE ROYALE AND ENVIRONS

As you walk down the sloping Côte de la Montagne from the upper city, you'll find yourself on eye level with the second and third stories of the ancient houses built beneath the embankment on rue Notre-Dame. "One wanders by Norman roofs with Norman gables and Norman chimneys, relics of a past when human beings would seem to have come into the world with a sense of beauty as naturally as they arrived with a right hand," Henry Beston wrote in *The St. Lawrence* (1942).

Painstaking restoration has fixed the leaning walls and sagging rooflines of those seventeenth- and eighteenth-century houses that Beston praised. On one towering brick wall, the trompe l'oeil mural **la Fresque des Québecois** pays tribute to the men and women who made Québec what it is. Here are Cartier and Champlain; Jean Talon, who put New France on a sound financial footing as its first *intendant* (chief administrator); Marie Guyart (Marie de l'Incarnation), first leader of the Ursuline order in New France; François de Laval, the first Catholic bishop of

La Fresque des Québecois *depicts the movers and shakers of Québec history.*
(left) The Saint-Louis gate is one of the few fortified entrances to Québec City.

Canada; Lord Dufferin, the governor-general of Canada who was instrumental in saving Québec's fortifications from destruction; Alphonse Desjardins, founder of the credit union movement; and Félix Leclerc, the popular musician identified as the "founder of French singing." Each left an indelible mark.

Rue Notre-Dame continues into **Place Royale.** Québec began here in 1608, when Champlain built his fortified "habitation," described in seventeenth-century accounts as a wooden dwelling house and storerooms surrounded by a wooden palisade mounted with small arms. Inside the palisade was a moat, and inside the moat a garden where Champlain eventually cultivated roses and carnations. Perhaps he would have been better advised to grow cabbages or another crop high in vitamin C; during the first winter twenty of his company died of scurvy.

Known first as the community's market square, or Place Marché, the plaza embodied the public world of the little outpost. Community meetings all took place in the square, traders and trappers exchanged furs for cloth and kettles, and settlers bought their subsistence goods. Here, too, the head of Jean de Val stood on a pike in 1609 for plotting Champlain's assassination. As the community grew and

Rue Saint-Jean, looking toward the city gate, ca. 1890.

flourished, merchants expanded their offerings to include wine, wheat, fine furniture, and brocaded fabric. And when the courts decreed public hangings and floggings, the square was packed for the spectacle. As Québec assumed the role of capital of New France, the homes and shops of wealthy merchants sprang up along the square's perimeter. In 1686, they erected a bust of Louis XIV and renamed the spot Place Royale. The original bust was lost over the centuries, but in 1928 the city of Paris presented Québec with a replacement, installed three years later. From his flowing locks and frilly garments, it seems clear that the Sun King was not cut out for life in the colonies.

Place Royale flourished as the city's trade center for nearly two and a half centuries, beginning its decline around 1860 when Montréal surpassed Québec as a port. Over the next century, the place where New France was born fell into decrepitude, and only a sluggish economy kept it from the wrecker's ball in the 1950s. But as Québecois pride began to swell in the 1960s, a movement to preserve Place Royale took hold, and in the 1970s the derelict neighborhood was spruced up to showcase its history.

The stone building of the **Centre d'Interprétation de Place-Royale** demonstrates the resilience of the merchants and business people of the lower city. The ground level and cellar date from 1684–85, when Place Royale was rebuilt after the fire of 1682 destroyed most of the wooden structures. Lined with limestone blocks, the high-vaulted cellar—originally a storehouse—is set up as a series of rooms that illustrate domestic life during the French regime. If you're of a mind to fantasize, you can sit down at a table and imagine eating dinner surrounded by your dozen children. The furnishings and artifacts are either commonplace antiques or modern reproductions, and visitors are encouraged to handle them.

The second floor shows the reconstruction of the building after the bombardments of 1759, when forty thousand English cannonballs and five thousand fireballs rained on the lower town in two months. The third floor is a late-nineteenth-century addition. More traditional displays fill the upper levels. Objects retrieved from archaeological digs are displayed under glass. Dating from the seventeenth century into the twentieth, the quotidian refuse of daily life—chipped and cracked plates and saucers, old bottles, and other discards—relates a tale of continuing habitation, even as fashion and technologies changed. Drawings and historic photographs show the evolution of trade in timber, fish, and fur at Place Royale. Absent a useful currency, standard equivalencies were developed for

THE MISSIONARY DEPARTS

Laforgue knelt in the narrow canoe.... Behind him a Savage woman steadied the canoe with light strokes of her paddle. Three dogs sat on skins which covered the cargo, and at the front a male Savage held the craft in midstream, waiting, looking back to where the other canoes were moving off from shore. On the riverbank, Fathers Bourque, Bonnet and Meynerd lined up in a row, waving their hats in a gesture of farewell. There were five canoes in all: the Savages traveled in family groups, the children and dogs sitting on the goods, the women paddling in the middle, the men in front and at the rear, steering and guiding the craft.... The canoes, incredibly light and fragile for their heavy burdens, glided swiftly into the slipstream, using the ebb flow to avoid moving against the main current. Laforgue looked back at the huddle of wooden settlements, at the steep cliffs and, above them, at the earth and timber ramparts enclosing the modest stone edifice of Champlain's fort.... As he did, from the ramparts came a puff of smoke and the roar of cannon. Alarmed and astonished, the Savages looked up. Neehatin, standing in his canoe, called out that the cannon fire was an honor, a salute from the Normans for their journey. Delighted, laughing, the Savages bowed to their stroke. The canoes sped on.

—Brian Moore, *Black Robe*, 1985

exchange. In 1665 one beaver pelt was worth two axes, two pounds of sugar, or eight knives. Six pelts were worth one gun; three pelts were worth one long coat. *27 rue Notre-Dame; 418-646-3167.*

Back outside in the square, the buildings have been restored as much as is practical to their original appearance and continue to function as a market, selling film, souvenirs, and crafts to tourists. Depending on how one measures antiquity, the picturesque **Notre-Dame-des-Victoires** is the oldest stone church in North America. Constructed in 1688 of gray limestone, the original church was smashed by shellfire in the siege of 1759 and has been twice restored. The highly decorated altar resembles a beige-and-gilt castle, and the nave is filled with ex-votos given by ships' captains to express thanks for safely reaching land. The large ship's model hanging from the ceiling represents *Le Brézé*, Québec's equivalent of the *Mayflower*. In 1664, the vessel brought over the soldiers of the Carignan Régiment—the direct ancestors of much of the population of Québec. Many couples choose Notre-Dame-des-Victoires for their weddings, and tourists gather and snap photos as the happy couples pose in the square. *32 rue Sous-le-Fort; 418-692-1650.*

If you continue through the old quarters down rue Sous-le-Fort, the conjunction of history and tourism can sometimes prove jarring. Maison Morin, for example, built in 1753 with a splendid view of the harbor even then, is now the ever-popular restaurant La Place du Spaghetti. Literally just across the street, the **Maison Chevalier** takes its history far more seriously. This pioneer of historic preservation in the lower city—it was restored in 1956—was the 1752 home of merchant Jean-Baptiste Chevalier, but passed through an assortment of owners before being transformed into an inn in 1806. Later known as the London Coffee House, it was a landmark for sailors and tourists alike. The exhibit "A Sense of the Past" uses furniture from the collections of the Museum of Civilization to re-create the rooms as they might have been used in the eighteenth and nineteenth centuries. *50 rue de Marché-Champlain; 418-646-3167.*

Costumed actors portray early colonists in Québec City's "middle ages" festival.

The **Atelier du Patrimoine Vivant** (Living Heritage Workshop) occupies the cellars of the Maison Chevalier, reached by a separate entrance. You can never tell who will be demonstrating a Québecois craft or art form in this folk arts center. You could stumble on a knitter or a lacemaker, a fiddler or a carver. Another day you might encounter an accordionist playing jigs and reels while someone demonstrates lumberjack dances. *5 rue du Cul-de-Sac; 418-647-1598. Open May–Oct.*

As you come out the door, the Batterie Royale, a small park with ancient cannons, stands on the left. The battery was installed in 1691 and functioned as a first line of defense in the siege of 1759. On occasion, interpreters in historic costume put on shows here, but most of the time it is one of the few quiet places near Place Royale to repair and eat an ice-cream cone in peace.

■ QUARTIER PETIT-CHAMPLAIN AND ENVIRONS

Tucked into the base of the hill directly below the Dufferin Terrace, Petit-Champlain is possibly the busiest souvenir-shopping district in Québec. As viewed from *l'escalier Casse-Cou,* or "Breakneck Stairs," the length of the pedestrian rue de Petit-Champlain seems to telescope into a colorful montage of signs with a swirling crowd flowing in both directions on the pavement. Restaurants, crafts shops, and boutiques are shoehorned into the restored ancien régime buildings. Street musicians, clowns, and magicians perform in every nook, giving the district the feel of a wholesome, family-oriented carnival. Not all is ticky-tacky in the quarter, which includes the parallel boulevard Champlain. Along with shops selling Québec keychains, shot glasses, and beer steins are upscale folk art galleries, boutiques with clothing by Canadian designers, and even a glassblower's shop.

The quick route between the lower and upper parts of Old Québec is the funicular, or cable car, which has been running since 1879. At the opposite end of Petit-Champlain, a ferry crosses the St. Lawrence to Lévis. Established as a commuter service, the ferry also carries many tourists, most of whom never disembark on the far shore, but simply ride back and forth to enjoy the view. To appreciate how Québec rises dramatically out of the river on the abrupt bluff of Cap-aux-Diamants, you really have to see it from the water.

Rue de Petit-Champlain is now the busiest street of Old Québec's lower city.

■ VIEUX PORT

Québec's Old Port district begins just north of Place Royale, under the rim of the fortifications. Rue Notre-Dame ends at Côte de la Montagne; its continuation into Vieux Port is the colorfully named rue Sault-au-Matelot, or "fall of the sailor." Tradition has it that the street was named for Champlain's dog, Matelot, who took a header off the cliff here. But given the proximity to the port and the fact that taverns used to line the street, the sailor in question might well have been human rather than canine. Whatever the origin of its name, Sault-au-Matelot and parallel rue Saint-Pierre have emerged as a chic district of nineteenth-century commercial buildings converted into swank bars and restaurants and design-conscious boutique hotels. Côte de la Montagne functions almost as a boundary between the pieties of Québec history and the pleasures of the moment.

Even the dominant museum in the Old Port, the **Musée de la Civilisation,** trades as heavily in popular culture as in history, emphasizing its many temporary and often quirky exhibitions ("Dogs in Art," for example, or "Skin"). Two permanent exhibitions do address historical Québec, but not the Québec of famous explorers or famous clerics or famous anybodies. "Memories" plays off the *"je me souviens"* motto, which was added to the provincial coat of arms in 1883, as a catch-all of popular culture. The clever "I remember" theme allows curators to group any number of objects with nostalgic associations—from farm tools to hockey sticks to schoolbooks—while a century of popular music plays in the background. "Encounter with First Nations" emphasizes the native cultures of Québec, principally through fine crafted objects, such as baskets, handwoven cloth, snowshoes, beadwork, and Inuit carving in stone, bone, and ivory. One of the most striking objects is a large bark canoe, or *rabaska,* typical of those used in the fur trade between Montréal and the Great Lakes. It was crafted in 1985 by a native artisan who died in 1995 at age 92. "Rabaska," the museum carefully points out, is an Algonquian word that has entered the French language. *85 rue Dalhousie (back entrance on rue Saint-Pierre); 418-643-2158.*

Rue Saint-Pierre runs into the principal plaza of the Old Port, the **Place de la FAO,** which commemorates the fiftieth anniversary of the United Nations Food and Agriculture Organization, founded in Québec in October 1945. Appropriately for the neighborhood, the statue of La Vivrière follows the form of a ship's masthead

Cap-aux-Diamants looms over Québec's lower city.

and is surrounded by flowing waves of water. In her arms she bears foodstuffs from around the globe.

The construction of the plaza in 1995 capped a two-decades-long transformation of a run-down dock district into one of Québec's liveliest neighborhoods. The first wave of gentrification came from antiques dealers on rue Saint-Paul, which begins at the Place de la FAO. **Antiquités Zoar** (112 rue Saint-Paul; 418-692-0581) opened in 1964, and a decade later other dealers began buying up the old houses along the street to open their own small shops. Then came the artists, who discovered the neighborhood's open light and the then-cheap rents of its often-derelict buildings. Soon galleries sprang up to represent their work. By the time Place de la FAO was installed, hoteliers and restaurateurs had colonized the neighborhood as well, and the Old Port was on its way.

But even as rue Saint-Paul continues the inexorable process of gentrification, the street retains an old-fashioned neighborhood ambience. Luthier and bow maker **Hans Peter Beer** (209 rue Saint-Paul; 418-694-1263) is usually at his bench just inside the door, carving away on pieces for a new violin and seemingly grateful to be interrupted. Benches line the sidewalks and antiques dealers sit outside their shops, shooting the breeze with each other and with visitors willing to spend the time. "This was the underused and abandoned part of the city," recalls one pioneer in the antiques trade. "Every other building was empty or a rooming house for winos. But we got smart and didn't tear the buildings down. Now look at it!" He gestures down the street, where tourists are clustered around the menu of the day just posted outside a small bistro. Then he excuses himself. A customer has a question about an antique hooked rug with a traditional Québec country scene.

So far, the bus tours ignore rue Saint-Paul, but the proliferation of smartly designed boutique hotels and the proximity to Place Royale bring increasing numbers of visitors to the street. Outside the walls, the weight of Québec's gray stone and its lengthy history seem to vanish in the open air. Sidewalk cafés and snug bistros proliferate, offering plates of sausage in mustard sauce or all-you-can-eat meals of *moules-frites* (steamed mussels and french fries).

With its small-scale world of tiny shops and tinier bistros, rue Saint-Paul hardly seems like a port district—until you turn down rue des Navigateurs and cross rue Saint-André to the quays along Bassin Louise, a safe harbor off the main flow of the St. Lawrence River. The **Centre d'Interprétation du Vieux-Port-du-Québec** is devoted to the historical role of the port, which was one of the five largest in the world in the mid-nineteenth century. The ground level is a favorite with children.

The life-size model of a ship being unloaded even includes a terrified horse coming off the deck in a sling. The upper levels of the center tell the story of the integrally linked shipbuilding and timber industries.

Québec's first shipyard opened in 1712, but shipbuilding truly rose to a frenzy under British rule. When Britain and France were at war between 1793 and 1815, Napoleon blockaded the Baltic. Needing eighty thousand loads of timber to build five hundred new vessels a year, the British Admiralty turned to Canada for logs. Even when the blockade was lifted in 1812, Britain established preferential tariffs that made Canadian timber competitive with European sources despite the cost of transatlantic shipping. More than two thousand log rafts of pine and oak were floated 1,280 kilometers down the Ottawa and St. Lawrence rivers each year for shipment to Britain.

Between 1820 and 1899, Québec shipyards produced seventeen hundred vessels, employing up to five thousand men at a time—ten percent of the city's population. Consequently, the port became a center for working men, many of whom lived alone in boardinghouses and took their pleasures where they could. In 1830, the city had more than four hundred licensed "beverage rooms" mostly frequented by sailors, soldiers, and shipyard laborers. Québec was also a major port of entry for immigrants from the British Isles during the mid-nineteenth century. At the peak in 1854, 53,183 people landed at Québec—half of them Irish, the rest mostly English and Scottish. Many moved on to Montréal and farther west, but the steady flow kept Québec's port a crowded, rowdy district.

Although Québec was among the first ports to build an oceangoing steamship—in the 1830s the *Royal William* crossed the Atlantic without the aid of sail—the transition to iron ships at the end of the nineteenth century spelled the end of the city's shipbuilding and timber-export industries.

With all that history in mind, you can climb to the top level of the interpretation center, where an observation room faces the walled city on one side and overlooks the recreational boat basin on the other. An open-air deck on the water side is a good place to catch some rays. In the distance, the Laurentians rise from the horizon, their peaks as rounded as a soft meringue. *100 rue Saint-André; 418-648-3300. Open May–mid-Oct.*

(following pages) Portraitists and caricaturists ply their trades on rue Sainte-Anne.

Bicycle and walking paths follow the water's edge at Bassin Louise and along the St. Lawrence, although the naval base on the point between them is off-limits. Small restaurants and bars crouch along the landings going west toward the head of Bassin Louise. The **Marché du Vieux-Port** (160 Quai Saint-André; 418-692-2517) is especially busy from mid-June into October, when the bounty flows in from the farms and orchards on the Île-de-Orléans, just downriver from Québec. The island's microclimate causes its soils to warm early and its first frost to come late, making it one of the few places in the province where long-season crops can be grown in open fields. The small, somewhat misshapen, deeply red Île-de-Orléans strawberries are some of tastiest in the world. Their brief season comes at the end of June. Along the riverbanks east of the city, cidermakers, beekeepers, and cheesemakers all ply their trades, and farmers raise ducks, geese, and lamb to bring to the market. Much of the produce at Marché du Vieux-Port is fit for the cover of a cooking magazine—large and leafy heads of brilliant green lettuce with red fringes, golden new potatoes as handsome as a heap of smooth river cobblestones, veined melons that split open to marigold-orange centers.

■ HAUTE-VILLE

Secure within the fortified walls, the upper city of Vieux Québec consists of narrow streets lined with stone houses and ancient cloisters tucked away on back lanes. It is the stronghold of French tradition, of Catholic religion—and of tourism. Penetrating into the central keep today is far easier than Wolfe's armies found it. You need only hop the funicular from rue de Petit-Champlain, or huff and puff up the steep wooden stairs or winding sidewalks. Or you can come overland, as invading armies did. Several of the city's largest hotels stand just west of the walls, and many visitors make their first foray through the Saint-Louis gate.

Draft horses swish their tails and nuzzle their feed bags on Grande Allée, just outside the gate at Québec's equestrian equivalent of a taxi stand. One by one, sightseers engage the carriages, drivers jiggle the reins, and the horses dutifully clip-clop down the pavement. The calèche wheels rattle and squeak as the carriages whirl around to proceed downhill into the heart of the old city. The eighteenth-century stone dwellings of rue Saint-Louis are resplendent in the summer, their window boxes spilling over with petunias. Rue Saint-Louis was originally the quarter of

Restaurants and sidewalk cafés line Grande Allée.

Stone carving remains one of the chief forms of artistic expression among the Inuit. *(top left)* Man Hunting Seal *by Isa Oomayoualook, Inukjuak. (top right)* Hunter *by Oomaaaiuk Tikinik. Kimmirut. (bottom)* Whale hunter, *artist unknown.*

CLERICAL CITY

As I wander about Quebec this pleasant morning after rain, it is of the clergy I think first, for this is much their city. No street seems to be without its ecclesiastical figures; everywhere they come and go in soft hats and shovel hats, black coats and black capes and "the wind in their gowns." Nuns, too, are passing in the sunlight in their decorum of black, and every now and then strides by, with younger step, one of the teaching brothers who wear the broad French hat, the French eighteenth century *souane*, and the white neck cloth of the *abbés* of old France. Habits and gowns, orders and brotherhoods, metropolitan dignities and parish simplicities, no part of the picture of Quebec is more native to the canvas than this sense and awareness of the church.

—Henry Beston, *The St. Lawrence,* 1942

Québec's haute bourgeoisie, but real estate is too precious for these foursquare houses to remain as private residences. Bright doorways announce restaurants and bars, a smattering of B&Bs occupy the upper levels, and shops proffer everything from shiny plastic souvenirs to Inuit art.

As the narrow street begins to widen into the shady park of Place d'Armes, the **Musée d'Art Inuit Brousseau** displays stone, bone, and ivory sculptures carved by Inuit artists. The museum, which grew from the personal collection of a single distinguished dealer, claims to be the first institution south of the Arctic devoted exclusively to Inuit art and culture. Temporary exhibitions, sometimes showing contemporary graphic art as well as sculpture, augment the permanent collection. The museum's excellent, if expensive, gallery will spoil you for cheap imitations. *39 rue Saint-Louis; 418-694-1828.*

Directly across the street from the museum, Maison Jacquet was built in 1677. The small house, with a steeply pitched red roof, is said to be the oldest dwelling still standing in Québec City. The novelist Philippe-Aubert de Gaspé, the author of *Les Anciens Canadiens,* lived here from 1815 to 1825; the restaurant that has occupied the structure since 1966, **Aux Anciens Canadiens**, takes its name from his book. The menu is as old-fashioned as the house, offering both traditional Continental cuisine and such Québecois specialties as meat pies and grilled caribou. *34 rue Saint-Louis; 418-692-1627.*

Aux Anciens Canadiens stands on the corner of a small street that leads down to tiny rue Donnacona, lined by the blank-faced buildings of the Ursuline convent. The teaching order arrived in Québec in 1639 under the direction of Marie Guyart, best known as Marie de l'Incarnation. Her letters—278 of them were published in 1876—paint vivid images of the early years of the colony. When she arrived, she wrote, "There weren't six houses in the whole area and just two of them were made of stone; even the fortifications were wooden."

Although the Ursulines have not been cloistered since Vatican II (1962–1965), the convent is not, strictly speaking, open to the public. About sixty sisters still live at the facility, teaching between four hundred and five hundred grade-school girls. The **Musée des Ursulines,** however, pulls back the veil a bit with a good recounting of the order's history in Québec as well as some detail on the lives of the nuns (who rise at 4 A.M. and pray at 4:40 and 7 A.M., noon, and 3 and 7 P.M. before retiring at 8:30). The museum is straightforward about the French crown's intention to claim the New World for Catholicism. As chief minister to Louis XIII, Cardinal Richelieu made sure that New France was at least as well endowed with clergy as with soldiers, sending the Sulpicians in 1615 and the Jesuits in 1625. The king and the cardinal also authorized two cloistered orders of nuns, the Ursulines and the Hospitalières de Saint-Augustin, to open schools and hospitals respectively. The Ursuline sisters initially enrolled both native as well as French girls between the ages of six and sixteen, but native pupils stopped attending the school by the end of the seventeenth century. Women were few in the early years of New France, but thanks to the Ursulines, they were generally literate.

The Ursuline order attracted some of the smartest and most talented women born into the colony, and the museum's exquisite needlework and religious paintings show how many of them channeled their creativity. The Ursuline convent also became a repository for many cultural artifacts. Most of one room is devoted to Father Paul Lejeune's ink and watercolor drawings of the Montagnais tribe, made between 1632 and 1634. Lejeune, who was superior of the Jesuits at the time, was a passionate missionary. Although he is often depicted today as a zealot with suspect motives, there's no doubting his intense curiosity about "les sauvages," whose culture he studied and described in minute detail. *12 rue Donnacona; 418-694-0694. Open Feb.–Nov.*

The adjacent **Chapelle des Ursulines** can be viewed in late morning and midafternoon. The current chapel is a 1902 reconstruction on the site of the 1723 chapel; the heavy gilding of the altars, which are original, was applied by the nuns in the eighteenth century. The religious paintings are a legacy of the French

Marie de l'Incarnation brought the Ursuline nuns to Québec in 1639.

Revolution, purchased for the Ursulines during the "spoilation" that followed the confiscation of church property. The French commander of Québec in the Seven Years War, Gén. Louis-Joseph de Montcalm, is entombed in the north wall of the chapel. Although the spot now has a properly ceremonial formality, tradition says that when his body was brought to the Ursulines after the Battle on the Plains of Abraham, the nuns placed him in a crater in the wall inflicted by British bombardment. Thus, the hero's epitaph reads, "Galli lugentes deposuerunt et generosoe hostium fidei commendarunt" (in mourning, the French buried and commended him to the generosity of the enemy). *12 rue Donnacona; 418-694-0413. Open May–Oct.*

■ CHÂTEAU FRONTENAC AND THE DUFFERIN TERRACE

Bristling with turrets and capped by multiple peaks of verdigris copper, the **Hôtel Château Frontenac** dominates the landscape like a medieval castle. Indeed, for two centuries this prime spot atop the cliff of Cap-aux-Diamants at the foot of rue Saint-Louis was reserved for the lord of the land. Champlain built Fort Saint-Louis on the spot, and his successor as governor of New France, Charles Jacques de Huault de Montmagny, replaced the fort with a castle that served as the governor's residence until it burned in 1834.

It's hard to imagine that the official residence could have equaled the Château Frontenac for sheer grandeur. The nineteenth-century hotel was the brainchild of William van Horne, general manager of the Canadian Pacific Railway. As passenger service expanded from coast to coast, Canadian Pacific constructed grand hotels to accommodate passengers. Van Horne was particularly enamored of the Richardsonian Romanesque merger of medieval and Renaissance influences and engaged New York architect Bruce Price, father of Emily Post, to hammer out the signature "CP Château" style.

The Frontenac, named for another governor of New France, was inaugurated in 1893 and has been enlarged at least four times. Virtually every head of state or celebrity who has visited Québec has stayed here, and the hotel hosted the 1943 and 1944 Québec Conferences, which brought together Franklin Delano Roosevelt, Winston Churchill, and the phlegmatic Canadian prime minister William Lyon Mackenzie King. The hotel offers "behind-the-scenes" tours by guides in nineteenth-century period dress. *1 rue des Carrières; 418-692-3861.*

Behind the Frontenac, an obelisk rises from the sloping park known as the Jardin des Gouverneurs. In the country of the two solitudes, the single finger pointing to the sky memorializes the opposing generals who both perished in the cataclysmic clash on the **Plains of Abraham**. The Latin inscription on the **Monument Wolfe-Montcalm** neatly evades making a choice between French and English: *Mortem virtus communem, famam historia, monumentum posteritas dedit* (usually translated as "Destiny gave them a common death, history a common fame, posterity a common monument").

Tout le monde turns up on the **Dufferin Terrace**, the 671-meter walkway between the hulking mass of the hotel and the airy edge of the Cap-aux-Diamants cliff. The planked promenade was built at the instigation of Frederick Temple Hamilton-Temple-Blackwood, mercifully known as Lord Dufferin. During his service as

Two men ski down the toboggan run above the Dufferin Terrace, ca. 1900.

governor-general of Canada in 1872–1878, Lord Dufferin was also instrumental in saving Québec's walled fortifications. He laid the cornerstone for the terrace in October 1878. The city's most prominent Victorian architect, Charles Baillairgé, endowed the kiosks and lampposts with flowing lines that prefigure art nouveau.

In a gentler era, couples promenaded arm in arm on the terrace and the world moved at a more stately pace. Today, people stroll along with ice-cream cones in hand, clustering periodically around the street performers who make the terrace their outdoor stage. The crowd can be unpredictable, and its tastes questionable. A fourteen-year-old with a backward baseball cap doing unicycle stunts may command the attention of a few hundred people, while only a few friends circle around a middle-aged woman who sings Edith Piaf songs accompanied by a balding friend on an electric keyboard. A pots-and-pans drummer may draw a crowd while a classical violinist plays nearly alone. An escape artist asks a volunteer to handcuff him, tie him up, and stuff him in a bag fastened with a bicycle cable lock. Acrobats do their flips, magicians snatch bouquets from the air, and, before the night is over, an Andean pan-pipe and string band will almost certainly play their Peruvian folk-rock. The terrace is just as lively in the winter, when the city floods one portion to

LES FILLES JOLIES

One of the first questions a Canadian lady proposes to a stranger is whether he is married? The next, how he likes the ladies of the country, and whether he thinks them handsomer than those of his own country? And the third, whether he will take one home with him? There are some differences between the ladies of Quebec and those of Montreal. Those of the last place seemed to be generally handsomer than those of the former. Their behaviour, likewise, seemed to me to be somewhat too free at Quebec, and of a more becoming modesty at Montreal. The ladies at Quebec, especially the unmarried ones, are not very industrious. A girl of eighteen is reckoned very poorly off if she cannot enumerate at least twenty lovers. These young ladies, especially if of a higher rank, get up at seven and dress till nine, drinking their coffee at the same time. When they are dressed they place themselves near a window that opens into the street, take up some needlework, and sew a stitch now and then; but turn their eyes into the street most of the time. When a young fellow comes in, whether they are acquainted with him or not, they immediately lay aside their work, sit down by him, and begin to chat, laugh, joke, and invent *double-entendres;* and this is reckoned being very witty....

In Montreal the girls are not quite so volatile, but more industrious. They are always at their needlework, or doing some necessary business in the house. They are likewise cheerful and content; and nobody can say that they want either wit or charms. Their fault is that they think too well of themselves.... The girls at Montreal are very much displeased that those at Quebec get husbands sooner than they. The reason of this is that many young gentlemen who come over from France with the ships are captivated by the ladies at Quebec, and marry them. But as these gentlemen seldom go up to Montreal, the girls there are not often so happy as those of the former place.

—Peter Kalm, *Travels in North America*, 1770. This excerpt from *Canadian Types of the Old Regime 1608–1698*, by Charles W. Colby, Henry Holt and Company, New York, 1908.

make a glassy skating rink. A toboggan slide parallels the steps of the Promenade des Gouverneurs, providing an exhilarating one-kilometer run from the Plains of Abraham down to the terrace. Samuel de Champlain, standing tall at the foot of the Dufferin Terrace, might even crack a smile if he could.

■ PLACE D'ARMES AND ENVIRONS

The city founder's effigy faces the leafy circle of **Place d'Armes,** where an orna-mented fountain erected in 1915 commemorates the tercentenary of the arrival of the Recollet fathers, the first of Québec's clerical orders. Face painters work their artistry on youngsters, while teenage girls opt for hair wraps. Carriage drivers patiently stand by as their horses drink from large buckets of water. At the foot of the square, caricature artists set up their stands along rue Sainte-Anne, while painters and printmakers turn rue du Trésor into an outdoor art gallery. In the Anglican church courtyard, jewelers, potters, weavers, wood carvers, and even shoemakers offer their wares.

The **Cathedral of the Holy Trinity** (Cathédrale de la Sainte-Trinité), the first Anglican cathedral built outside the British Isles, took over the former garden of the Recollets. Modeled on Saint-Martin-in-the-Fields in Trafalgar Square in London, the church was begun in 1800 and consecrated in 1804. King George III funded the construction and provided the communion silverware and folio Bible. A royal box is still reserved in the balcony for the reigning sovereign or her representative. The cathedral runs a strong program of choral music, both at Sunday services and special concerts. The bell ringers practice English change ringing on Tuesday evenings dur-ing the summer. *32 rue des Jardins; 418-692-2193. Open for visits mid-May–mid-Oct.*

■ PLACE DE L'HÔTEL-DE-VILLE

The small shelf of a park at Place de l'Hôtel-de-Ville is filled with bleachers for much of the year—all the better to watch the street performers in front of city hall. The small park essentially divides the upper streets of Haute-Ville from the valley formed by Côte de la Fabrique and **rue Saint-Jean,** where some of the best bars, restaurants, and boutiques of the Haute-Ville are located.

Facing the park, **Basilique-Cathédrale Notre-Dame de Québec** is less grand in scale than Notre-Dame de Montréal but makes up for its modesty with history. As the home church of the oldest parish in the Americas north of Mexico, the cathe-dral has accreted nearly four centuries of relics and art. The remains of most of the governors of New France and the bishops of Québec rest here. Severely damaged in the 1759 siege, the original basilica was destroyed by fire in 1922. The current church is a 1925 replica rebuilt from the original plans. Visits are free except dur-ing the thirty-minute multimedia "Heavenly Lights" show, which animates Québec's religious history with hovering images and special effects. *20 rue de Buade; 418-694-0665. Open daily for services year-round, for visits May–Oct.*

The **Musée de l'Amérique Française** occupies the historic buildings of the Séminaire de Québec—appropriately enough, since the French experience in North America is intimately entwined with the missionary efforts launched, in great part, from the Séminaire. François de Laval, who became archbishop of New France, founded the Petite Séminaire (a religious school for boys) in 1677 and the Grand Séminaire (for training of priests) in 1681. The Université Laval, the first Catholic, French-language university in North America, was also established here in 1852 with faculties of law, arts, theology, and medicine. The university and its associated seminary moved out of the cramped downtown quarters to a spreading campus in suburban Sainte-Foy in the 1950s, but Laval's architecture school returned in 1987 and shares the site with the museum.

The budding architects study within a stone matrix of history. The white-washed structure with the bell tower dates from 1678, and a sundial from 1731 warns passersby that "Our days pass like shadows." Some windowpanes, miraculously still intact, came from France in barrels of molasses.

Over the centuries, conflagrations have pared the campus down to stone. Even interiors burned. After two chapels were consumed by fire, the Jesuits took no chances when they built the next replacement. Inaugurated in 1900, much of the chapel interior is constructed of sheet metal masterfully painted to look like marble and even tapestry. The desanctified chapel is a popular site for wedding receptions and for classical music concerts that take advantage of the acoustics of the metal surfaces.

True to its name, the Museum of French America takes a broad, all-inclusive view of the French adventure in North America, noting that more than nineteen million inhabitants are of French descent. Galleries display the objects that accrued to the church over centuries of exploration of the continental interior— everything from native beadwork to chalices once used to serve Mass in remote missions. A film gives a capsule history of the Acadians in Nova Scotia and New Brunswick, the Métis of Manitoba, and the Cajuns of Louisiana. The French adventure continues as the narrative walks a fine political line to address the 1980 and 1995 referenda on sovereignty for Québec—giving French-Canadians the hard choice between the Canada they helped to build or the dream of their own country. *2 Côte de la Fabrique; 418-692-2843.*

Ornate interior of the Basilique-Cathédrale Notre-Dame de Québec.

■ PLAINS OF ABRAHAM AND PARLIAMENT HILL

Some historians call the battle between the English troops under James Wolfe and the French defenders under Louis-Joseph de Montcalm the "half hour that changed the world." Others call it the "birth of Canada." And many Québecois still refer to it as "the Conquest." Strictly speaking, it was one battle among many, and Québec was never "conquered" in the usual meaning of the term. All of French Canada was handed over to Great Britain in 1763 in the Treaty of Paris, which ended the Seven Years War. But that doesn't diminish the significance that the Québecois place on the September 13, 1759, encounter on the Plains of Abraham, pasturelands immediately west of the city walls.

Sailing from Fort Louisburg on Cape Breton Island in June, Wolfe brought a formidable force of twenty-two thousand men to Québec. He anchored in the harbor and bombarded the city for two months. Already in frail health and concerned that his fleet would have to set sail before winter locked up the river, he chose to attack the French where they least expected it—by scaling the cliff face to put an army on the high pastures just west of the city walls. Wolfe and his men began climbing in the dark; by the time the first pre-dawn light reached the plains at 5:30 A.M., his army was in battle array. Montcalm sent his troops out of the city to meet them, and the first shots were fired at 10 A.M. By 10:30 the battle was over, with 250 dead and another 2,500 wounded. Both of the young, brilliant generals were casualties. Wounded three times in battle, Wolfe expired on the field after learning that victory was his. Montcalm was wounded and died just hours later. Five days later, Québec City surrendered.

When the snows of that winter melted, the French made one last desperate attempt to regain their capital. In April 1760, François-Gaston, Chevalier de Lévis won a decisive battle west of the city in Sainte-Foy and laid siege to Québec from the Plains of Abraham. Bruised from his Sainte-Foy defeat (442 dead, 1,500 wounded), Gen. James Murray chose not to repeat Montcalm's mistake. Although the British garrison was wracked with disease and hunger, Murray stayed within Québec's fortifications in a waiting game to see which army would get reinforcements. On May 9, the lead vessel of a British fleet sailed into the harbor and Lévis withdrew.

The struggle between Wolfe and Montcalm became the stuff of legend, the subject even of a tune still popular among French-Canadian, New England, and Cape Breton fiddlers—"Wolfe and Montcalm" or "Wolfe et Montcalm," depending on who's playing. In 1908, the rolling fields were solemnly inaugurated as **Parc des Champs-de-Bataille,** or Battlefields Park.

There is no shortage of commemorative plaques, monuments, informational panels, and ancient artillery to recall the events in this 108-hectare (267-acre) park, but the desperate armies that clashed for control of a continent have become dim shades obscured by the sheer vivacity of the living. The Plains of Abraham are both park and playground, with footpaths through woodlands and gardens, and natural amphitheaters for summer concerts. Bird-watchers prowl the fields through much of the year and cross-country skiers enjoy five groomed trails in the winter. Some of the best views of the St. Lawrence River can be had atop the very cliffs scaled by Wolfe and his men.

The park's visitors center—the **Maison de la Découverte des Plaines d'Abraham**, which even French speakers call the Discovery Pavilion—shows "Canada Odyssey," a multimedia presentation that mixes film, still images, holograms, and soundtracks to tell the tale of greater Québec history. Actors impersonating historical figures add a bit of levity. (Montcalm, for example, comes across as a real whiner; Abraham Martin, the original owner of the pastures, is portrayed as an eccentric geezer. Wolfe writes home to his mother, complaining about the weather.)

Artist's depiction of the British capture of Québec in the Battle of the Plains of Abraham, 1759.

The center contains a useful scale model of the Battlefields Park and serves as the departure point for summer bus tours. *835 avenue Wilfrid-Laurier; 418-648-4071.*

Military buffs might prefer the **Centre d'Interprétation du Parc des Champs-de-Bataille,** or National Battlefields Park Interpretation Center, located within the park at the provincial art museum. The multimedia show and model armies supply the details of troop movements, strategy, and struggles. Exhibits also chronicle the transformation of the battlefields into a national park. *Baillairge Pavilion, Musée National des Beaux-Arts du Québec, Parc des Champs-des-Bataille; 418-648-5641.*

The sculptures outside the **Musée National des Beaux-Arts du Québec** have a refreshing modernism that contrasts with the memorial sculptures of most of the rest of the park. In an unusual adaptive re-use, part of the museum is housed in the former Québec prison, designed by the same talented architect, Charles Baillairgé, who created the kiosks and light poles of the Dufferin Terrace. The building preserves one original cell block and has other exhibits relating to penal history. Another building, created as a fine-arts center in 1933, holds Québec's "national" art collections. These range from exquisite folk art to seventeenth-century devotional images to the "Automatistes" of the mid-twentieth century, including the famous Jean-Paul Riopelle. *Parc des Champs-des-Bataille; 418-643-2150.*

■ COLLINE PARLEMENTAIRE

If the French lost Québec on the Plains of Abraham, they have thoroughly saved face on Parliament Hill, where the 125 members of Québec's National Assembly meet amid maximum pomp and considerable circumstance in the **Hôtel du Parlement.** Constructed between 1877 and 1886 from plans by Eugène-Étienne Taché, a Québec City engineer-architect, the Parliament building indulges in a riot of symbolism so extensive that it even satisfies politicians brought up in the ceremonial formality of the Catholic Church. The Main Hall sets the tone: its decorative motifs include fleurs-de-lis (for France), three lions (Great Britain), harps (Ireland), a single lion (Scotland), and maple leaves (Canada). Stained-glass panels relate the history of the French regime.

The National Assembly Chamber is purely Québecois—blue walls with white and gold trim. The members sit at wooden desks in straight-back padded chairs, the majority and the official opposition facing each other. The throne at the front is reserved for the president, an unelected nonpartisan "referee of the room." The United Kingdom coat of arms crowns the throne. Below it is a crucifix installed in

1942 by Maurice Duplessis, the Union Nationale party leader and longtime Québec premier. The staunchly conservative and fervently Catholic Duplessis compelled the members of the assembly to pray before each session. Separation of church and state has since become the law of the land, but the crucifix remains as a symbol of Québecois heritage. The large painting above the throne depicts *Le Débat sur les Langues,* the debate on languages that occurred on January 21, 1792, in the Legislative Assembly of Lower Canada. Of the fifty members, thirty-five spoke French and fifteen spoke English. In contrast to modern "solutions" to language use, the members decided that they could use either tongue but that no oral translation would be provided. The rule still applies to the National Assembly. *1045 rue des Parlementaires; 418-643-7239.*

In addition to guided tours of the building, the public can rub elbows with the legislators at the **Restaurant Le Parlementaire,** which serves three meals a day when the legislature is in session—from March to late June and October to Christmas—and breakfast and lunch during the summer. Meals at the restaurant require a reservation (418-643-6640). Otherwise, you can dine more casually with the staffers in the cafeteria.

Statues of Québec prime ministers stand on the grounds of Parliament Hill like so many bronze soldiers of Québecois defiance. Those who sought to bring the province into closer alliance with the rest of Canada are conspicuously absent, while those who fought to maintain Québec's "special status" within the Confederation are prominent: Honoré Mercier, the fervent advocate of Québec autonomy who led from 1887 to 1891; Jean Lesage, architect of the Quiet Revolution and prime minister from 1960 to 1966; and the mordant Réné Lévesque, whose administration (1976–1985) established the cleanest campaign-finance reforms in North America as well as the French-primacy language laws.

But the hill rises above the weight of its symbols. Broad formal plantings cover the front lawn, and meticulously tended shrubs and trees give the seat of provincial government the beneficent demeanor of a lord's country estate. When the structure is bathed at night in blue and white lights, the scene calls to mind the fleur-de-lis—the floral emblem a people chose over the trappings of might.

EASTERN TOWNSHIPS

Summer is short and almost unbearably sweet in the Eastern Townships, a cluster of hill-country villages snuggled up against the Vermont and New Hampshire borders less than 100 kilometers southeast of Montréal. Fall is shorter and sweeter yet. Waves of high pressure flow one after another off the Canadian Shield and the sky assumes an endless, nearly cobalt blue. The first frost snaps everything into focus. Lobo and McIntosh, Empire and Paula Red, Delicious and Wolf River—the apples pile up in sheds, in baskets, in bags, in heaps beside the road. Beekeepers extract the late wildflower combs from their hives, and kitchens from Phippsburg to Hereford bubble with the sweet scent of jam.

The Eastern Townships are the Anglo end of Québec, mostly settled during and just after the American Revolution by Loyalists whose allegiance remained with the British crown. For the first hundred years or more, the settlers tried farming, but the Appalachian mountain topography and thin glacial soils made traditional agriculture difficult. By the 1930s, farmers switched to dairy herds and apple orchards, making spreads in the Townships virtually indistinguishable from those across the border in Vermont. Farms that didn't survive were snapped up by well-off Montrealers as summer and retirement spots.

Many Montrealers still favor the southwest corner of the Eastern Townships—from the Missiquoi Bay of Lake Champlain to Lake Memphremagog—for a bucolic getaway. If they are blessed with a country house, they go for days at a time to decompress with no more nighttime disturbance than crickets and starlight. But even more make the Townships a day trip or long weekend—a jaunt to picturesque Victorian villages, a harvest-time drive from orchard to orchard, a casual tour along the Wine Route, or an extended cycling outing through a landscape as rumpled as an unmade bed.

The most direct route from Montréal is to leave the island by the Champlain Bridge and follow Autoroute 10 east. At exit 29, Route 133 snakes through the broad farms along the Rivière Richelieu to enter the Townships at Stanbridge, a few miles north of St. Albans, Vermont. The route described in this chapter is essentially a taste of the Townships—a land of crisp apples, tart cider, surprising wine, delectable duck, and some of Québec's most exquisite cheeses.

Despite the challenges of the weather, wine grapes grow in the Eastern Townships.

■ FRELIGHSBURG

The Chemin des Patriotes, as Route 133 is called in memory of the Québec rebellion of the 1830s, winds along a series of river valleys. Church spires, power-line stanchions, and the occasional mountain are all that puncture the distant horizon. Long and tangled rows of cucumber vines and swaying fields of wheat, oats, and barley line the road. By mid-July, farmstands post signs for *mais sucre*, or sweet corn.

The township of Stanbridge was originally a seigneury, a French land grant; its long strip reaches back from the Rivière des Brochets. In 1801, the Montréal merchant and McGill College founder James McGill purchased the Stanbridge seigneury and on his death deeded it to the Rivières family.

A detour into Notre-Dame-de-Stanbridge provides a peek at history written on the land. As you enter the village limits, watch on the left for a sign to a covered bridge. The red-painted, queen truss structure, Pont des Rivières, cuts straight through the fields of the Rivières farms—now divided into slivers after having been parceled up by each generation of heirs. This was a fate typical of the seigneuries. Farms were divided again and again until they were no longer viable.

The road concludes at the end of the riverbank land grant; turn right onto rue des Duquette, which passes the narrow frontages of farms that stretch back to the river. In addition to corn or tomatoes, many of these farms offer pick-your-own raspberries in July. At the end of the road, follow Route 235 south until it intersects chemin Saint-Armand, which rolls and dips eastward through orchard country to Frelighsburg.

Barely over the border from Vermont, the town nestles in a hollow along the Rivière des Brochets beneath Mont Pinnacle. The combination of quiet country roads and hillside farms makes Frelighsburg the nexus of cycling and agricultural tourism in the region. Adélard Goudbout, the premier of Québec in 1936 and again from 1939 to 1944, grew up here, and his name appears on various public works. Many artists and craftspeople live in town, and each Labour Day weekend the main streets are converted into an open-air gallery for Festiv'Art.

The bakery café at **Les Sucreries de l'Érable** occupies the former general store, and the old wooden floors, antique cash register, and ceiling fans evoke the era between the world wars. The bakery specializes in maple pie (*tarte au sirop d'érable*) and creamed maple butter (*la beurrée d'érable*), but the hordes of cyclists who descend on the tables on weekends are just as likely to chow down on big cookies and slabs of cake. In addition to baked goods, the shop sells honey, maple syrup, salad dressings, vinegars, and jams from local producers. *16 rue Principale; 450-298-5181.*

Anyone not snacking at Les Sucreries is probably dining at **Aux Deux Clochers Bistro/Restaurant,** a classic small Québec farmhouse, with a gallery and bell-cast eaves on the front, and a back porch that hangs above the river. The seasonal menu is drawn from local farms—Lac-Brome duck with honey and lemon, lamb cutlets topped with chèvre. *2 rue de l'Église; 450-298-5086.*

Orchards cover the hill above the village, and the proprietors at **Domaine de Pinnacle** produce an apple specialty found almost solely in Québec. Ice cider is made by harvesting apples after a frost, pressing them for juice, and letting the juice freeze. This final step removes about eighty percent of the water. After fermentation, the resulting ice cider is luscious and thick, a perfect match with strong cheeses and foie gras—both of which are also produced in the Townships. The unassuming farmhouse at Domaine de Pinnacle dates from 1859. Only six miles

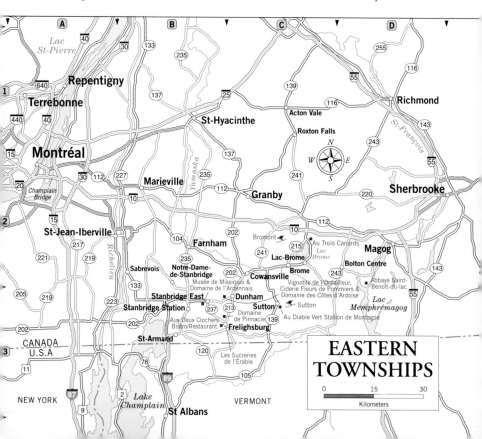

EASTERN TOWNSHIPS

0   15   30

Kilometers

DAIRY DREAMS

There's no denying that the Québecois have a love affair with cheese. Every country gas station and *depanneur* (corner store) sells bags of fresh curds near the check-out counter for munching in the car, and those same rubbery, bland bits of newborn cheese are a key ingredient in *poutine*—French fries drenched in brown gravy and topped with melted curds.

But Québec cheesemakers also craft superb artisanal cheeses. A relative handful of these—including the spectacular Bleu Bénédictin of Saint-Benoît-du-lac in the Eastern Townships—are made from pasteurized milk. But most of the world-class cheeses described below are labeled *fromage de lait cru*, or raw-milk cheese.

Two of the most exquisite soft cheeses of Québec hail from l'Île-aux-Grues, near the mouth of the St. Lawrence River: Riopelle and Mi-Carême are soft-rind, brie-style cow's milk cheeses with strongly nutty overtones and a melting richness. Ferme Piluma in Saint-Basile, just west of Québec City, also produces soft-rind cheeses—including the gentle, slightly tangy Saint-Basile sheep's milk cheese—that are rarely seen outside of a few shops in the province. La Suisse Normande, operating northeast of Montréal in Saint-Roch de l'Achigan, fashions a creamy soft-rind goat cheese with an explosive pungency, La Sablon de Blanchette.

Firm goat cheeses abound in Québec as well, with the aged Tomme des Joyeux from the Beauce region between Québec City and Maine leading the pack with its sweetly round flavor and slightly ashen aftertaste. Québec is well-known for its aged cheddars—one of the most successful products of the large industrial cheesemakers. But some of the more delicate, aged cow's milk cheeses, like the Victor et Berthold Réserve from Notre-Dame-de-Lourdes, northeast of Montréal, are winning over the palates and plates of Québecois.

You'll have to enjoy most of these raw-milk cheeses while in Québec. The young ones don't travel well, and the U.S. Food and Drug Administration does not allow unpasteurized cheeses to be brought into the country unless they have been aged a minimum of sixty days.

from the Vermont border, it was reputed to have been both a lookout station on the Underground Railroad and a base for Prohibition-era rum-runners. The back porch has views of Vermont's Green Mountains—Jay Peak to the southeast, Mount Mansfield and Camel's Hump due south—and New York's Adirondacks. *150 chemin Richford; 450-298-1222.*

■ STANBRIDGE EAST AND THE ROUTE DES VINS

Less than five kilometers northeast of Frelighsburg on Route 237, the **Musée de Missiquoi** in Stanbridge East documents local history. The same colonists who were denounced as Tories in New York and New England during the American Revolution were welcomed as United Empire Loyalists in Québec and Nova Scotia. The majority settled in the St. John's Valley in what is now New Brunswick, or north of Lake Ontario in what is now Ontario. But a few thousand moved into the previously unsettled hill and lake country that became the Eastern Townships of Québec. The Missiquoi Museum chronicles this early settlement—and the role of the Loyalists in putting down the 1866 and 1870 Fenian raids by Irish nationalists—with a wealth of official papers and more personal artifacts. (The Fenian Brotherhood, based in the United States, dreamed of capturing Lower Canada and holding it hostage until Great Britain gave Ireland its freedom.) Temporary exhibitions recount later episodes in Stanbridge history, such as the activities of liquor smugglers during Prohibition. The museum's main building is a restored three-story, redbrick mill built by Zebulon Cornell in 1830 that operated

Vineyard tours as well as tastings are available along the Route des Vins.

until 1963. The dam and mill pond behind the museum have also been restored, and the lawns make a perfect spot for an al fresco picnic along the Pike River, as locals have long called the Rivière des Brochets. *2 rue River; 450-248-3153. Open last Sunday in May to second Sunday in October.*

The east–west ridgelines and the proximity of Missiquoi Bay on Lake Champlain give the south-facing slopes of the Pike River valley a marginally warmer microclimate than surrounding areas, and many a farmer has taken a crack at viticulture. Wine making has a spotty history in Québec. Samuel de Champlain must have had high hopes when he planted French grapevines in 1608, only to discover them frozen in 1609. The Sulpicians continued to try to grow French wine grapes with little success, and the ever-practical Jesuits resorted to making sacramental wine with native varieties. But the French clearly missed their wine: in 1739, New France imported the equivalent of 775,166 bottles for a population of less than twenty-five thousand—about thirty-two liters per person. John Molson almost single-handedly switched Québecois taste to beer, but attempts to make indigenous wines continued through the nineteenth century. Varietals from New York and Ohio were introduced but simply did not produce satisfactory wine.

With the introduction of sturdy French-American hybrid varietals in the 1980s, Québec wine making finally got off the ground, and the vineyards now produce wines that are more than mere novelties. Many of the wineries, however, hedge their bets by crafting other fruit-based alcoholic beverages, including fortified apple cider and aperitifs.

More than a dozen wineries make up the Route des Vins along Route 202. West of Stanbridge East off Route 202, chemin Ridge has long south-facing slopes with sufficient elevation to avoid early frosts. The fields are planted with such brash grapes as chancellor, Maréchal Foch, and seyval, making for an incongruous scene of cold-climate sugar maples framing heat-loving wine grapes. Since 1995, **Domaine de l'Ardennais** has made a number of varietal wines from the hybrids as well as one of the traditional cold-climate noble wine grapes, Riesling. L'Ardennais also adds black currants, peaches, strawberries, or raspberries to some of its wine to produce aperitifs. *158 chemin Ridge, Stanbridge East; 450-248-0597.*

Three of the most successful Québec vintners lie along Route 202 east of Stanbridge East heading toward Dunham. The largest of the group is **Vignoble de l'Orpailleur,** which has educational displays that show the history of Québec wine

Outside of ski season, the Bromont countryside looks pastoral.

making, illustrate the cycle of the growing year, and explain the processes of vinification. Visitors are encouraged to walk through sections of the vineyard and to bring picnics, though the winery also operates a terrace restaurant for lunch and dinner from late June through mid-October. In addition to table wines, l'Orpailleur produces a crisp méthode champenoise sparkling wine that takes advantage of the acidity of Québec grapes. One compensation for the hardships of the climate is that l'Orpailleur, like most Québec vineyards, can count on making ice wines in any year when the grapes reach full maturity. Ripe Riesling and seyval grapes are left on the vines until they begin to pucker and dry. A heavy frost will further concentrate the sugars, allowing the winemakers to quickly pick and press the desiccated grapes to ferment an intensely flavored dessert wine that fetches a premium price. The ice wines are so sought after that most vineyards sell them only on the premises. *1086 Route 202, Dunham; 450-295-2763.*

Almost directly across the road, the **Ciderie Fleurs de Pommiers** takes a more traditional Québecois approach to producing alcoholic beverages, concentrating

Carnival rides come to town for the Brome Fair …

on a range of sweet, hard, and fortified apple ciders. In what is traditionally a male domain, cider-maker Marie-Andrée Tremblay excels at producing finely blended Normandy-style dry ciders as well as sweeter, fruited hard ciders flavored with strawberry, blackberry, raspberry, and black currant. The star of the lineup is Pommeau d'Or, a fortified aperitif cider that can be used in the kitchen in lieu of Calvadós. A separate facility makes cider vinegars and all manner of mustards, chutneys, relishes, jams, and jellies. *1047 Route 202, Dunham; 450-295-2223.*

The pioneer winery of the Townships, **Domaine des Côtes d'Ardoise,** remains one of the more modest producers. While most Québec wineries follow the California model of bottling single varietals, Côtes d'Ardoise blends most of its wines, using seyval as the backbone of the whites and chancellor as the main grape for the reds. In recent years the winery has taken advantage of the maturity of its early Riesling plantings to make select vintages and to produce ice wines. This is one of the lovelier wineries, with beds of flowers, cross-country ski trails, and a small terrace restaurant that offers light meals in the summer and early fall. The

… and livestock growers display their prize goats.

farm also has pick-your-own raspberries, strawberries, and apples. *879 rue Bruce (Route 202), Dunham; 450-295-2020.*

The small and tidy village of Dunham is the frontier of gentrification in the Townships, lying as it does between farm country and both the vacation retreats of the Lac-Brome villages and the ski centers of Sutton and Bromont. Several roadside shops deal in country antiques, with an emphasis on Québec pine furniture. Art galleries and cafés cluster in the village center.

Route 202 leads north from Dunham to connect to Route 104, which leads east into the villages of Brome and connects to Route 241 north to Bromont or Route 139 south to Sutton. Although the Laurentians have better and more challenging skiing, these two centers also provide excellent downhill options. **Bromont** (450-534-2200) is essentially a cluster of condominium complexes around a ski hill with forty-three trails and a maximum vertical drop of 385 meters. **Sutton** (450-538-8455) is an old-fashioned dairy-farming village where a ski center was built in 1960 and has grown to include fifty-three trails with a maximum drop of 416 meters.

Warm-season mountain activities are more varied at Sutton. The outfitter **Au Diable Vert Station de Montagne** runs guided excursions for biking, mountain biking, hiking, canoeing, kayaking, bow-hunting, off-trail skiing, snowshoeing, and fly-fishing on its three-hundred-acre mountain spread. Less strenuous outdoor activities also take place, including lessons on map and compass orientation, mushroom identification, and nature photography. Chalet lodging and primitive wilderness camping are both available. *168 chemin Staines, Glen Sutton; 450-538-5639 or 888-779-9090.*

■ LAC-BROME (KNOWLTON)

Seven villages on the shores of Brome Lake were subsumed when the town of Lac-Brome was created in 1971, but the road signs for Lac-Brome point the way to the largest and most intentionally picturesque of them: a Victorian fantasy that still sometimes goes by its maiden name of Knowlton. The sheer preponderance of boutiques showing English country-style furniture, china, fabrics, and toiletries might convince you that you'd taken a wrong turn and ended up in some quaint corner of Ontario. Golden retrievers wander the streets, and many of the summer people affect a uniform of shorts and sandals with plaid socks.

Skier takes a back-country trail at Mont Sutton.

In the mid-nineteenth century, the concentration of flour mills and sawmills, the presence of the region's only inn and general store, and the establishment of a telegraph station and post office made Knowlton the de facto business center of Brome County. The village flourished, and it soon became one of the first in Québec where Montréal's upper middle class spent their summers. The Pettes Library, the first free public library in Québec, was inaugurated in 1894, and still holds a place of pride in the village center, next to the shallow lake at Coldbrook Park.

Lac-Brome has been justifiably famous for raising ducks since Canards du Lac Brome—the oldest duck farm in Canada—was established in 1912. During the last two weekends of September and the first weekend in October, Knowlton goes all out to celebrate Le Canard de Lac-Brome en Fête—essentially a harvest festival built around tastings of duck treats prepared by chefs from around the province. But it's not necessary to wait. The small restaurant **Au Trois Canards** occupies a cheery yellow farmhouse with blue shutters and a large porch that overlooks Colebrook Park. There are two menus, one standard country-French and the other an "express menu" that is all duck, all the time—duck terrine, duck baked in a casserole, duck sausage, duck foie gras, duck cassoulet, Alsatian duck choucroute . . . *78 Lakeside Road; 450-242-5801.*

■ LAC MEMPHRÉMAGOG

It's clear by the poor quality of the dirt roads over the hills that Brome County and the region around Lake Memphrémagog have little historic connection, but it's not hard to reach the jewel of the lake, the Benedictine abbey, by following signs from Lac-Brome to Bolton Centre and turning onto chemin Nicolas Austin toward **Abbaye Saint-Benoît-du-lac.**

This French order has been in residence on the lake since 1912, and the abbey is a popular retreat for Catholic laymen, as is the neighboring Saint Scholastica's villa for laywomen. The order's motto is "Pray and Work," and visitors come both to join the monks in worship and to enjoy the fruits of the brothers' labors. The morning Mass and afternoon vespers are sung in Gregorian chant, with portions of the services also in French.

In 1943, the Saint-Benoît-du-lac brothers began making cheeses, and in an increasingly competitive cheese-making world, their blue cheeses repeatedly have won the prize as best overall cheese in Canada. The Bleu Bénédictin, produced in

LOOKING FOR MEMPHRÉ

Ever since 1798, people along the shores of Lake Memphrémagog have reported see-ing some sort of large creature swimming around. Documented sightings involving more than one person go back to 1816, and during the 1850s, a Newport, Vermont, resident named Uriah Jewett entertained passengers on the lake's first steamboat with sea serpent tales. More recent sightings led in 1986 to the creation of an association of witnesses—the International Dracontology Society of Lake Memphrémagog. Skeptics note that many of the sightings have taken place from the deck of the East Side Restaurant in Newport, usually around happy hour. But others swear that something's out there—something with big brown eyes, a horse-shaped head, large body like a whale, long neck, big hump, and front and back flippers. They call her "Memphré."

two-kilo rounds, is the flagship of the abbey's fourteen cheeses, all produced from local cow's, ewe's, and goat's milk. The monks also ferment sweet and dry alcoholic ciders, which they package in champagne bottles—the perfect complement to some cheese and bread for a picnic. The cheeses and ciders—and recordings of the monks singing Gregorian chants—are sold in a small shop downstairs from the church. *Saint-Benoît-du-lac; 819-843-4336.*

The resort community of **Magog** stands at the head of Lake Memphrémagog, a forty-four-kilometer-long finger of water sometimes likened to the lochs of Scotland, right down to a supposed sea serpent. Two-thirds of the lake lies in Québec, one-third in Vermont, and you can see both ends on the seasonal excursion boats of **Croisières Memphrémagog** (Public Landing, Magog; 819-843-8068).

As the largest town on either end of the lake, Magog is a magnet for shopping and dining and has been a center for summer visitors since the mid-nineteenth century, when lake sailing was the big attraction. Its several small inns, motels, and B&Bs often offer extra beds, suites, and other flexible sleeping arrangements to accommodate family vacations. Magog is one of the more francophone communi-ties in the Eastern Townships. Clothing in the small boutiques along rue Principale (literally, "Main Street") has a French sense of style, and the little bistros and restaurants honor the tradition of fine French country cooking. The lake is so large that it even enjoys significant wave action, and the sandy stretch at Parc Baie-de-Magog throngs with parents and children in the summer.

THE LAURENTIANS

Friday evenings on Autoroute 15 have all the decorum of a cattle drive as Montrealers flee northward en masse to the Laurentians—an ancient mountain range that begins just forty kilometers from the city. Vast tracts in the northerly reaches, crossed only by rivers and woodsmen's trails, have been set aside as wilderness parks and wildlife refuges. But most rusticators pine for the domesticated woods in the heart of the Laurentians, where ski trails slice down the slopes of round-topped mountains and silver lakes gleam in the valley bottoms. Montrealers aspire to own a little cottage on one of those six thousand Laurentian lakes, where balsam scents the air and early risers are treated to deer coming to the edge of the water to drink. Days pass all too swiftly in a blur of mornings on gentle trails, sunny afternoons in a canoe, rainy evenings playing cards at the kitchen table, and weekends puttering around the antiques shops and flea markets in quest of Québec country furniture. The alternative is a little chalet—or, failing

(above and following pages) Mont Tremblant is eastern Canada's premier ski mountain.

that, a townhouse condo—on a ski mountain where the garage has an extra bay for the family snowmobile.

Seasons in the Laurentians are vivid, even exaggerated. Summer seems more summery, winter more wintry. For every foot of snow that falls in Montréal, two feet fall in the Laurentians. A late spring snowmelt may delay the vegetation—spring flowers don't bloom until June—but the long days let every growing thing catch up. Summer, then, seems sudden and profuse. Rivers, streams, and lakes ameliorate the heat, and the shadows of deep woods prove a cool respite.

The lakeside cabin or ski slope condo is hardly a prerequisite for enjoying the region. These gentle mountains are so close to Montréal that they developed as a vacation destination even when travel was more arduous. Today, Autoroute 15 shoots from the urban center all the way north to Saint-Agathe-des-Monts, bypassing the villages in between. The parallel "local" Route 117 strings the valleys together and meanders through all the historic villages.

■ SAINT-JÉRÔME

Saint-Jérôme is sometimes called the Gateway to the North, because it sits on Route 117 at the transition from the flat St. Lawrence River valley to the Laurentian foothills. The region's first village, Saint-Jérôme was settled in 1834, during a period of tremendous economic hardship in Québec. Agriculture, which for two centuries was organized on a feudal model, was no longer viable. The original land grants, or seigneuries, had been divided so many times among large families that it was no longer possible to make a living off the land. Tens of thousands of French Canadians were forced to seek work in the mills of Montréal, or even in New England. To stem the depopulation of the countryside, the government of Lower Canada (as Québec was still called) offered large new land grants in the Pays-d'en-Haut, or High Country of the Laurentians, but found few takers. By 1849, only three families had staked their claims in the vast reaches north of Saint-Jérôme.

Antoine Labelle would change that. He arrived in Saint-Jérôme as parish priest in 1868 with the dream of creating a resurgent French northland that would stretch from the Laurentians across northern Ontario all the way to Winnipeg. A towering figure more than six feet tall and weighing more than three hundred pounds, Labelle hauled his substantial bulk over the mountains within a two-hundred-kilometer radius of Saint-Jérôme to identify potential village locations based on

soil fertility, access to waterways, and proximity to the railroad line he was determined to see built. According to his contemporaries, the curé would not take "no" for an answer, and by 1880, about ten thousand French Catholics had settled on their own plots of land. All told, Labelle helped found twenty-nine villages and opened twenty parishes in the wild.

Le Roi du Nord, or "King of the North," as he came to be called, was also instrumental in opening rail service. During the bitter winter of 1871–1872, Labelle took wood from the Laurentians to distribute to poor families in Montréal. The humanitarian act proved a brilliant political gesture, underscoring how the city could benefit from the nearby mountains. Montréal ponied up $1 million to help fund the rail line that finally reached Saint-Jérôme in 1879. In 1892, the year after Labelle's death, *Le P'tit Train du Nord,* the narrow-gauge Little Train of the North, pulled into Sainte-Agathe-des-Monts. Mont-Laurier, at the head of the Laurentians, finally welcomed service in 1909.

Saint-Jérôme today is a prosperous community. An oversized bronze **statue of Labelle** by Alfred Laliberté stands high in the center of the village park. He faces the **Cathédral Saint-Jérôme** (355 rue Saint-Georges; 450-432-9741), built in 1899 when the archdiocese elevated the parish church to a bishopric in recognition of the church's role in colonizing the Laurentians. For all its Old World references, the soaring Roman-Byzantine edifice is unmistakably Québecois in its gray stone blocks and shining metal roof. The old courthouse on the park has been converted into a visual arts center, **Centre d'Exposition du Vieux Palais** (185 rue de Palais, 450-432-7171) with free expositions of contemporary art. It also serves as a venue for concerts and plays. Across from the park, a large amphitheater serves a similar purpose for summer evening concerts. Below it, children cast worms for perch, and lovers stroll in the moonlight along the boardwalk promenade on the bank of the Rivière-du-Nord.

Saint-Jérôme's tourism office holds down the historic train station at the edge of town. In its heyday, the **P'tit Train du Nord** transformed the Laurentians. Labelle's fantasies of verdant agriculture and industrial cities never materialized, because the mountains lacked both arable land and significant minerals. What they did have was wood, but the forests were quickly depleted. The train gave the region a second life as a tourist destination. Train service reached its peak between 1920 and 1940, when the Canadian Pacific Railway introduced the Snow Trains, allowing skiers to party in the close quarters of the cars as they sped to the slopes.

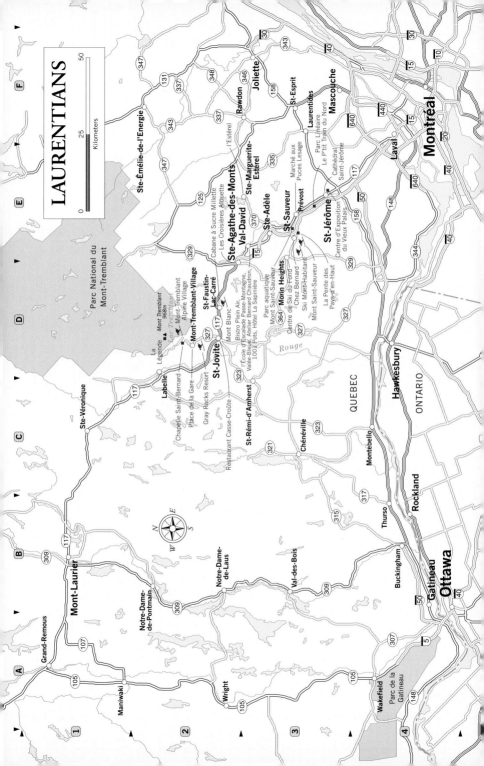

Every time it snowed, CP sent out a spunky snowplow engine equipped with an oversized cow-catcher that cleared the tracks by throwing up twenty-foot drifts on each side. Auto roads eventually siphoned passengers off the trains; the last passenger run was in 1981, the last freight train in 1989. The tracks were removed, the rail bed was paved, and the right-of-way opened for bicycling, snowmobiling, and cross-country skiing in 1996 as the **Parc Linéaire Le P'tit Train du Nord** (Place de la Gare; 450-432-0767). Saint-Jérôme is kilometer zero in the two-hundred-kilometer ribbon that follows the banks of lakes and rivers to Mont-Laurier. Because it was surveyed for a train, the average inclination is only two degrees, making the path easy to pedal. For an even easier ride, many cyclists start at the northern end and ride downhill.

■ SAINT-SAUVEUR TO SAINTE-AGATHE

Autoroute 15 is for travelers in a hurry. Route 117 north from Saint-Jérôme is by far more interesting, stringing together the Laurentian villages like beads on a rosary. Commercial skiing in the lower Laurentians got started just north of Saint-Jérôme when the Maple Leaf opened in Prévost in 1932. Skiers quickly tired of walking back up the slope, so in 1933 the ski center installed a mechanical chairlift, said to have been the first in North America. The mountain has since closed; travelers flock to Prévost instead for the antiques shops that line both sides of Route 117 and the year-round flea market **Marché aux Puces Lesage** (2845 boulevard Labelle; 450-224-4833). In the summer, the weekend-only market has more than three hundred merchants indoors and out.

■ SAINT-SAUVEUR

Saint-Sauveur was the first full-fledged ski resort town in the Laurentians. It remains a popular destination, because it is close to Montréal, less expensive than the larger Mont-Tremblant, and emphasizes night skiing. The two local ski mountains have forty-nine trails between them, all but ten of which are lit. The smaller **Ski Mont-Habitant** (12 boulevard des Skieurs; 450-227-2637) has a higher proportion of trails for beginners, while **Mont Saint-Sauveur** (350 rue Saint-Denis, 450-227-4671) has four black-diamond trails as well as glade skiing. Not everyone goes downhill on skis or snowboards. Sliding over the snow on inner tubes is an exhilarating, distinctly Québecois pastime. One area on Mont Avila (part of the Mont Saint-Sauveur operation) is devoted exclusively to this activity: **La Pente des**

A locomotive pushes a snow plow to clear the tracks in Rivière-du-Nord, 1869.

Pays-d'en-Haut (440 chemin Avila; 450-224-4014) maintains thirty-eight slides for tubing and snow rafting.

If the Québecois can't be skiing, they'd just as soon be splashing—or so it sometimes seems from the preponderance of water parks. **Parc aquatique Mont Saint-Sauveur** features two high-speed water slides, six giant spiral water slides, and a giant wave pool that mimics the surf of an ocean beach. *Route 117; 450-227-4671. Open mid-June–August.*

The village of Saint-Sauveur itself has a certain sprawling charm, as if it had settled into a valley surrounded by ski hills the way water seeks a low spot. Restaurants along the strip of rue Principale serve Italian, French, Szechuan, Vietnamese, and Mexican fare along with crepes and hot dogs. The foil for this we-are-the-world ski-town gastronomy is the grocery store and delicatessen **Chez Bernard** (411 rue Principale; 450-240-0000), which stocks its coolers with ready-to-heat dishes such as coq au vin and offers a wide range of Québec cheeses and other local products.

Tree-lined Route 364 heads west from Saint-Sauveur to **Morin Heights**. Much to curé Labelle's dismay, the town was founded by Protestant anglophones in 1855. Regional tourism literature notes only that this enclave of private cottages is considered to have "Anglo-Saxon architecture," which is to say that it looks more like Ontario's lake country than Québec's. It is the eastern terminus of an "aerobic corridor"—a hiking and biking path that doubles as a cross-country ski trail—that stretches about sixty kilometers west to Saint-Rémi-d'Amherst. The trailhead is at 50 chemin de Lac Écho. The town also maintains more than 150 kilometers of interconnecting cross-country ski trails along with a warming lodge, the **Centre de Ski du Fond** (612 chemin du Village; 450-226-2417).

■ VAL-DAVID

On warm days, Val-David feels like a fashionable gym. Tanned and trim young men and women strut around in Spandex bicycle pants, their calf muscles bulging, their washboard abs rippling. They seem to travel in packs with long poles topped with pennants extending from their knobby-tired mountain bikes. Eavesdropping on their conversations quickly reveals that "dude" is the same in both English slang and Québecois *joual*. Possibly no community in the Laurentians has been so transformed by the P'tit Train du Nord park as Val-David. Most towns built their train stations on the outskirts. But in Val-David, the railroad right-of-way went through the middle of the village, and the bike path makes this artistic and outdoorsy community the locus of social and athletic activity in the Laurentians. On most summer nights, the outdoor terrace of **Bistro Plein Air** (2510 rue de l'Église; 819-322-7348) entices crowds to the edge of the bike path with live bands as the fireflies glimmer just beyond the reach of the streetlights.

AlthoughVal-David lies in an almost perfectly flat valley of the Rivière du Nord, it is surrounded by mountains. Rock-climbing got its start as a Québec sport here in the 1980s, and it's still the perfect place to learn the basics or to tackle difficult ascents with other experienced climbers. Classes at **l'École d'Escalade Passe-Montagne** match three to six students with an experienced instructor who demonstrates security measures and proper technique. Make reservations on weekdays; everyone on staff is out scaling the hills on weekends. *1760 Montée deuxième rang; 819-322-2123 or 800-465-2123.*

Saint-Sauveur is dotted with dozens of charming cafés and small restaurants.

If you don't pull into town with your own bicycle or canoe on top of your car, there's no shortage of places to rent them. Both **Pause Plein Air** (1381C rue Dufresne; 819-324-0798) and **Phénix Sports et Aventures** (2444 rue de l'Église; 819-322-1118) rent canoes for the two-hour trip down the Rivière du Nord to Lac Raymond, where they'll pick you up. Both shops also rent bicycles. In the winter, Phénix rents cross-country ski equipment, kick sleds, skating skis, snowshoes, and ice skates. Although the major ski resorts are farther north, mellow Val-David skiers and snowboarders favor the sixteen trails of **Valée-Bleue** (1418 chemin Valée-Bleue; 819-322-3427).

Artists and craftspeople discovered Val-David in the 1920s and happily coexist with the jocks. Several art galleries and boutiques in the village center feature local work. Two dozen artists banded together to produce a walking-tour map of galleries and ateliers that they call La Route des Arts. One of the best-established is **Atelier Bernard Chaudron** (2449 chemin d'Île; 819-322-3944). Chaudron makes functional pieces in pewter and gladly explains the process to visitors as he shows them around the studio. The quirky annual exhibition **1001 Pots** (2435 rue de l'Église; 819-322-6868) was launched by ceramist Kinya Ishikawa in 1989. From mid-July to mid-August, about a hundred artisans from around Québec show their works on his property, located just west of the village center, and celebrate with a monthlong roster of activities, including chamber music concerts.

Jean-Baptiste Dufresne arrived in Val-David in 1849, making it one of the earliest settlements in the Laurentians. His grandson, Léonidas Dufresne, served as the first mayor and shaped the community into a resort by damming a small river and building the peeled-log **Hôtel La Sapinière** next to the resulting pond in 1936. In the ensuing years, La Sapinière has expanded from twenty rooms to seventy, but it retains much of the air of an early-twentieth-century rustic lodging. The first-class classic French dining room and good French wine cellar, however, make La Sapinière the genteel choice among more than twenty lodgings in the little village. *1244 chemin de-la-Sapinière; 819-322-2020.*

■ SAINTE-AGATHE-DES-MONTS

Like a sun-bleached picture postcard on a drugstore rack, the post–World War II tourism boom town of Sainte-Agathe-des-Monts poses the cheerful dreams of summer yesteryears. The town had developed as the marketplace of the central

ROCK OF AGES

The Laurentians are mountains of a comfortable house-broken sort. Not one of them importunes you with peaks and pinnacles to assault. Not one confounds your senses or twists your reason with a hurly-burly grandeur. They are the kind of mountain that you like to have just beyond the garden. They are as cozy as a kitchen, often— old and magnanimous and worn with the weathers of all time. Most geologists agree that they are the oldest ranges of the globe, and even the counter-geologists, who mumble about recent infusions from below, put the period far enough back to be impressive. Certainly they wear their age as becomingly as an old lady her wrinkles.

— T. Morris Longstreth, *The Laurentians,* 1922

Laurentians, because it sits just below a mountain pass that long stymied road-builders. But the long sandy beaches of Lac au Sables destined it for resort development, and in the late 1940s and early 1950s, Sainte-Agathe became, as Mordecai Richler wrote in *O Canada! O Quebec!*, a "minor-league Catskills. Indigenous comics played a flourishing hotel circuit. . . . Children's camps proliferated. . . . A Jewish baker set up in town, and there was of course, a synagogue and a kosher butcher. On Saturdays in July the rue Principale and the rue Tour de Lac swelled with noisy Jewish families parading in their finery, tooting the horns of their newly acquired Buicks, lining up for a midnight medium-fat smoked meat on rye at the local deli."

Those vintage ethnic pleasures of Sainte-Agathe have faded. The comedy circuit is gone, and SUVs have replaced the loud-horned Buicks. But the main streets are still lined with tiny souvenir shops; restaurants, cafés, and bars (each hardly bigger than a front parlor); and an inordinate number of places to get your hair and nails done. The three municipal beaches still pack in the summer people, and old-style lakeside hotels still have canoes for their guests. Young and old alike line up for the narrated fifty-minute lake cruises of **Les Croisières Alouette** (town dock; 819-326-3656), and parking is no easier to find than it ever was. In the winter, when the ski crowd packs the town, a portion of the lake is cleared for ice-skating.

■ LAC MASSON AND ESTÉREL

Lac Masson—a classic multi-lobed alpine lake dotted with islands and surrounded by hemlock forest—is one of the most fabled resort regions of the Laurentians. It lies northeast from Sainte-Adèle on the Route 370 spur off Route 117, the main highway. The tiny village of Sainte-Marguerite-du-Lac-Masson, founded in 1855, blossomed as a woodsy getaway early in the twentieth century; at one time it boasted five hotels and several inns and boarding houses. One of the most famous visitors was the Belgian writer Georges Simenon, author of the Inspector Maigret mystery novels, who spent 1945 and 1946 on the lake. Leaving his wife and son to fend for themselves in a log cottage, he went to Manhattan for a few weeks and promptly fell in love with the French Canadian Denyse Ouimet, whom he later married. Returning to Lake Masson, Simenon set up his mistress in another cottage and, even as he shuffled between the two abodes, managed to write two novels, *Maigret in New York* and *Three Rooms in Manhattan*.

Simenon wasn't the first Belgian of note to discover the lake. Baron Louis Empain so fell in love with the setting that he acquired three thousand acres on the southeast lobe in 1935, christening his estate Estérel (starry sky) after the mountain range west of Cannes. Over the next three years, the baron constructed an art deco hotel, sports center, and ski chalet. Although it was the middle of the Great Depression, he also sponsored a commercial mall with a movie theater, dance hall, upscale boutiques, stables for saddle horses, and a service station. A showman above all, Empain hired Benny Goodman to entertain his guests on opening night in 1938. The mall now houses the town hall of Sainte-Marguerite–Estérel (as the merged villages of Sainte-Marguerite-du-lac-Masson and Estérel have been called since 2001) and the community theater. The adjacent log structure, formerly the baron's private lodge, is a small inn.

But the bulk of the estate was transformed into a lakeside resort by Fridolin Simard, an industrialist who discovered Lac Masson when bad weather forced him to land his small plane and take shelter in the baron's old stables. The next day Simard learned that the land was for sale and snapped it up to build the principal lodging on the lake today, **l'Estérel** (39 chemin Fridolin-Simard; 450-228-2571 or 888-378-3735). The rounded balcony extending out over the lake gives the 125-room resort something of the feel of a classic ocean liner. The resort's boat club (450-228-4722), a separate concession, rents jet-skis, canoes, pontoon party boats, pedal boats, motorboats, and water skis. L'Estérel has a busy winter season as well.

The shallow lake freezes early and solidly, making it ideal for skating and snowmobiling. Guests can also bundle up and step right outside the door for snowshoeing, cross-country skiing, and dogsledding.

■ MONT TREMBLANT REGION

Autoroute 15 ends at Sainte-Agathe-des-Monts, but Route 117 broadens to press northward across the mountains, closely following the route laid out for the P'tit Train du Nord. This part of Québec routinely receives up to four meters of snow per year, making it ideal for winter sports. **Saint-Faustin-Lac-Carré** offers the first intimation of Québec's premier ski country. This sleepy pair of recently amalgamated villages are an alternative for skiers who wish to avoid the crowds up the road at the Mont-Tremblant megaresort. The comparatively diminutive slope (a three-hundred-meter vertical drop) of **Mont Blanc** (Route 117; 819-688-2444) has thirty-five trails for skiing minus the hubbub.

Saint-Faustin is also the home of one of the premier sugarhouses in the Laurentians, **Cabane à Sucre Millette.** The Millette family has been tapping these maple groves since 1877, when the town was first settled, and four generations

Ski trails crisscross Mont Tremblant.

later, they have expanded the operation to include a gift shop, indoor and outdoor exhibits, and a group restaurant. If you visit in March and April, you might smell the wood smoke and the faint aroma of boiling maple syrup before you see the sugarhouse. With luck, you'll catch one of the Millettes leading a horse-drawn sled burdened with a big barrel for collecting sap. At the very least, you can watch the "sugaring off" process, in which sap is reduced to syrup in open evaporator pans. During the active sugaring season, the Millettes also offer daily lunches and dinners of traditional Québecois country cuisine sweetened with maple syrup. Fiddlers rosin their bows and spoon players set up a clacking rhythm for traditional French-Canadian music during the sugaring season's Saturday night suppers. More than three hundred old farm and woods tools—from wooden hay rakes to huge crosscut saws—line the walls of the year-round gift shop. Follow the line of small maples planted by Japanese tourists—up to ten thousand visit each year—to the boiling hut. *1357 rue Saint-Faustin (off Route 117); 819-688-2101.*

■ **MONT-TREMBLANT**
Since the 1990s, the Québec government has been combining previously independent villages into amalgamated towns and cities. In the case of Mont-Tremblant—where the name denotes the superimposed municipal entity, a small village, a huge alpine ski resort, and (without the hyphen) the mountain itself—signage can be thoroughly confusing. To add to the muddle, the formerly independent village of Saint-Jovite is also part of the larger municipality. But the mountain subsumes everything. Mont Tremblant may rise only 968 meters above sea level—and only 736 meters from base to summit—but it's the biggest rock around and the largest ski region in eastern Canada.

Saint-Jovite's short main street, rue Ouimet, is tightly packed with restaurants, cafés, boutiques, art galleries, and even a *salon de thé* (tearoom). Because the town's old buildings, many of which have front porches with welcoming chairs and benches, have been preserved, Saint-Jovite escapes the cookie-cutter look of so many ski towns around North America. Plaques along the street proclaim the year a given structure was built, who erected it, and what it was used for; one farmhouse, for instance, became first a general store before morphing into a florist shop. Among all the jovial new bars and fern-bedecked restaurants is one survivor of old-fashioned snacking, **Restaurant Casse-Croûte** (995 rue Ouimet; 819-425-2466). Its indoor tables are a welcome respite from the winter cold, but during the summer most customers take their burgers, hot dogs, fried fish, *poutine,* and soft-serve ice cream to the picnic tables at the edge of the parking lot in back.

The first recreational getaway in the Mont Tremblant area was the Gray Rocks Inn, now the **Gray Rocks Resort,** on Lake Ouimet a few kilometers north of Saint-Jovite on Route 327. With only eighty-four rooms, it seems almost cozy compared to most resort developments. Gray Rocks opened the first ski trails and first golf course at Mont Tremblant in 1920, and Herman "Jack Rabbit" Johansen launched the ski instruction program in 1938. Credited with introducing alpine skiing to the Laurentians, Johansen was a walking advertisement for an active lifestyle and fresh air. A regular on the slopes until age 103, he died January 5, 1987, at the age of 111. *2322 rue Labelle; 819-425-2771 or 800-567-6767.*

The original Mont-Tremblant-Village barely hints at the alpine resort farther up the hill. If you pause in the village at the **Place de la Gare**—the former rail station in the P'tit Train park—you'll get a hint of the excitement that ran through these parts in the 1940s. A display of old, mostly amateur snapshots captures a can-do spirit that turned a mountain into a way of life. The snowplow train comes roaring out of the 1940s, black smoke curling from its stack as the plow sweeps the rail bed like a snowblower on a sidewalk. Other ancient black-and-whites show pioneers of Mont-Tremblant's tourist days grinning for the camera, including Jack Rabbit Johansen in his prime, and Charles Hector Deslauriers, the parish priest of the village from 1929 to 1979 who helped develop the ski industry. (A small park honoring the curé stands about fifty meters uphill.) The station also exhibits paintings by contemporary local artists; in warm weather, you'll find the artists themselves gathered outside at their easels, putting finishing touches on mountain scenes. *1886 chemin Principal; 819-429-5529.*

Prosperity didn't always smile on Mont-Tremblant. Times were tough in 1938—the lumber tract was timbered out, sawmills were shut down, and the town's only remaining industry, a factory that made denatured wood alcohol, had closed. Curé Deslauriers was on the verge of pleading for financial assistance from the provincial government when young Joe Ryan from Philadelphia came to town with money in his pockets.

When Ryan visited the Laurentians in 1938 to do a little gold prospecting, he stayed at Gray Rocks—which, at the time, was the best place around. Like many a

(following pages) The condos and shops of Tremblant village stand right next to the ski lifts.

vacationer before him, he climbed the summit of Mont Tremblant, though few other adventurers hiked up in the company of journalist Lowell Thomas, who made the mountain famous when he wrote about it. Local legend has it that Ryan was spellbound by the snow-covered slopes and vowed to build a world-class alpine village. By February 1939, his Mont-Tremblant Lodge was ready, and the ski mountain was on its way. In 1991, IntraWest (owner of, among other ski resorts, Blackcomb and Whistler in British Columbia) bought out the Ryan heirs and transformed the successful resort into the biggest and most extensive ski center in eastern Canada.

The winding road between the modest village and the resort is lined with little *gîtes* and *auberges*—B&Bs and inns. The horizon suddenly opens at the southern tip of the ten-kilometer-long Lake Tremblant, a Scottish-style loch that wraps around the western slope of Mont Tremblant. The scale of everything seems to double, as if you had entered the valley of the giants. Large sail craft and power boats bob on the lake, and every hillside not blazed with ski trails is dotted with condo developments. From June into mid-October, **Les Croisières Mont-Tremblant** (2810 chemin du Village; 819-425-1045) offers seventy-minute cruises of the lake.

On the lakeshore drive, just below Joe Ryan's pioneering ski run, the Flying Mile, stands the **Chapelle Saint-Bernard**—one of the favorite subjects of the painters who hang their work in Place de la Gare. Joe Ryan and his wife, Mary, were so taken with a 1678 church on the Île d'Orleans near Québec City, that they asked curé Deslauriers's blessing to replicate it in Mont-Tremblant. Every detail of the seventeenth-century church was faithfully copied, including the cock on the spire and the red roof. The Ryans scoured Québec for old chandeliers, statues, and wooden crucifixes to furnish the interior, and the chapel was dedicated in March 1942 to the patron saint of skiers. Old photographs show vacationers of the 1940s and 1950s attending Mass in their ski gear while their skis stand outside in the snowbanks. Even curé Deslauriers was said to have worn ski boots under his robes.

Mont-Tremblant Alpine Village (1000 chemin des Voyageurs; 800-461-8711) is the recreational resort at the foot of the lifts. The usual mix of multicolored mountain-slope architecture is tempered by mansard roofs that nod to Québec's French heritage. The construction parallels a medieval mountain redoubt, with a circle of ring roads instead of a moat and high towers of large hotels instead of crenellated walls. Inside, developers have conjured a rather charming pedestrian village, with several tiered levels packed with boutiques, bars, and restaurants. For the most dramatic meals, though, you'll have to take a nine-minute ride on a bubble-enclosed chairlift to **La Légende** (819-681-5500) at the summit of Mont Tremblant.

The Disneyesque qualities of the village take nothing away from the ski facility, which boggles the imaginations of most East Coast skiers with more than six hundred acres of skiing and snowboarding terrain on ninety-two trails stretching seventy-five kilometers. Average natural snowfall is 382 centimeters (150 inches), and snow guns augment that on the busier trails. As a result, Mont-Tremblant enjoys a seven-month ski season.

When the skiing gets grassy, there's always golf. The resort area has no less than seven courses, of which the eighteen-hole, par seventy-two **Le Géant** is the flagship. The challenging course, consistently ranked in Canada's top ten, features striking views of Lake Tremblant and more than fifty devilish sand traps. Fans of older-style courses with mature growth might head back down the hill to Gray Rocks; its original eighteen-hole **La Belle** course calls for finesse with its side hill and uphill lies.

■ LABELLE

History, vision, and tenacity all come together in Labelle, just eleven kilometers from Mont-Tremblant village by the back road along Lake Tremblant's western shore. The curé had great hopes for his namesake community when he founded it in 1880 at the impassable Iroquois Rapids on the Rivière Rouge, figuring correctly that the settlers could saw the lumber coming down the river from the north woods. Moreover, there were gems in the ground. But Labelle's garnets proved to be the industrial sort used as sandpaper grit, and once the timber was gone, the sawmills closed. If nothing else, the town has pluck: it serves adventurers, outdoorsmen, and snowmobilers as a base camp for ventures into the broad wilderness tracts of Rouge-Matawin, Papineau-Labelle, and Mont-Tremblant parks and wildlife preserves. The recently restored train station (180 rue de Dépôt) on the P'tit Train du Nord path proudly displays photographs of the last log drives and the old coal-burning snow trains, as well as an account (in French only) of curé Labelle's campaign to populate the north with good French-Canadian Catholics.

PRACTICAL INFORMATION

■ AREA CODES AND TIME ZONE

The entire province of Québec lies within the Eastern time zone. The area code for Montréal is 514, for Québec City 418. Area code 450 applies in parts of the Laurentians and Eastern Townships near Montréal; farther away, the area code is 819.

■ METRIC CONVERSIONS

1 foot = .305 meters   1 mile = 1.6 kilometers   1 pound = .45 kilograms
Centigrade = Fahrenheit temperature minus 32, divided by 1.8

■ CLIMATE

Montréal enjoys four distinct seasons. The climate is cool-temperate, according to meteorological temperature averaging, but is prone to extremes in both winter and summer. Annual rainfall averages 736 millimeters (29 inches) and annual snowfall averages 214 centimeters (84 inches). In January, highs average -6°C (21°F) and lows -15°C (5°F). April highs average 11°C (52°F) and lows 1°C (34°F). In July, highs average 26°C (79°F) but often soar above 30°C (86°F). October highs average 13°C (55°F) and lows average 4°C (39°F).

■ GETTING THERE AND AROUND

■ BY AIR

Montréal–Pierre Elliott Trudeau International Airport (YUL) on the west end of the island of Montréal is served by most major international and domestic carriers. Before 2004 the airport was known as Montréal International Airport–Dorval. It is located about twenty kilometers from downtown. Some European and charter carriers use the alternate Mirabel airport (YMX), about fifty-five kilometers northwest of downtown but under the same airport authority. *514-394-7377 or (from Canada, Vermont, and Albany, New York only) 800-465-1213; www.admtl.com.*

■ **By Train**

VIA **Rail Canada** handles all passenger rail service to Montréal, including connecting service with Amtrak; *514-989-2626 or 888-842-7245; www.viarail.ca.*

■ **By Car**

Several limited-access superhighways (autoroutes) funnel into Montréal. Autoroute 40 is the swiftest approach from Ottawa and the north-shore route from Québec. Follow Autoroute 20 for the south-shore route from Québec. Drivers coming from New England enter Canada on I-89 to Route 133 and Autoroute 35 north. Transfer to Autoroute 10 west to Montréal. From New York, drivers enter Canada on I-87, which becomes Autoroute 15 to Montréal.

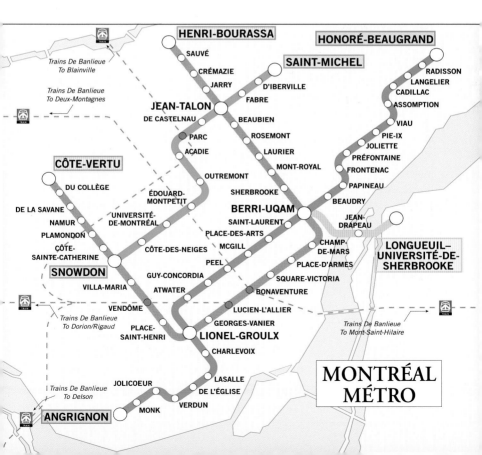

MONTRÉAL MÉTRO

■ **By Bus**

All bus services to Montréal use the Terminus Voyageurs (505 boulevard de Maisonneuve est; Métro: Berri-UQÀM). **Greyhound USA** (800-229-9424; www. greyhound.com) and its **Trailways** (www.trailways.com) affiliates offer service from the United States. Canadian bus service includes **Greyhound Canada** (800-661-8747; www.greyhound.ca) and **Orleans Express** (514-842-2281; www. orleansexpress.com).

■ **By Riverboat**

Les Dauphins du Saint-Laurent offers four-hour hydrofoil service between Montréal and Québec City with a stop at Trois-Rivières. Boats operate twice daily from mid-May to mid-October. *514-288-4499 or 877-648-4499; www.dauphins.ca.*

■ **Local Transit**

An extensive network of Métro (subway) lines covers most of central Montréal and some of the more distant neighborhoods on the island. Where the Métro doesn't go, the buses do. Service operates from 5:30 A.M. to 1 A.M. One-way fares, in Canadian dollars, are $2.50, or $10 for a strip of six tickets. The Tourist Card for unlimited bus and subway travel costs $7 for one day, $14 for three days. *514-288-6287; www.stm.info.*

■ **Language**

By law, French is the official language of public services, signage, and legal transactions throughout Québec. English is widely spoken, though with varying fluency. English-speaking visitors are unlikely to have any communications difficulties in areas covered in this book, but a smattering of French can come in handy in small towns and residential neighborhoods.

■ **Customs/Tax Rebate**

Nonresident visitors to Canada can apply for a rebate of the seven-percent federal goods and services tax (GST) on short-term accommodations (less than one month) and on goods taken out of the country. Proof of export is required, so receipts must be validated by a Canada Customs official as you leave Canada, either at the airport or the border. Each receipt must be for at least $50 (Canadian) and receipts must total at least $200 (Canadian). Receipts must be originals. Tax rebate forms are available in shopping malls, stores, and at Canada Customs and Revenue Agency desks at airports and border crossings. Québec does not rebate provincial sales tax.

■ Food

With more than five thousand bistros and restaurants representing at least eighty national cuisines, Montréal is a great city for eating out. Humble Québecois comfort food has suffered in this health-conscious era, but you can still find the occasional neighborhood greasy spoon serving homemade *soupe aux pois* (green pea soup), *tourtiére* (meat turnover), and *cretons* (a pâté of ground pork cooked in lard with onions). Traditional breakfast items include *fèves au lards* (baked beans with salt pork) and almost anything doused with *sirop d'érable* (maple syrup). The classic breakfast drink is *un bol de café au lait* (a large bowl filled half with dark coffee and half with frothy hot milk).

French and contemporary Québecois cuisines dominate among fine-dining establishments, but thousands of small ethnic spots represent Montréal's francophone immigrants over the last quarter century: Lebanese, Cambodian, Thai, Vietnamese, North African, West African, and Haitian specialties await. Many of these "newcomer" cuisines are found on rues Prince-Arthur and Duluth and avenue Rachel. You can also find good Portuguese seafood and roast chicken restaurants on the Plateau, the cuisines of the old Hapsburg empire around Mile End, and pastas and southern Italian cooking in Little Italy. Many of these restaurants do not serve alcohol but have a BYOB policy, which helps keep prices down.

In the 1990s, fine dining modeled on French provincial cooking but using Québec ingredients swept Montréal, making it possible to eat as well in Montréal as in, say, Lyon. Local specialties include foie gras, succulent duck, salt-meadow–fed lamb, caribou, salmon, oysters, scallops, and mussels. Foragers supply a wonderful array of mushrooms, from the morels of spring to the autumnal hen-of-the-woods. Fruits begin with almost impossibly sweet strawberries of June that announce the arrival of summer and progress through the seasons with tangy raspberries, explosive blueberries, and a wide range of fall apples. A critical mass of talent and competition has developed among the city's chefs, each vying to outdo the others.

Montrealers tend to make an evening of dining out, pacing themselves between courses, lingering over dessert, conversing over coffee. As a result, outside of tourist areas, service tends to be measured and decorous rather than rushed. "Smart casual" clothing will get you in the door of most establishments, but Montrealers tend to be more European than American in their dining attire—i.e., better-dressed—and at many top restaurants, especially in exclusive hotels, gentlemen are expected to wear coats and ties.

■ FAVORITE RESTAURANTS

Prices below are per person, in Canadian dollars; they include an appetizer, main dish, and dessert, but exclude drinks, taxes, and tip. U.S. citizens should keep in mind that when the rate of exchange is favorable, dining out in Canada is a true bargain.

MAIN-COURSE PRICES PER PERSON

$ = under $20   **$$** = $20–$35   **$$$** = $35–$50   **$$$$** = $50 or more

---

MONTRÉAL

Au Pied de Cochon. Lusty bistro-brasserie cooking of Martin Picard draws the smart set on the Plateau. Reserve far ahead. *536 rue Duluth est; 514-281-1114. Contemporary.* **$$$**

Bistro L'Entrepôt. Classic neighborhood bistro emphasizes Lyonnaise dishes. BYOB. *1622 rue Hôtel-de-Ville; 514-845-1369. French.* **$$**

Chez Claudette. Outside the mainstream dining areas of the Plateau, Chez Claudette serves breakfast all day (it's open 24 hours) as well as such Québecois home specialties as *pâté chinois*—ground beef, corn, and potatoes topped with browned mashed potatoes. It's also known for *poutine,* the Québecois concoction of french fries topped with brown gravy and sprinkled with fresh cheese curds. *351 avenue Laurier est; 514-279-5173. Traditional Québecois.* **$**

Chez l'Épicier. Nouvelle Québecois cuisine gets an Asian accent and light treatment emphasizing salads, vegetables, and fish. The restaurant's grocery store also sells fabulous take-out dishes. Even lunch can be busy, so make a reservation. *311 rue Saint-Paul est; 514-878-2232. Contemporary.* **$$$**

La Colombe. Clean contemporary Québecois cuisine rules at this extremely popular BYOB restaurant sandwiched in among the *brochetteries* on Duluth. Fresh fish, raw milk cheeses, and game are all featured on the menu, and the tiny room is bright and celebratory. *554 avenue Duluth est; 514-849-8844. French.* **$$**

La Gargote. Like something out of a circa-1948 French movie, this mom-and-pop bistro in Old Montréal has a very limited menu and even more limited list of wines, but offers good value and great atmosphere. Outdoor tables on the square are available in the summer. *351 Place d'Youville; 514-844-1428. French.* **$$**

Visual panache is a hallmark of Montréal events.

Le Caveau. If you long for the great French restaurants of yesteryear, look no farther. All modern quirks are banished in favor of classic cuisine bourgeoisie—cassoulet, entrecôte bordelaise, rack of lamb, and even a rich cauliflower soup. *2063 rue Victoria; 514-844-1624. French.* **$$$**

Leméac. Chic and gleaming, this stylish room on the Outremont edge of the Plateau is a treasure box of delights, from the salmon and beef tartars to the unctuous raw-milk cheeses (with plenty of stops in between for roasted veal chops or lemony sole). Pricey Leméac offers a bargain three-course menu after 10 P.M. *1045 avenue Laurier ouest; 514-270-0999. Contemporary.* **$$$$**

L'Entrecôte Saint-Jean. Fixed-price meals of steak-frites with soup, salad, and dessert make up the entire menu of this bargain-priced bistro in the midst of a chichi district. *2022 rue Peel; 514-281-6492. French.* **$**

Les Halles. Montréal's pioneer of the fresh-market approach to dining, Les Halles has been one of the city's top restaurants since it opened in 1970. Executive chef Dominique Crevoisier has developed a long and complex menu—with lots of daily specials. *1450 rue Crescent; 514-844-2328. French.* **$$$$**

Rôtisserie Laurier. It doesn't get more down-home than this roast chicken house, which has been in business since 1936. Pierre Elliott Trudeau used to stop in for the half chicken and a slice of *tarte au citrón-crème* (lemon-cream pie). *381 rue Laurier ouest; 514-273-3671. Traditional Québecois.* **$**

Schwartz's. Smoked meat is a Montréal thing—less peppery than pastrami, more subtle than barbecue. This Plateau institution didn't invent smoked meat; it only perfected it. Expect a line, especially for takeout. *3895 boulevard Saint-Laurent; 514-842-4813. Deli.* **$**

Toqué! Chef Normand Laprise has won international accolades for his interpretations of local fish, meat, and produce and his redefinition of Québecois cuisine. Reserve far ahead and consider the chef's tasting menu to enjoy Laprise's latest discoveries. *900 place Jean-Paul-Riopelle; 514-499-2084. Contemporary.* **$$$$**

EASTERN TOWNSHIPS

Au Trois Canards. The village of Knowlton is part of Lac-Brome, and to a gourmet, Lac-Brome translates as "great duck." The menu here exhausts virtually every classic preparation for the tasty fowl. *79 rue Lakeside, Knowlton; 450-242-5801. French.* **$$**

QUÉBEC CITY

Laurie Raphaël. Daniel Vezina is one of the brightest young stars of innovative Québecois cuisine, and this destination restaurant, named for his children, is Québec City's gourmet temple. Think flash-fried quail breasts with prunes wrapped in prosciutto and served with a salad of tangy bitter greens and candied lemon. *117 rue Dalhousie; 418-692-4555. Contemporary.* **$$$$**

L'Entrecôte Saint-Jean. Fixed-price meals of steak-frites with soup, salad, and dessert make up the entire menu of this pioneering bargain bistro. Expect long waits on weekend nights. *1011 rue Saint-Jean; 418-694-0234. French.* **$**

Le Saint-Amour. Chef Jean-Luc Boulay takes such local specialties as caribou and lobster and gives them beautiful, intense treatments—wrapping the steak in a mushroom-blueberry crust, serving the crustacean with saffron-steamed fennel. The glass roof makes the dining room bright and cheerful all year round. *48 rue Sainte-Ursule; 418-694-0667. Contemporary.* **$$$**

Rue de Petit-Champlain as seen from the Breakneck Stairs, ca. 1905.

■ LODGING

Like most large cities, Montréal has an extensive range of convention and business hotels—which often have very good leisure travel rates on weekends. In recent years, there's been a trend toward creating fine B&Bs in historic buildings and carving out boutique hotels by refitting Old Montréal warehouse and factory structures with state-of-the-art furnishings. New hotels in Montréal tend toward chic, ultramodern design with splashy glass showers, custom-made furniture, and high-speed Internet connections. A similar trend prevails in Québec City outside the walls of Old Québec. Within the walls, lodgings tend to be cozy inns with a Victorian warmth. Lodgings in the Laurentians and Eastern Townships run the gamut from rural farm-stay B&Bs to all-inclusive resort hotels. Room availability in the countryside is limited in July and August, when most Québecois take their summer vacations.

■ RESERVATION SERVICES
Eastern Townships. *800-355-5755; www.easterntownships.cc.*
Laurentians. *800-561-6673; www.laurentians.com.*
Montréal. *800-267-5180; www.bbmontreal.qc.ca; or 800-738-4338; www.bbmontreal.com.*
Québec City and Province. *877-266-5687; www.bonjourquebec.com.*
Québec Provincial Parks. *800-665-6527; www.sepaq.com.*

■ HOTEL AND MOTEL CHAINS
Best Western. *800-780-7234; www.bestwestern.com.*
Comfort Inn. *877-424-6423; www.choicehotels.com.*
Crowne Plaza. *800-227-6963; www.crowneplaza.com.*
Days Inn. *800-329-7466; www.daysinn.com.*
Delta. *877-814-7706; www.deltahotels.com.*
Fairmont. *888-499-9899; www.fairmont.com.*
Hilton. *800-445-8667; www.hilton.com.*
Holiday Inn. *800-465-4329; www.holiday-inn.com.*
InterContinental. *800-327-0200; www.intercontinental.com.*
Loews. *800-235-6397; www.loewshotels.com.*
Marriott. *800-228-9290; www.marriott.com.*
Novotel. *800-221-4542; www.novotel.com.*

Omni Hotels. *800-843-6664; www.omnihotels.com.*
Quality Inn. *877-424-6423; www.qualityinn.com.*
Radisson. *800-333-3333; www.radisson.com.*
Ritz-Carlton. *800-241-3333; www.ritzcarlton.com.*
Sheraton. *800-325-3535; www.sheraton.com.*
Sofitel. *877-285-9001; www.sofitel.com.*
Travelodge. *800-578-7878; www.travelodge.com.*
Westin. *800-228-3000; www.westin.com.*
Wyndham. *877-999-3223; www.wyndham.com.*

■ FAVORITE LODGINGS
Room rates swing widely in Montréal and Québec, with frequent bargain promotions in early spring, mid-winter, and late fall. Rates given here are in Canadian dollars and represent rooms for two people during the high seasons of summer and early fall. Visitors from outside Canada can receive rebates on national hotel taxes.

> PRICE DESIGNATIONS FOR LODGING
> **$**= most rooms under $150 **$$** = most rooms $150–$300 **$$$** = most rooms $300–$400

MONTRÉAL
Auberge du Vieux-Port. One of Montréal's first warehouse conversions, this inn facing the Old Port proves that chic styling need not be expensive. *97 rue de la Commune est; 514-876-0081 or 888-660-7678; aubergeduvieuxport.com.* **$$**

Delta Montréal. This solid business hotel in the Canadian Delta chain is the base for media and performers during the Just for Laughs Festival, with live broadcasts every day. The bar is a late-night hangout for comedians. *475 avenue du President-Kennedy; 514-286-1986 or 877-286-1986; www.deltamontreal.com.* **$$**

Hostellerie Pierre du Calvet. As romantic as the story of the *filles du roy* (who, tradition says, came here to meet prospective husbands), this Old Montréal inn features a superb indoor-garden dining room. *405 rue Bonsecours; 514-282-1725 or 866-544-1725; www.pierreducalvet.ca.* **$$**

Hôtel Le Germain. Sister hotel to Québec's Dominion 1912, le Germain carries the modernist styling to an even higher level with design that's ergonomic as well as beautiful. The convenient downtown location is pleasantly quiet. *2050 rue Mansfield; 514-849-2050 or 877-333-2050; www.hotelboutique.com.* **$$$**

Hôtel Nelligan. This quintessential boutique hotel in the heart of Old Montréal takes its name from the mad poet who was Montréal's answer to Baudelaire. A trendy bar and restaurant complement the property. *106 rue Saint-Paul ouest; 514-788-2040 or 877-788-2040; hotelnelligan.com.* **$$$**

Hôtel Wyndham Montréal. Set across rue Sainte-Catherine from Place des Arts, this fine business hotel turns into the hottest spot in town during the Montréal Jazz Festival, serving as the headquarters for performers and media. *1255 rue Jeanne-Mance; 514-285-1450 or 800-361-8234; www.wyndham.com/montreal.* **$$**

Les Passants du Sans Soucy. Sharing an eighteenth-century warehouse with a small art gallery, this smart Old Montréal B&B has stylish, if sometimes small, rooms. *171 rue Saint-Paul ouest; 514-842-2634; www.lesanssoucy.com.* **$–$$**

QUÉBEC CITY

Hôtel Dominion 1912. Clean deco styling, artisan furniture, and free espresso in the lobby set the chic tone for this relaxing getaway in Québec's Old Port district. *126 rue Saint-Pierre; 418-692-2224 or 888-833-5253; www.hotelboutique.com.* **$$–$$$**

Hôtel Le Clos Saint-Louis. This B&B is a perfect example of Victorian style with a French accent. Despite the location in the heart of Québec's Haute-Ville, the spacious rooms are surprisingly quiet. They are also well heated in the winter and well cooled in the summer. *69 rue Saint-Louis; 418-694-1311 or 800-461-1311; www.clossaintlouis.com.* **$$**

L'Hôtel du Capitole. Attached to a restored beaux arts theater, this stylish hotel at Place d'Youville offers special packages that include theatrical and musical events. *972 rue Saint-Jean; 418-694-4040 or 800-363-4040; www.lecapitole.com.* **$$**

LAURENTIANS

Hôtel La Sapinière. The peeled-log exterior has a definite rustic appeal, and the modern, air-conditioned rooms offer pure comfort in this outdoorsy getaway in the northern Laurentians. The classic French restaurant with lake view draws gourmets from miles around. *1244 chemin de la Sapinière, Val-David; 819-322-2020 or 800-567-6635; www.sapiniere.com.* **$$**

L'Estérel. This destination lodging features a full complement of water sports in the summer and snow sports in the winter. It's built a little like a stationary ocean liner. *39 chemin Fridolin-Simard, Ville d'Estérel; 450-228-2571 or 888-378-3735; 1888esterel.com.* **$$–$$$**

■ OFFICIAL TOURISM INFORMATION

Association Touristique des Laurentides. *800-561-NORD; www.laurentians.com.*
Office du tourisme et des congres de Québec. *418-649-2608; www.quebecregion.com.*
Tourisme Cantons-de-l'Est. *800-355-5755; www.easterntownships.cc.*
Tourisme Montréal. *514-844-5400; www.tourisme-montreal.org.*

■ USEFUL WEB SITES

Art and Antiques. Listings of antiques dealers and art galleries in and around Downtown Montréal. *www.antiqueartmtl.com.*
Artisans Québecois. Listings of artisans. *www.artisansquebecois.com.*
Canada Customs and Revenue Agency. How to obtain a refund of federal sales tax on goods and hotel accommodations. *www.ccra-adrc.gc.ca/visitors.*
Disability Access Information. Resource listings for people with disabilities. *www.keroul.qc.ca.*
La Maison des cyclistes. Cycling resource center. *www.velo.qc.ca.*
Meteorological Service of Canada. Weather forecasts for all parts of Canada. *www.meteo.ec.gc.ca.*
Montréal Design Guide. Listings of commercial establishments recognized for design excellence. *commercedesignmontreal.com.*
Montreal Gazette. Online edition of the city's only English-language daily. *www.montrealgazette.com.*
Parks Canada. Information about Canada's National Parks and National Historic Sites. *parkscanada.pch.gc.ca.*
Société de Transport de Montréal. Public transportation routes and schedules. *www.stm.info.*
Transports Québec. Updates on road conditions. *www.mtq.gouv.qc.ca.*

■ FESTIVALS AND EVENTS

■ JANUARY

Winter Carnivals. The Québecois prove that even a daunting winter can be an excuse to celebrate. Parades, snow sports, and general merriment prevail. *Fête des Neiges, Montréal; 514-872-6120; www.fetedesneiges.com. Carnaval de Québec, Québec City; 418-626-3716; www.carnaval.qc.ca.*

■ FEBRUARY

Festival Montréal en Lumière/Montréal High Lights Festival. Eleven days of festivities include outdoor light displays, cultural events, and special restaurant menus. *514-288-9955; www.montrealhighlights.com.*

■ MARCH

St. Patrick's Day Parade, Montréal. About forty floats and forty-five marching bands take over rue Sainte-Catherine in a tradition dating back to 1824. *514-815-2180; www.montrealirishparade.com.*

■ APRIL

Festival de la Gastronomie de Québec/Québec City Gastronomy Festival. Wine and beer tastings and friendly competitions among local chefs highlight this three-day festival. *418-683-4150; www.coupedesnations.com.*

■ MAY

La Féria du Vélo de Montréal/Montreal Bike Fest. Eight days of events, including a tour of the island, showcase Montréal as a cycle-friendly city. *www.velo.qc.ca.*

Pays-d'en-Haut Tour, Laurentians. Val-David is the starting point for this 100-kilometer cycling circuit in the Upper Laurentians. *819-326-6037; www.valdavid.com.*

■ JUNE

Air Canada Grand Prix, Montréal. This eighth stage of the Formula One world championship attracts some of the world's top drivers to the Gilles-Villeneuve Circuit on Île Notre-Dame. *www.grandprix.ca.*

The Tour de l'Île bicycle ride in June follows a different route each year.

La Fête Nationale/National Day. It's a toss-up which city puts on a bigger show of Québecois patriotic fervor on June 24—the feast of John the Baptist, and the "National Day" of Québec. Traditionally, it's the launch of summer. *La Fête Nationale, Montréal; www.cfn.org. La Fête Nationale des Québecois, Québec City; 418-640-0799; www.snqc.qc.ca.*

■ JULY

Arts Tours, Eastern Townships. Artists open their studios to visitors in the Lac-Brome–Sutton region (800-565-8455; www.tourdesarts.com) and Magog-Orford (800-267-2744; www.circuitdesarts.com).

Divers/Cité, Montréal. This weeklong celebration of gay pride features films, theatrical performances, and a massive parade. *514-285-4011; www.diverscite.org.*

Festival d'été/Summer Festival, Québec City. More than a thousand musicians and street performers entertain the city for eleven days. *418-529-5200; www.infofestival.com.*

The Montréal Alouettes represent the city in the Canadian Football League.

SIDEWALK TO BIG TOP

With several troupes touring internationally and several more performing at fixed sites in Las Vegas and Orlando, hardly a night passes on the planet without a **Cirque du Soleil** performance. The world's leading "new circus" may have regional headquarters in Orlando, Singapore, Amsterdam, and Las Vegas, but the international home remains in Montréal, where in 1996 the company built a new complex next to an abandoned quarry in the Saint-Michel neighborhood. With the province's great tradition of street performance, Montréal is also the company's spiritual center. The troupe's modest beginnings date from 1982, when a group of street performers organized as le Club des Talons Hauts (High Heels Club), so named because most of the founding members were stilt walkers. Two years later they refocused the troupe as Cirque du Soleil and created the first of their signature shows, which merge acrobatics, New Age music, and colorful costuming. All productions are conceived, developed, and rehearsed at the Montréal headquarters, and new shows generally debut in Montréal. L'École Nationale de Cirque (the National Circus School) moved from its Old Montréal headquarters in late 2003 to the campus of Cirque du Soleil, where many of its graduates work. The school has a few nights of "graduation" shows each June. *Cirque du Soleil, 8400 avenue 2e, Saint-Michel, Montréal; 514-722-2324 or 800-361-4595; www.cirquedusoleil.com. L'École Nationale de Cirque; 514-982-0859; www.enc.qc.ca.*

Festival International du Blues Tremblant/International Blues Festival, Tremblant Resort, Laurentians. Musicians from around the world perform for ten days. *888-736-2526; www.tremblant.ca.*

Festival International de Courses de Bateaux-Dragon/International Dragon Boat Race Festival, Montréal. More than a hundred teams compete in the Olympic Basin at Parc Jean-Drapeau. *514-866-7001; www.montrealdragonboat.com.*

Festival International du Jazz de Montréal/Montréal Jazz Festival. This eleven-day festival, beloved by performers and audiences alike, includes more than 500 concerts, of which about 350 are free. *514-871-1881; www.montrealjazzfest.com.*

Festival International Nuits d'Afrique/Nights of Africa International Festival, Montréal. Traditional and contemporary African music and dance take center stage on the streets and in the dance clubs. *514-499-3462; www.festivalnuitsdafrique.com.*

Festival Juste Pour Rire/Just for Laughs Festival, Montréal. World's largest comedy festival proves that humor is an international language. *514-845-2322; www.hahaha.com.*

Le Mondial SAQ, Montréal. This international fireworks competition features ten shows between mid-June and late July. *514-397-2000; www.lemondialsaq.com.*

Les FrancoFolies de Montréal, Montréal. This ten-day festival is devoted to French-language—and other non-anglophone—music from around the world. *514-876-8989; www.francofolies.com.*

■ **AUGUST**

Brome Agricultural Fair, Brome, Eastern Townships. This traditional agriculture fair was launched in 1856. *450-242-3976.*

Festival des Films du Monde/World Film Festival, Montréal. Screenings of films from several dozen countries take place from late August through early September. *514-848-3883; www.ffm-montreal.org.*

Elaborate snow sculptures add to the fun of Carnaval de Québec.

Marathon des Deux Rives/Two Banks Marathon, Levis/Québec. A marathon, half marathon, 10K race, team challenge, and mini-marathon for youth are all part of this major running event. *418-694-4442; www.marathonquebec.com.*

■ **SEPTEMBER**

Festival des Canards du Lac-Brome/Brome Lake Duck Fest, Knowlton, Eastern Townships. Menus featuring local duck are the highlight of this fall celebration. *450-242-6886; www.cclacbrome.qc.ca.*

Festival International de Nouvelle Danse/Festival of New Dance, Montréal. One of the largest festivals of experimental dance, this biennial event is held in odd-numbered years. *514-844-2172; www.find-lab.com.*

■ **OCTOBER**

Québec designer labels sale, Montréal. Locals head to Bonsecours Market for great buys on samples and surplus stock from about forty Québec designers. *514-866-2006.*

■ **DECEMBER**

Bal de 31 Décembre/New Year's Eve Ball, Montréal. A heated dance floor warms revelers at Place Jacques-Cartier. *514-874-0485.*

Delices de Noël/Christmas Delights, Montréal. Christmas trees and other holiday decorations fill the main exhibition greenhouse at the Botanical Garden. *514-872-1400; www.ville.montreal.qc.ca/jardin.*

RECOMMENDED READING

A Yankee in Canada (1850), by Henry David Thoreau. The Concord curmudgeon proves a virtual raconteur in this account of a journey to Montréal and Québec City.

The Alley Cat (1986), by Yves Beauchemin, translated by Sheila Fischman. Mishaps befall the new owner of the Beanery, a classic Plateau eatery.

Black Robe (1985), by Brian Moore. Tale of fur traders and missionaries in the Great Northwest incorporates all the sex and violence that the history books leave out.

Exploring Old Montreal (2002), by Alan Hustak. Exhaustive and sometimes amusing account of the most historically dense part of the city.

The Fat Woman Next Door Is Pregnant (1981), by Michel Tremblay, translated by Sheila Fischman. The noted playwright brings his fine sense of detail to this novel about the interwoven lives of French-Canadian families living in the Plateau's triple-deckers.

The Favourite Game (1963), by Leonard Cohen. The poet and songwriter's semiautobiographical account of growing up rich, Jewish, and libidinous in Westmount.

Flavourville (2002), by Lesley Chesterman. The *Montreal Gazette* restaurant critic surveys the city's dining scene.

Jump (2000), by Marianne Ackerman. Members of Montréal's artistic community confront their own identities as the third referendum on Québec sovereignty looms.

Memoirs (1993), by Pierre Elliott Trudeau. The intellectual mandarin of Canadian politics recalls his life, from a Montréal childhood to the reins of power in Ottawa.

Montreal: Seaport and City (1945), by Stephen Leacock. Engaging history of the city through the mid-twentieth century.

Smart Shopping in Montréal (annual editions), by Sandra Phillips. Guide to the best bargains. Details on www.smartshopping.net.

Sainte-Anne-de-Beaupré *(1897), by James Wilson Morrice.*

The Street (1969), by Mordecai Richler. Perhaps Montréal's best-known anglophone author, Richler gives an entertaining account of growing up in the world of Jewish immigrants on the Plateau.

The Tin Flute (1947), by Gabrielle Roy, translated by Hannah Josephson. A sympathetic outsider's view of working-class French-Canadian life at the start of World War II.

Two Solitudes (1945), by Hugh MacLennan. This saga of French-Canadian and Scots-Irish families introduced the widely used term for the separation of language and culture in Québec.

I N D E X

ACKNOWLEDGMENTS

■ From the Authors

The authors wish to thank Gilles Bengle of the Greater Montréal Convention and Tourism Bureau, Siegfried Gagnon of Tourisme Québec, Richard Seguin of the Québec City and Area Tourism and Convention Bureau, and Nicolle Dufour of the Association touristique des Laurentides for their invaluable assistance. We are indebted to guides Ronald Poiré and Suzanne Bonin for insight into Montréal life and history; to the librarians of the Westmount, Mont-Royal, and main research branches of the Montréal library system for help with research; and to Suzanne P. Leclerc for her first-hand understanding of the evolution of Québecois cuisine. We're also grateful to innumerable rangers, guides, and interpreters at museums and historic sites, as well as to Jean and Monique Dontigny, the most hospitable landlords that tenants could ask for. Thanks, too, to mapmaker Mark Stroud for so beautifully obviating the need for bread crumbs, and to Benoît Aquin for his evocative imagery, restaurant tips, and advice about microbrewed beers. We want to express our continued gratitude to Fodor's visionary creative director, Fabrizio La Rocca, and to designer Tina Malaney. Finally, we wish to thank Daniel Mangin for originating the project at Compass American Guides and for his enthusiastic encouragement and unstinting support, and editor Paula Consolo and senior editor Paul Eisenberg for shepherding it to completion.

■ From the Publisher

Compass American Guides would like to thank Rachel Elson for copyediting the manuscript and Ellen Klages for proofreading it. All photographs in this book are by Benoît Aquin unless otherwise noted below. Compass American Guides is grateful to the following individuals and institutions for the use of their photographs and illustrations.

Old Montréal
Page 37, McCord Museum of Canadian History (Notman Photographic Archives) (MP-0000.3130)

Lachine Canal and Rapids
Pages 68–69, Samuel McLaughlin/National Archives of Canada (PA-147588)

Parc Jean-Drapeau
Page 79, National Archives of Canada (e 000756917) ▪ Page 82, National Archives of Canada (C-030085)

Downtown
Page 130, Daniel Choinière/Montréal Tourism

Hochelaga-Maisonneuve
Page 178, Canada Science and Technology Museum (Image No. CN002282)

Québec City
Page 185, Yves Tessier/Tessima ▪ Page 186, North Wind Picture Archives ▪ Page 188, Library of Congress Geography and Map Division ▪ Page 191, Yale Collection of Western Americana, Beinecke Rare Book and Manuscript Library ▪ Page 194, Yves Tessier/Tessima ▪ Page 196, McCord Museum of Canadian History (Notman Photographic Archives) (MP-1983.63.1) ▪ Page 201, Yves Tessier/Tessima ▪ Page 202, Yves Tessier/Tessima ▪ Pages 206–207, Yves Tessier/Tessima ▪ Page 209, Yves Tessier/Tessima ▪ Page 210, Paul Dionne/Musée d'Art Inuit Brousseau ▪ Page 213, National Library of Canada, Rare Books Division ▪ Page 215, McCord Museum of Canadian History (Notman Photographic Archives) (MP-1984.147.10) ▪ Page 218, Yves Tessier/Tessima ▪ Page 221, North Wind Picture Archives

The Laurentians
Page 245, McCord Museum of Canadian History (Notman Photographic Archives) (MP-0000.1452.93)

Practical Information
Page 264, McCord Museum of Canadian History (Notman Photographic Archives) (MP-1990.39.84)

Recommended Reading
Page 277, Montreal Museum of Fine Arts, William J. Morrice Bequest (1943.785)

■ About the Authors

A writing team for more than two decades, Patricia Harris and David Lyon have published extensively on travel, food, the arts, and popular culture in magazines, newspapers, and on the Web. They are the authors of more than a dozen books, including *Escape to Northern New England* and the *Boston* and *Cape Cod* volumes in the Compass American Guide series. When not on assignment, they can usually be found in a third-floor walk-up in Cambridge, Massachusetts.

■ About the Photographer

Having studied at the New England School of Photography in Boston from 1985 to 1987, Benoît Aquin has developed a prolific career in photography, with his work showcased in Canadian and foreign publications, notably the weekly *Voir*, as well as *Maclean's*, *Canadian Geographic*, *Wired*, and *Time* magazines. Although he is above all a photojournalist, Aquin has photographed countless personalities: filmmakers, actors, musicians, singers, and writers from around the globe. His photographs have been shown in many galleries and museums in Canada and other countries and are included in numerous public and private collections. He lives in Montréal.